THE JOURNEY TO MIDNIGHT

An undercover officer's path from suicide to redemption

MATT GRIFFIN

THE JOURNEY TO MIDNIGHT

An Undercover Officer's Path

from Suicide to Redemption

Written by Matt Griffin

Copyright ©2021 Matt Griffin

ISBN: 978-1-7367298-0-9

ISBN: 978-1-7367298-1-6

Developmental Edit by Becky Blanton

CONTENTS

TESTIMONIALS

"*I sincerely appreciated the opportunity to meet Matt and understand his journey; Matt's passion for the wellbeing of the professionals that protect our Country, at home and abroad is evident. This book is a roadmap that accurately describes the dangerous road of unattended trauma but more importantly, the pathway to successful recovery. It is a must-read for practitioners in public safety and military wellness programs, including policing leaders at all levels.*"
— **Ramon Batista, Retired Police Chief, and Co-Author of the best-selling book** ***Do No Harm***

"*We MUST change the stigma in LE that it is not ok to hurt. We must tell our people that it is ok to ask for help because we are all human. We are getting better, but there's still a long way to go. Matt, I pray that your book reaches those who might be in that dark place and shine that needed light. Proud of you brother!*"
— **Detective Joe Pannullo (Retired), Narcotics / Crisis Negotiator Las Vegas Metropolitan Police Department**

"*I am so happy and proud to be a part of this book. The things that Matt*

shares are things that every first responder should hear. I hope what is in this book helps others that may be going through valleys in their life."
— **Det. Paul Gifford, Lebanon Police Dept.**

"*We cannot continue to expect the acts of heroism that result in horrific trauma if we do not provide a safe space to put it. Matt's enduring courage is demonstrated in his resolution to give his comrades permission to ask for those spaces. Trauma bleeds over the Thin Blue Line everyday. Matt courageously reminds us of the importance of addressing the demons that stay in the hearts and minds of our heroes—when the armor comes off.*"
— **Deanna Axe**

"*For 20 years I've always known Matt as a strong person both physically and mentally. But what he's doing with this book showcases his real courage. Suicide is a delicate subject to understand and tackle; suicide among men and women in uniform compounds that complexity. As the brother of a suicide victim who wore the badge, this book highlights the ones left behind and how we can stop, listen and help.*"
— **Cole Hyland, USN Veteran, Apt 300 roommate, and brother of Graham Hyland, Cook County Corrections Officer EOW July 5th, 2019**

"*Over the years I have transitioned through multiple careers as a Professional Athlete, Photojournalist and First Responder. I have been brought face to face with the detritus which physical and emotional trauma imprint on those involved in trauma. Some of it is horrific and glaring in the level of intensity. Some subtle. Each type is dangerous and can lead to an ending no one should ever have to face alone.*

Matt's thorough look at the challenges we face in trauma is thorough and incredibly generous. It offers safeguards, a pathway to resolution, and healing. It may help repair damaged hearts and lives in more ways than I can write here.

In the Maritime Rescue group I work in, we have a motto we all hold high, which was penned by RWC pioneer Shawn Alladio. "The Life that you save, may be your own"

Read this book. Learn the lessons in it, apply them and share this book. It will matter.

— **David Pu'u: Filmmaker, Photojournalist, CEO, First Responder**

DEDICATION

This book is dedicated to Brian, and to all the men and women, mothers and fathers, sons and daughters, law enforcement, first responders, firemen and military alike, who didn't get a chance to see the light at the end of the tunnel, or know just how much they were loved—and to those who did, and to those who may need reminding in the future.

ACKNOWLEDGMENTS

This book wouldn't have been possible without the courage, and willingness of so many people to share their personal stories, losses, and pain around the topic of suicide, mental health, and loss. Thank you for coming forward and sharing your stories, your tears, your pain, and your hope with me.

Kendra, without you I wouldn't have the sons and family I hold so dear, and live for, now. It's been a rough journey, but a healing one.

Finn Wentworth, who knew that your generosity, foresight, and support of a 14-year old lacrosse crazy kid would result in this book and this movement. Thank you for believing in me all these years.

Brian, Thank you for being with me every day along this journey. You're my Lighthouse and 111 is in everything I do.

To my sons. Every minute of every hour I am thankful for each of you. You all are the best thing that has ever happened to me.

Rick Smith, Steve Tuttle and Axon, Thank you for taking a chance on me and being so supportive and believing in my mission to change the culture of mental health awareness in Law Enforcement.

For all those officers, psychologists and therapists, mothers, fathers, and survivors I interviewed, thank you for sharing your stories with me. Whether the interview made it into the book or not it was valuable background information and only served to reinforce how critical this information is to those living under the shadow of PTSD, depression, and suicidal thoughts.

Seth Godin, Thank you for "sowing seeds for trees you might never sit under, flowers you may never smell, and stories you may never read," and for Triiibes.com.

Last, but not least—Becky Blanton, my collaborator and editor— We did it. From the first phone call to the last typed word, we've shared so many tears and even more laughs! From the bottom of my heart, thank you!

To all those I didn't name, please don't feel left out. You matter. You are loved. You aren't forgotten.

WARNING

There may be parts of this book that are triggering if you have PTSD, or a history of on or off the job trauma. It's not the details that may trigger a reaction, I am not graphic here, but the sheer number and stories and tragedies of those who have died at their own hand may come up as you read and remember your own trauma history.

Not everyone I interviewed for this book, or that I mention, shares my belief in God or Jesus Christ, but all were gracious and mature enough to agree to disagree and to contribute their experiences, thoughts, and stories.

For that I am eternally grateful, and will keep praying for all!

The stories that sound familiar or echo your own experience or isolation may evoke a reaction, sadness, or depression. You may recall incidents that you thought you'd processed or forgotten. That's normal. If you need help, get help. If you need to cry, cry. Reach out to someone to talk about the book, if nothing else. Know that you are not alone. At the end of the book are several pages of resources we've found to be focused on veterans, LEOs, and first responders. Please reach out to any of them for help if you need to. The names and some details of my stories have been changed to protect the people involved.

FOREWORD

I first met Matt Griffin during the week of May 10, 2015 during an undercover survival training course that I was conducting in Boston, MA. He was not very interactive during that course, but that would soon change.

I returned to Boston in March of 2017 to conduct a different training course. After the first hour, Matt quickly approached me and said that he was interested in becoming an instructor for my company (Professional Law Enforcement Training — (PLET.)

As he spoke, I immediately noticed his eyes because they were watery. Matt continued by saying he had intended to take me to lunch to share his idea about a Fentanyl training course. At that time, I had no idea how Fentanyl was destroying communities in New England. Before I could accept his invitation to lunch, Matt broke down and said that his police chief had committed suicide earlier in the week and that he had a close relationship with him.

He shared their last conversation and then told me that he had to leave class to attend his police chief's funeral. Before I could gather my words to respond, Matt said he was *already* struggling that day because it would have marked his 15th wedding anniversary, but that he was divorced.

Matt provided me his cell phone number and email address and asked me to give him a shot at speaking on the National stage for PLET.

I remember thinking how important it must have been for him to show up to class the day of his police chief's funeral just to get an opportunity to talk to me face to face. That left an amazing impression on me.

After a few weeks, I conducted a phone interview with Matt and was impressed with his passion for wanting to educate officers on the dangers of fentanyl. So, I hired him as a contract instructor and I sent him to El Paso, TX for his first class.

I asked him what size PLET shirt he needed because all our instructors teach in our PLET Polo Style shirts. Matt laughed and said, "That's not me bro. I need a suit with a bow tie."

Thinking he was joking, I laughed with him, waiting for him to tell me what size polo shirt he wore. I very quickly realized he was serious, and I immediately questioned what I was getting myself into with this clown!

But, Matt went to El Paso in June 2017 and taught a phenomenal course. After reading the end of course evaluations, I knew he was special. Matt would become PLET's first full-time instructor traveling the United States weekly, teaching various narcotic-related courses. His unique style of teaching, the passion that he exhibited, and that crazy looking bowtie made him one of the most beloved instructors that PLET had.

I eventually learned about Matt's struggle with depression and his near suicide attempt. I thought back on my interaction with Matt in 2017 and wondered, how I did not pick up on the fact that he was suicidal or struggling?

In my mind I questioned my own investigative skills for not recognizing any clues. Matt's ability to mask his pain was second to none. He personified the warrior culture in his demeanor—never letting anyone see him sweat or cry.

Police officers are really equipped to elicit information from victims, witnesses, and suspects. They dig and dig until they get to the truth or obtain a confession. However, when talking to our own, we rarely dig deep into the soul because oftentimes we do not want to offend that person, or we think it's none of our business.

Suicides are one of the leading causes of deaths for active/retired law enforcement officers. Matt is using his unique speaking abilities on the national stage to educate officers on the signs and symptoms of officer suicide. He has connected with thousands of officers on a personal level and hundreds of those officers have reached out to him directly in their time of need.

Initially, I was leery that police officers would be receptive to Matt's story. I thought that he would be viewed as a "weak cop" who could not handle the stress. I was completely wrong. I have witnessed firsthand the power of his suicide presentations. I was so impressed with the responses he got that I asked him to make a video segment that our instructors could play during their training so that more officers could be reached.

Matt is one of my closest confidants and we talk daily. I admire him taking a stand and tackling the negative stigma associated with police officers needing help. We will never know how many lives he is saving by writing *Journey to Midnight*, but we know that his powerful message during speaking engagements has already saved at least one life.

The most powerful statement I learned from watching Matt's presentation on this topic was when he said, "I wasn't committing suicide, I was making a sacrifice, so my boys didn't have to see me struggle any longer." That was the first time I had ever heard some one compare "suicide" to a "sacrifice" and it gave me a different perspective on how to communicate with officers that may be struggling. As Matt told me, if this book only helps one person turn away from suicide, it's been worth writing. Read it, share it, and believe it.

— Byron Boston
PLET (Professional Law Enforcement Training)
https://www.pletraining.com/byron-boston

PROLOGUE

Have you ever had that sick sinking feeling? You know the one. The one where everything and everyone is against you. Like, whatever you touch or look at immediately breaks or turns to shit? Well, that was me on March 17th, 2017. My chief, mentor, and partner had just committed suicide two weeks earlier, my ex-wife froze my bank accounts and I was sleeping in my car. I had nothing to live for and I had too much pride to ask for help. I was physically and emotionally exhausted and I could not find a way out. That's when I wrote my suicide note;

To my sons:

You won't understand, I know this. But please understand that I love you more than anything in the whole world. You are my light in bad times and my sunshine every morning. I'll be watching over you every minute. Continue to make me proud.

Life is funny, You're on top then you're under the rock. Financially, emotionally they never coincide. My demons have finally won. The skeletons have become more of me than the person I'm proud of. Let go of me. I've shamed many and harmed a few. I hope that in my time I've at least made a couple of lives better.

Even when the curtain closes for us all, the show will live on. I've lived

1

the best life I could but it wasn't good enough. Not for you, and not for anyone.
Signing off 10-2 at midnight.
Without hope,
Matthew A Griffin

So there I sat. In an empty parking lot. With an empty heart. I know it sounds cliche, but my life actually did flash before me. It had been, for the most part, a good life—a scholarship to a prestigious private high school that took me out of a poor, ghetto neighborhood at the age of 14. I became an all-state lacrosse/football player, president of my senior class, and after high school, a US Navy Search and Rescue swimmer (SAR), and a wildly successful undercover police officer...I had all the accomplishments, accolades and awards others would kill for.

Yet, none of it helped me see the value in myself. All the struggles and demons and secrets and lies I'd been living finally caught up with me.

I remember that day very well. I made up my mind that I was going to leave this earth. I was going to be strong for my boys and take myself out like a wounded animal suffering on the side of the road. Because I WAS wounded. I was not only hurt and hurting, I was hurting immensely, beyond anything I'd ever experienced in my life.

I was done with people, and police work, and being strong. I was tired. I was exhausted. And most of all, I was done with this life. Gazing out the front window of my Yukon, I thought about each of my four sons.

"Be tough! Be strong!" I kept saying to myself. I was doing this for them. I knew they wouldn't understand but I couldn't let them see their dad continue to fail. And all I had done was fail. When the clock read all 0000s, I was going to be strong, I was going to finally have peace! There was something about that midnight hour and the zeros on the clock that felt right, that gave me strength and an unusual sense of calmness.

2

People say your mind can't unsee something. I wish I'd known that before I became a police officer because right now all I could see was my future, where my lifeless body would be slumped over the steering wheel for some other officer to find and see — just like so many other suicides I'd seen in my police career. And I wondered, just for a second, whose mind and eyes my lifeless body would be burned in when they found me.

Obviously, I didn't pull that trigger. I didn't make it to midnight. An unknown officer and responding crew would have one less trauma to deal with that night.

There was another journey, another path for me. This is about that other journey and about how I came to be on that "less traveled" path. It's a true story about my journey *to* that dark moment and my journey *from* that moment into the light, and into hope.

For me, there is only a before and an after. Others before, and after me, did make it to their own midnight and pulled their own triggers. I feel deeply that there was no one there to tell them what people told me—that they were loved, and there was a light at the end of the tunnel if they'd just hold on. If you're one of the men or women considering that same dark path I hope you'll wait until you read this book to make your decision. I've been on that path, minutes away from pulling that trigger. I get it.

I hope that you will embark on this journey with me and you'll allow me to share my life and struggles with you. And by the end of this journey, it is my hope that you will know the two things that kept me from making the worst decision of my life:

One, that there is light at the end of the tunnel and...and two,

That you are loved.

— Matt Griffin

Why this book? Why now?

Throughout time there have always been people running into burning buildings while others were running out. These first responders put themselves in harm's way, often risking or giving their lives to save others. They are the first people to see and deal with death. They are the first on the scene of traumas so severe that the average citizen could not function after seeing what these men and women see on a daily basis.

In 1995, Oklahoma City and nearby military police were first on the scene in the bombing of the Oklahoma City Murrow Building. They carried 168 bodies from the rubble, including almost two dozen dead children.

When James Alex Fields, Jr. deliberately drove his car into a crowd of people who had been peacefully protesting the Unite the Right rally in Charlottesville (C'Ville), Virginia, on August 12, 2017; it was police officers and first responders who were on scene at the downtown mall where Heather Heyer was killed that dealt first-hand with the carnage. Thirty-five other people were injured, and hundreds more traumatized by the events and what they witnessed, either in person or on the news.

In spite of the public criticism and Monday morning quarterbacking by the local and national news and social media over the events, C'Ville police and first responders were there to deal with the crowds and the aftermath for months on end. They were the ones tasked with dealing with the blood, the assaults, the victims, and the media onslaught that continued for months, even years. I studied the C'Ville case extensively. It has a lot of elements of other cases I've seen, including mental trauma to some of the officers.

On the 20th anniversary of 9/11 in NYC, let's not forget the LEO and first responders who died rushing into those burning buildings. Of the 2,977 victims killed in the September 11, 2001 attacks, 412 were police, firemen, and first responders. They were at the scene of the World Trade Center saving lives when the planes hit and the buildings fell. But it was a firefighter who joined the NYFD *after* 9/11, and *because* of 9/11 that got my attention.

After joining the New York City Fire Department because of the tragedy of 9/11, joining being a feat in itself, thirty-four year old Matt Byrne fought a seven-alarm fire which killed two firefighters and injured more than 100 others. Later in his career, two children "died in his arms" after being run over in Chinatown. The fires he could handle. It was, as his father Edward Byrne told the *New York Times*, and later, my editor, "the constant deaths that he struggled with."

Like many Law Enforcement Officers (LEOs) and first responders, a knee injury started Matt Byrne down the road to opioid abuse, then to various treatment programs. He left the fire department in March 2014, then lost a longtime job as a Jones Beach lifeguard and was later charged with driving while intoxicated.

"He lost everything that mattered to him," his father told me. "He lost his career, his longtime lifeguard job, his girlfriend. He lost everything but his family, and he lost it all in a very short time." In August, Matt Byrne died when he hung himself from a swingset in his parents backyard. Years later his father, a New York attorney, wrote a memoir about Matt, entitled, *In Whom I Am Well Pleased,* wanting to keep his son's memory alive. As of the writing of this book he hasn't published it yet, but I pray he will. He's looking for an agent to ensure the book gets the exposure he wants.

"People forget. I don't want him to be forgotten," he said. There are so many people whose loved ones don't want them to be forgotten, especially if they go out by their own hand. It staggers the imagination.

The 2017 Las Vegas Convention Shootings left 58 people dead and more than 500 wounded. I know a bit about the shooting because my friend Joe Panullo was there and let me interview him about his experience.

"I was off work," he said, "I heard it on the radio and I got up to go back, despite being off-duty and a couple of weeks away from retirement. It's what we do. I didn't want to. I was afraid I wouldn't come home. My wife was crying, I was crying, we were both afraid I wouldn't come home if I turned around and went to the scene. But I went. It's what I signed up to do, so I did," he told me. Joe came home but many others at the scene—58 to be exact, did not. Many survived the shooting and came back, but haven't been the same since.

PTSD respects no one. The veteran officer as well as the rookie can succumb at any time for any trauma, large or small.

One of the most notorious school shootings of all time was Columbine High School. In the aftermath 12 students and one teacher were dead, and 21 other people were wounded by gunfire before the two shooters committed suicide.[1]

The first SWAT team members to enter the school stepped around bodies and were forced to ignore a wounded and panicked student's plea for help as they searched for the shooters. What they didn't know at the time was that the shooters had already taken their own lives.

"What if?" I can hear them asking. "What if we'd gone in immediately instead of waiting?" The active shooter protocols have changed since Columbine, but the question still echoes in the minds of many who were there. "What if?"

According to ABC news reports, the impact on the SWAT team after Columbine was palpable. *"Amid the emotional toll of what it experienced, the Jefferson County Regional SWAT team began to fall apart. By 2002, only three members of the 10-person team remained. The others were reassigned or left the department."* [2]

As a result of Columbine, four states have now passed legislation, including The Law Enforcement Mental Health and Wellness Act of 2017 (LEMHWA) to help law enforcement officers deal with trauma on the job.

The LEMHWA was signed into law in January 2018, recognizing that law enforcement agencies need and deserve support in their ongoing efforts to protect the mental health and well-being of their employees as well as the public. Good mental and psychological health is as essential as good physical health to ensure law enforcement officers are effective in keeping our country and our communities safe from crime and violence.[3]

The bill directs the Department of Justice (DOJ) to report on the Department of Defense and Department of Veterans Affairs mental health practices and services that could be adopted by law enforcement agencies. We can't get it active in all 50 states soon enough. Additionally, the DOJ's Office of Community Oriented Policing Services must report on programs to address the psychological health and well-being of law enforcement officers after critical incidents. Is this the ultimate solution? No, but it's a start.

Moving to the eastern U.S....Shortly after 2:02 a.m. on June 12, 2016 the Orlando Police Department began receiving calls of an active shooter at The Pulse Nightclub in Orlando, Florida. Before the day was out, police, SWAT teams, and first responders would respond to the popular gay nightclub and deal with 50 dead men and women, and dozens of other wounded club attendees.

This was not a shooting that was over quickly. Police arrived on scene within six minutes and entered the club, guns drawn and taking immediate action. The shooter, Omar Mateen, 29, called 911, pledging allegiance to ISIS. He began shooting, then later barricaded himself in a bathroom for more than three hours, threatening to put explosive vests on hostages and detonate them.

While officers pulled, carried or directed victims out of the club the threat of bombs remained, but they acted anyway. Officers knocked down walls, put themselves in harm's way during the event, then stood over and worked tirelessly to recover bodies, document the deaths, and process the crime scene afterwards.

In 2018, in the aftermath of the shooting, survivors of the massacre, along with family members of those killed, sued the club's security guard, thirty police officers, the police department and the city of Orlando for "not acting quickly enough, not doing their duty, or violating their civil rights."

In other words, victims who survived the shooting because of police actions, blamed the police, not Omar Mateen, the shooter, for their ordeal. A federal appeals court later sided with U.S. district judge U.S. District Judge Paul G. Byron, in throwing out the lawsuit.

You read that right. Victims blamed, not thanked officers for risking life and limb and injury to save them. That kind of litigous response only adds to the psychological trauma officers face.

Gerry Realin, 37, part of the Hazmat team who spent four hours tending to the dead inside the club, told reporters that he wishes he had never become a police officer because of the things he saw at The Pulse shooting. He was not the only officer who developed PTSD from responding to the scene. Others in the department, news reports say, remain silent in order to keep their jobs and avoid the stigma of mental health issues.[4]

From what I have been told, the scene with the wounded, along with 49 dead bodies that the officers and first responders tended to, was so traumatic that one of the responding SWAT team members stayed on the scene for 16 hours so as to not let anyone else have to see what he went through inside the club.

This was the second most horrific killing on American soil since 9/11. I think about how the officers who were there risking their lives, knowing the shooter was threatening to blow up hostages and the club, while they were doing their damndest to save lives, handled so much trauma. I can imagine how they must have felt, or still feel about the incident. I wonder how they responded to the trauma, and then to the lawsuit. Again, the question, "What if?"

Hollywood makes all this "shoot 'em up and be a hero," action look easy, but it's not. Every situation, every shooter, every call is unique. And no matter who you are, or how long you've been on the job, it impacts you and changes you forever.

You do the best with what you know, and what is happening in the moment. But, in the end, you still walk away with your pain, the strongest critic of what you could have done, should have done. Even if you do everything by the book, everything humanly possible, you still walk away asking, "What if?"

There are lots of dozens if not hundreds of studies on PTSD in civilian and victim populations, but not so many among LEOs and first responders. However, an estimated 7-19% of police officers do develop PTSD on the job. And, then they develop addictions as a result of self-medicating their pain to help them deal with their PTSD. They self-medicate so they can keep their pain a secret, and keep their jobs. They pose a risk to themselves, and others by doing so.

Ron Clark, a retired Connecticut State Police Officer, now works with *Badge of Life*, a police suicide-prevention group. In a 2017 NPR interview, he said that "when he started with the Connecticut State Police decades ago, people were told to just 'suck it up,' referring to the trauma and the reactions they developed as a result of what they saw and experienced on the job.

You can only stuff so much trauma before it begins to leak out and affect your daily life, your family, your job. There comes a time when you have to find some way to contain it, release it, deal with it and heal it. Officers use alcohol, drugs or sex to cope with stress because, if they spoke up, they were likely to get fired. "But," Clark says, 'Police officers are human beings. They're affected by what they see out there — decapitated children, families wiped out in car accidents, suicides — just name all the horrors you can think of.'"[5]

Suck It Up, Buttercup

Orlando firefighter Jimmy Reyes was at the Orlando Pulse shooting in 2016. He talked to FireRescue1.com about his experience. He said, "It was more about, 'suck it up and keep going, just ball your emotions and your feelings together,' Reyes said. "Sucking it up" describes the mentality that allowed him to keep working despite the horror around him.[6] But once the trauma was over, then what? What you see, feel, and experience doesn't go away as quickly as the media attention.

Reyes told FireRescue1 he kept his treatment for the trauma he experienced a secret from colleagues for two years. When he finally chose to share his treatment with them, he said he felt "relieved." He still suffers from anxiety and depression, and sees a counselor once every two weeks.[7]

More than 60 people who experienced trauma related to the Pulse nightclub shooting have received support from the University of Central Florida (UCF) Restores services, and the organization continues to provide support for firefighters.[8] Thank God for their program.

. . .

Abuse from Within

If trauma in the field, and from the job weren't enough, abuse from the public, and people inside the profession also contribute to the stress. Abuse from colleagues and supervisors, are also a factor in security, LEO, Veteran, and responder suicides.

On February 20, 2019, Transportation Security (TSA) Officer Robert Henry jumped to his death from the tenth floor of the Hyatt hotel inside the Orlando International Airport. The last line of his suicide note read: "Tell my managers I will be waiting for them in Hell. Especially the ones who feel this was necessary." Henry, and dozens of others, had complained of being bullied and harassed by their supervisors, but nothing was done.

I know first hand the effects of internal abuse. After Brian's death, I was pulled out of undercover work and placed on administrative leave pending an internal investigation over a timesheet discrepancy.

I went to a colleague, someone I thought was a friend/mentor, for advice on the situation. I sat down in Lt. JM's office and asked him what he would do. I later came to find out that he was the one who initiated the investigation because he no longer wanted me in the detective bureau.

During the course of the internal investigation that followed, I was training law enforcement officers around the country. I was deeply passionate about training other LEOS and as you'll read, I turned that passion into a company and career. Sometimes the people you trust with your back and your life are the last ones you should trust. That's another reason why officers are loath to share their feelings, fears, and doubts about the internal and sometimes the external political climate. It's ammunition for their competition and those who don't want them on the force. Not to sound paranoid, but who can you trust?

As the internal investigation was being completed, I received a phone call from Byron Boston (owner of PLET) and the company that gave me a shot at becoming a national training instructor.

He explained that he just received an anonymous email through his company's website. The email read "Are you aware that Matt Griffin just faced disciplinary action with the Keene Police Department and is no longer working for the Attorney General's Drug Task Force as a result?"

The email was sent from a fake email address whose IP address was tracked back to the area of the Keene Police Department. The results of the internal investigation had not been made public and had only been relayed to me earlier that same day.

Only a handful of people at the Police Department had knowledge of that information. It turns out one of that handful was Lt. JM, the same person who initiated the investigation and lied throughout it. I asked the Police Chief to investigate this policy violation and gave him my suspicions about who was behind it. Did he ever look into it?

Did he care that someone in his department was maliciously attacking me and attempting to derail my ability to feed my children or contributed to my PTSD? The answer unfortunately is no.

Yes. I am aware that I'm crossing that thin blue line of the brotherhood that says "Don't speak out against another officer, even if they're wrong, corrupt, or abusive." But that's part of the problem. When we don't speak out, we suffer. My outrage goes back to my lifelong awareness that so much of life is not fair. Until we speak out it will never be fair.

As police officers we are charged with upholding the law among the communities we serve. I believe we need to speak up about the corruption and crime within our own ranks. So, why does this thin blue line exist?

Because in the warrior culture, as in nature, anyone who is perceived as weak, whether they are or not, is fair game for those who want to climb to the top and don't care how many people they step on to do it. It's not just the Keene PD or the TSA. It's any department in any city that has a warrior culture, or even a remnant of one. This attitude of "shut-up," and hypocrisy has to stop. It shows up in racist remarks, in sexist remarks, and in other ways.

And, I believe it contributes to the suicides of officers and first responders, and even security guards, every year.

Two officers responding to a radio station WMFE survey, (WMFE is a non-profit, community-based public broadcasting company that operates in Orlando), claim two people responding to a survey about abuse from TSA officials, were hospitalized for suicide attempts or thoughts. They said abuse by the TSA was a major contributing factor in their own thoughts as well

Between five and 15 TSA officers commit suicide every year, some, like Henry, directly blaming TSA working conditions, bullying, and harassment for their suicides.[9]

I can't paint every agency or department with the same brush. Some are very supportive of their officers and responders mental health issues. Others, however, continue to contribute to the abuse and PTSD.

There's a broad spectrum of responses, but overall, I still believe the warrior culture and "don't ask, don't tell" mentality rules at most departments. When it comes to addressing mental health among law enforcement, veterans, and first responders and firefighters, that's the response I get the most. "It's not safe to admit you need help, even when you know you do."

When researching these events I noticed there's very little media coverage of the number of officers injured, or killed, or who commit suicide. Most don't want to talk about it, and even have policies against reporting private suicides (as opposed to public suicides where the victim kills themselves in a public venue, like on the street, or at their agency, in a park), but there are other ways to report on officer suicides.

There is also very little in-depth media attention paid to the people who risked everything to save those they could—one exception being the *Washington Post,* who reported on the death of one officer by a series of strokes, and the suicide of four Capitol Hill Police Officer's: Howard Liebengood, 51, and Jefferey Smith, 35, and just this week (August 4, 2021) Gunther Hashida, 43, and Kyle DeFreytag, 26. These four officers were at the January 6, 2021 protests in Washington, DC. The notices and news stories were brief and perfunctory.

What the media does not understand is that these suicides at home were "line of duty deaths" as much as being shot in an ambush, or killed in a traffic accident.

I could fill a book with the names of national tragedies where police, first responders, firemen, veterans and members of the US military have responded to natural disasters, crises, shootings, and trauma.

I could fill another bookshelf with the events that never make the national news where first responders die, or are tragically wounded or injured for life, or commit suicide long after everyone knew when they became mentally and emotionally wounded.

These men and women are, by anyone's definition, the brave, the courageous, and yes, the invisible when it comes to recognizing how profoundly these traumatic incidents impact them. But, they're not allowed to acknowledge that impact, and most would shun the coverage if given the opportunity to talk.

Blue Stigma

There's a stigma in LEO, veteran, and First Responder communities around mental health. It's a stigma that says we can't ask for help no matter how much we need it. We can't admit we're struggling, or affected, or suffering. The problem is first responders (and I include LEOs in that definition) see more trauma in one day than most people will see in an entire lifetime. Yet, for some reason it's looked upon as "weak" if we raise our hand and say "That event profoundly affected me too. I'm having panic attacks. I can't sleep. My nightmares keep me from going to bed every night."

In turn we suppress it. We bury it deep down and never let the emotions and pain surface. But it always surfaces. It surfaces in other ways—self medication, addiction, irritability, anger, domestic abuse, and the list goes on. The myth is we commit suicide because we're "weak." That's the lie.

We don't commit suicide because we are weak or afraid of "facing the music," or whatever. We don't even see killing ourselves as "suicide."

We see it as a SACRIFICE—a peaceful and triumphant end where we think we leave the world and our families in a better place without us. Call it a mental trick or whatever you like. But, PTSD plays with our minds, twisting our thinking to make us believe suicide is a good thing. Whatever it is, however it happens, it's real, and it's killing us.

That sacrifice ideation was why I was going to shoot myself. I believe it's why Brian, my good friend, partner, and the Chief of Police of my department killed himself two weeks before I wrote my own suicide note. Yes. The Chief of Police. I'll repeat it often— "No rank, no office, no service, no gender, race, or age is immune to suicide."

Brian didn't leave a note. He didn't talk to anyone. No one was privy to what was going on in his mind, but I believe, because of what I know about his situation, that Brian saw his suicide as a way to stand in the gap and protect his family from something worse than losing him. Financial or personal, or whatever was about to happen, was something he wanted to protect them from.

I have no proof of that theory. It's just the story I tell myself because it's the one I can best relate to. In the dark, twisted world I was in at the time, killing myself actually seemed like what I needed to do to keep my four sons from seeing me fail again, and lose their respect for me. Brian's death reinforced that for me.

Suicide was what I needed to do to ensure they had happier lives without me. Looking back I can see how wrong I was, but at the time it was so real to me. I thank God for the people and things that intervened and stayed my hand. Unfortunately, not every law enforcement officer, firefighter, veteran, or emergency service worker is as lucky as I was.

I do mean lucky. Police officers are at a higher risk of suicide than any other profession, and not by just a few deaths each year.

According to the Addiction Center, suicides of police officers are so high that the number of police officers who die by their own hand is *more than double and triple* that of officers who are fatally injured in the line of duty during the same time period. These are not cowardly men and women. Cops and law enforcement and emergency service workers are some of the bravest people I've met. I can't believe that they are trying to escape, or run away from something—trauma, the job, family, divorce, etc.. It goes deeper than that. They want away from the pain those things cause, but they remain devoted to helping.

Researchers are attributing these statistics to the unique combination of easy access to deadly weapons, intense stress, and human devastation that police are exposed to daily.[10]

Why are police officers at a higher risk than any other profession? There are numerous reasons, but I'm going to say a lot of it is personality. You have to care to be a good cop. Being a Type A, driven, passionate and devoted to your community kind of person is part of it. Yes, there are bad cops, and I'm sure they kill themselves too, but my experience has been that what officers who care see, experience, and deal with on a daily basis is a huge part of it. We see it all, from abused, beaten, raped kids to dead kids. We see bodies that have been dead for a while, suicides, horrific traffic accidents, domestic violence, and just plain odd, unexplainable tragedies. It takes its toll.

Policing isn't just a job. It's an identity you carry with you for life. Bound up with the trauma and depression you experience is the almost superhuman strength of the connections and bonds with your fellow officers who experience the same things.

It's who you are. Losing your job doesn't mean just moving on. You don't just lose the job. You lose your identity, your tribe, your connection, your brotherhood, your support. Losing or leaving police work is so much more than changing pay stubs. So the stress of that loss, plus the trauma you experienced, becomes a huge burden to bear.

John Violanti, a 23-year Police Veteran and a Professor at the University of Buffalo says, "*... what that (exposure to daily trauma) means*

is that the traumatic events and stressful events kind of build on one another...
If you have to put a bulletproof vest on before you go to work, that's an indica-
tion you're already under the possibility of being shot or killed. So all of these
things weigh heavily on the psyche and over time, they hurt the officers."

I agree with John. He's been there and lived it. He knows. But
I'm not going to give you a bunch of statistics and facts in this book.
I will point them out where appropriate. More than that I'm going
to tell you the story of my life, and the stories of real people, many of
them friends and colleagues of mine. They, like me, have stared
death and suicide in the face and lived to tell about it. Even as I
write this, I know of friends struggling with the urge to end it all,
but who fight it one day at a time, like I did.

The 28-year-old daughter of a colleague, a LEO, committed
suicide with a gunshot to the head just as I was finishing up the last
chapters of this book. Every day suicide claims someone and it
doesn't have to.

I'm going to tell you about things leading up to my decisions, and
share some graphic, but not gory, details of the kinds of stress officers go through—like Joe Pannulo, an officer at the Las Vegas concert
shootings in 2017.

That shooting left 59 dead and hundreds wounded. But, the
media never heard, or never shared, the story of one of the officers
who was there, and what he went through. As I mentioned earlier,
what was just as brutal as the scene at the convention center was
the scene Joe described where his wife begged him not to go.
Being off-duty and close to retirement, he briefly considered the
fact he might not come back. So did his wife. That possibility
didn't keep him from responding and turning around to go to the
shooting. He told his crying wife, "I have to go. I have to go. It's
what I do."

These are the kinds of stories more often shared during "choir
practice" than with family, friends or the media. The reason officers
rarely share with the media is because the media misses the message
—that we're strong, but we're not Superheroes. We want to shield
our families from the trauma we see. We don't want to give them any

more to worry about than they already do. They can't control what we see, or how we feel. So why burden them with the details?

And while the media has their moments, for the most part they don't understand what we do, why we do it, or how it affects us, and many don't seem to care. Is it any wonder police officers and first responders don't reach out for help? To do so would make them feel even more vulnerable than they already do.

And to those who would seek to defund the police and take us off the streets and out of their lives, I suggest you think twice. As George Orwell said, *"People sleep peacefully in their beds at night only because rough men stand ready to do violence on their behalf."*

I'm not supporting or encouraging violence to keep the peace. I am saying the average citizen is not ready, not trained, not emotionally, mentally or physically prepared to deal with the trauma, situations, violence, and people with which the police, fire, and first responders deal with daily. In some cities it's sometimes an hourly trauma.

In Chicago alone there have been 2,021 shootings so far this year (2021)—164 more than in 2020.[11] This is in a city with some of the strongest gun control laws in the country. Doctors and nurses and first responders treat these victims, but police officers respond to every incident as well. It's not just Chicago where violence runs rampant.

In June 2021, The Washington Post wrote, "New York City police reported 462 homicides last year, up from 319 the previous year. Police in Phoenix said there were 200 homicides last year, up from 139 in 2019. In Philadelphia, there were 499 homicides last year, up from 356 a year earlier, according to police."[12]

Those are just shootings. I'm not sure how to report all the incidents of child rape and abuse, sex trafficking, civilian suicide and murder, traffic accidents, and fires officers experience. If these events impact *us* as brutally as they do, and we train for years to deal with it, imagine what will happen when we're not there to be that buffer between evil and a civil society.

I'm going to tell you about one of the most dangerous contributors to police military, EMS, and firefighters' suicides. It's not the depth of evil, or the risks, or the harm we accept or deal with. It's not the gore, the trauma, or the bodies we see.

The biggest risk to any officer or responder, male or female, is the warrior culture we all both embrace and hate. It's the culture of "manliness." It's a culture that tells society that strong men, strong women, or "heroes" don't feel pain, fear, or doubt. We're so busy being brave, being there for others, that the fact we're human too gets lost in the narrative. It doesn't matter if you're male or female, it affects you. I'm writing this as a male to a predominantly male occupation, but women in these professions are impacted as well.

Don't take my word for it. According to Statisa, the folks who track the statistics of practically everything in the world, said, "In 2019, 67.1 percent of full-time *civilian law enforcement* employees [administrative staff, etc.] in the United States were female. But only 12.8 percent of *full-time law enforcement officers were female*, while 87.2 percent of law enforcement officers were male."[13] If you're one of that 12.8 percent I respect you more than you might imagine. I'm not slighting your role or experiences. You're just as critical as the men, there just aren't enough statistics or events I could find to share. What I did find was that male or female, we're all susceptible to the stress of the job.

According to the COPS *Law Enforcement Officer Suicide 2020 REPORT TO CONGRESS*, "...negative stress has a clear damaging effect on law enforcement officers. Studies on first responders in a variety of fields have shown that frequent requirements for overtime work, shift work, night work, and working conditions that are physically challenging or dangerous all increase the risk of damaging effects on first responders' physical bodies and mental health and wellness."[14]

As I talk to officers across the country I keep hearing that "Civilians and cops alike believe a "real" cop, or firefighter, or EMS responder, or Emergency Room doctor, or nurse would never feel or think about suicide, let alone carry through with it. They care too much about their jobs."

Just the opposite is true. We're in our professions because we do care about our communities, our job, and our duty. And, most of us care very much. So it does affect us when we see the trauma, the loss, and the deaths and the things we see everyday.

My story is unlike most, but very much like many. Most law enforcement officers (LEO) I know, or have met, have come from humble circumstances, or poverty themselves. They have decided to help their communities by being officers, deputies, first responders, firemen, EMTs, and serving in law enforcement in some way. They're not out to make a fortune—that's impossible to do in this field (legally anyway).

Most of the men and women I know and have worked with during my career tend to be Type A, Alpha male or female over-achievers. Then there are those people I call "RODS" (Retired On Duty) who are just putting in their time until they actually retire. But, I believe the majority of LEOs, and emergency responders, are people dedicated to the care and protection of their communities, families, and society.

They put themselves in harm's way and all they want is the same respect and treatment they give those in their care. That's why I'm writing this book. I want them, and society to know we care and care deeply for them and appreciate their service. But sometimes we need to care for ourselves as much as we care for our communities.

Why this book? Why now? Because change doesn't happen until people speak up, take action, and work for something different. If you're a law enforcement officer, fireman/woman, first responder, veteran, or in any way employed with an agency tasked with protecting your community or country, you deserve a more compas-sionate, realistic approach to mental health. I hope this book fans the flames of the agencies and organizations who are already looking into how to get us the mental health we deserve and need, while letting us keep our careers.

CHAPTER ONE

Closer to Midnight

"Who you're to be, you're now becoming."

I n both the civil and uncivilized world, anywhere there is a
clock or a watch, midnight marks the beginning and ending of
the day. Midnight traditionally signals the ending of one day,
and the beginning of another. It's associated with the hour 00:00.

Symbolically, if you're into those things (and I am), it means
you're leaving behind all the crap, the pain, the losses and failures of
one day, and greeting the possibilities and potential of the next day.
It's why every country in the world gathers to watch the ball drop or
celebrate midnight on New Year's Eve every year. New beginnings.

In a way it's a cleansing, a clean slate. Out with the old, in with
the new. Only in 2017, there wasn't going to be anything new for me.
Just the cleansing. Just O-dark 00:00, the click of the trigger of my
Glock, a muffled boom inside my Yukon, and then peace. Blessed,
blessed peace...

I put a lot of thought into the time and place where I planned to
kill myself, and how, and what I would tell my four sons in my suicide
note. I convinced myself that my suicide would be the best damn
thing to happen to all of us—including me, my ex-wife, my boys, and

my friends and family. I'm responsible that way—making sure everyone else was taken care of first. It's what I based my whole life on—being the best, doing the best, achieving the most I could with what I had.

I was a good father, a great provider, a solid, if overachieving cop, a great undercover guy, a great friend, a Navy SAR swimmer. I'd been a good friend to many, an athlete, a husband, but it wasn't enough.

On paper I had it all. In reality I had a loaded gun in my mouth and was counting down the last few hours of my life. Go figure.

All the way to the instant I died I was going to do the right thing. And I did. What I didn't count on was my best laid plans being interrupted by a force greater than my depression—a call from a friend, and a cold beer, a sympathetic ear. The light at the end of the tunnel began to look like hope, not an oncoming train.

Okay, that's where I was. But with all that I had going for me, how did I get to a point where I wanted to kill myself? A lot of guys, and women too, ask themselves the same question, "Wouldn't everyone, including me, be better off with me dead?

You may be one of the people who's asking yourself that now. Or, you've asked it in the past. Here's the answer. "No. No one is better off with you dead. No one."

Your story may parallel mine more than you know. Suicide is like that. It doesn't matter how great you are at anything you do. It doesn't care how good looking, talented, gifted, rich, or poor you are. It's all about the mental and emotional pain, the twisting, stabbing, searing pain you can't escape.

It's the pain that taps you on the heart, before taking you to your knees. I could deal with the physical pain. Hell. I was a Navy Search and Rescue Swimmer. I was one of the 19 out of a class of 80 who finished the physically brutal SARs course. I *know* physical pain.

After getting "kissed" hard by a car in 2015, I had a complete hip replacement in 2019. I was back on my physical routine, walking and running within a month. Doctors said the surgery would end my lacrosse playing. Nope. It improved it.

Physical pain? I got it covered. It's the mental and emotional pain that kicks your ass. Most officers would agree. Like the t-shirt says, "Physical pain is weakness leaving the body." Most of us can handle the physical demands.

I'm not talking about physical pain. You can heal from that. There's a pain that goes deeper and is sharper than anyone can fathom if they haven't felt it. It burrows into your heart like a hot lead spark and keeps smoldering until you can't stand it anymore. You can't drug it, drink it, sex it, or sleep it away. It lingers, flaming into fire when you least expect it. It might be a sound, a smell, a song, or even the way someone moves past you that triggers it. Then it's off to the races until you can distract yourself, or pass out from alcohol or drugs long enough to quiet the sound, the smell, the screams, the tears.

That secret pain no one else sees is why you hear people talking about suicides after the fact and saying things like, "But he had such a good life. No one saw it coming. Why would someone who had all *that* (fill in "that" with all the shiny, wonderful things like money, family, talent, accomplishments, awards, kids, potential and a great job etc. here) do that? Why didn't he reach out to someone? Why didn't he *say* something?"

I'll tell you why the cops who kill themselves don't say anything. That's the easy answer—Warrior culture. Because in the world I live in, the world that most law enforcement, military, emergency responders, doctors, medics, and special forces men and women live in, being mentally and emotionally weak, isn't an option. We don't get to say "No, that's too stressful." We're the ones people assume have all that emotional stuff under control.

We're not exactly what anyone would call weak to begin with before the academy we choose to attend. Police culture, first responder, firefighting culture, military culture — you name it. Whether you're male or female the culture is hypermasculine. The warrior culture is the hyper-testosterone culture. Responder culture is about strength and the warrior mentality on every level.

Remember the scene where Jack Nicholson is screaming, "You can't handle the truth!" at Tom Cruise in the movie *A Few Good Men*?

He gives this little speech where he talks about the men who stand guard on a dangerous wall while America sleeps peacefully, unaware of the cost of freedom and peace. I guarantee you every veteran in the audience is cheering, silently or not when they watch that movie. We get it. That's warrior culture.

I spent six years in the Navy as a SAR swimmer. If you haven't watched or heard about what military applicants to the various special forces go through, let me assure you it's absolute, total hell. You don't make it through special forces training if you're not one mentally tough SOB.

SAR Training has a 50 percent drop-out rate, and in my class there was an 80 percent drop out rate. You do not graduate if you are not made of some of the toughest stuff on the planet and chew nails like they're french fries.

When you enter SAR training you have to dig deeper than 99% of people ever do to find the mental and physical support that's going to keep you going through graduation. It's not just one week at the end of training that's "a crucible." Every day is a crucible.

All the instructors there *want* you to fail. It is their job to do their best to break you, and make you quit in training so you never quit on the job.

They're very good at making people quit. The attrition rate alone is proof positive they know what they're doing and they do it well.

What you learn at SAR, among the swimming and physical aspects of rescue swimming, is that it's okay to fail, in fact they encourage it at times. But it's *not* okay to break. Failing is just learning your limits and what you can and can't do. As long as you get back up it's part of the process.

Breaking is quitting and there is no room for quitters. There are no "safe" rooms in SAR where you can escape the stress and demands placed on you 24/7. You have you, your mental, physical, and emotional resilience, and your wits. If you "escape" anywhere during SARS, it is inside your head.

You learn your survival depends on being part of a band of brothers, of knowing and adhering to those brothers. Survival depends on not being last, of being able to consistently make the last hundred yards in any exercise, and to be and do more than you ever thought was possible. You have or have to develop the mental toughness to get through it, or you don't, and you drop out.

SAR, and all special forces, whether it's SEAL or DELTA training, or Army Rangers, your training comes down to two things: mental resilience and not ringing the bell signifying that you're quitting. Those two skill sets would later segue into my civilian life. Those two lessons were how I learned to take everything day by day. This mentality would eventually almost cost me my life, but it would also save my life.

That world, SAR, police work, the military, and undercover work...is a culture where it's not okay to have "issues."

It's not okay to hurt, feel lost, or scared. And if you do, you damn well keep it to yourself if you want to continue to be part of that culture. It's a tradeoff. The adrenaline high, knowing you're saving lives, protecting your community, being a hero, being part of a very male, very alpha, type A culture surrounded by other very male, very alpha, very strong brothers and sisters, is intoxicating. Making a difference, busting bad guys, it's a rush. Damn, it's such a rush. There is no higher high than adrenaline. But it comes with an insanely high price tag. Some of us pay it with our lives and at our own hands.

The high price for being a member of any special forces unit is often the ultimate one—suicide. You'd think we'd be better equipped to handle trauma because of our training, but that's a myth—a myth even the experts were shocked to discover.

The U.S. Special Operations Command (SOCOM) commissioned the American Association of Suicidology, one of the country's oldest suicide prevention organizations, to conduct a study of the United States most elite military forces. Until *The New York Times* invoked the Freedom of Information Act (FOIA) to get a copy of the results, the findings of this study had never been released to the public until June 2020.[1]

The study concluded in 2017, around the time I might have been one of their statistics. According to *The New York Times*, "The 46-

page report aggregates the findings of 29 'psychological autopsies' — detailed interviews with 81 next-of-kin and close friends of commandos who killed themselves between 2012 and 2015.

The *New York Times* article captured what I want to say in this book when they quoted an unnamed casualty who said,

"The job I love and have committed my whole being to is creating my suicidal condition, but I'd rather die than admit to having trouble and being removed from my unit and my team," he said often, according to someone close to him."[2]

The study acknowledged what anyone in police work already knows, that education regarding mental health and suicide is just a "check in the box." We all get the training, we all know the signs, and "the drill," and we all ignore it. It's just one more stage of training we "check off" in the box of official classes we complete.

All the suicides listed in the study had the required mental health training. They all knew what to do, but no one was going to do it. The reality is, leaders encouraging troops to seek help were seen as disingenuous. "He saw that individuals who shared having suicidal ideations were escorted like a criminal for evaluation," someone close to a S.O.F. member recalled.[3]

I'm praying that anyone reading this book doesn't just blow off my advice to get help for that very reason—the promises and reassurances supervisors and others offer are rarely genuine. They can be. There are departments out there who "get it," and others who are starting to "get it," about mental health and the need for it. In the meantime, I'm saying, your life is more important. You, your family, your loved ones, are more important than a job that pushes you into suicide.

Everybody loves it when we run into a shooting, or a burning building, or a drug house, or into harm's way. They love the television shows, the drama, the tension, the way we overcome incredible odds to save the day, or the moment. The media loves the photographs of police and firefighters, and men and women in uniform "saving a child" or carrying a victim away from danger. They win awards with those photos. They sway communities with those photographs.

What's not to love? We love saving people. It's what we do, what we want to do, and what most of us signed up for.

Everyone loves the depictions of us as heroes and saviors. So do we. It's a rush. The adrenaline high when you save a life, or you're the hero, can't be matched. And the low you feel when you can't, or don't save a life, or are pressured to keep it all inside is just as, if not more, intense.

People (including first responders and LEO supervisors) don't love it when you tell them that sitting next to the body of your first suicide or murder or accident victim is giving you cold sweats and nightmares. They're uncomfortable when they hear that what you saw on your last call is making you dread every time another death call comes over the radio.

They don't want to know that you, their hero, their officer, are scared, depressed and cracking under the strain of PTSD. If you're scared, then they wonder what happens to them if you've got a crack in your armor, or worse. The "don't break, don't fail" mentality isn't overtly taught. It's something you pick up as you go along.

In the academy or SARs school you're literally taught one thing about how to do your job. On the job, you learn the real way to do your job. You learn the sudden cold indifference when someone mentions they're struggling. You may feel the same way, but you don't talk about it. It's one of those unwritten rules. You both suck it up, joke about it and move along. Look the other way, have a cold one and choke it down.

It's not just civilians, our families, and our buddies that ignore the fact we're human. It's our chiefs, officers, supervisors, police unions and agency therapists. It's the men and women in control of the boots on the ground that don't take the mental health of their officers seriously. They don't want to hear you're struggling.

They say they do, but they don't. They may want to take it seriously, but they aren't trained to deal with it and they don't want to deal with it.

If they acknowledge their officers have mental health issues, or are struggling emotionally, or turning to substance abuse, that would mean admitting they might feel the need to do the same or they already have.

If they do listen, they nod like they "get it." They appear to understand you and your pain. They may share a time when they struggled just to show you they understand what you're going through. You begin to relax, to feel relief, maybe even open up a bit more because you're feeling safe. After all, they're part of the thin blue line too. They're making all the right noises and promises, putting a strong hand on your shoulder, and saying the things you hoped they would say. Maybe you were wrong. They do understand. They tell you it's okay. You relax. It's going to be okay.

Then one shift you're suddenly pulled off the streets, your gun and badge are taken away and you're put on paid leave. Or you find yourself driving a desk or on "light duty" for the rest of your career. So much for trusting anyone. You've just been thrown under the bus.

Once you have openly acknowledged your struggles, and your "weakness" gets out, you lose touch with your brothers and sisters on the force. An invisible wall goes up. Overnight you're poison, an "untouchable." You get looks of disgust or pity. You're gossiped about, talked about, shunned or avoided. Everything you hold dear and sacred is gone, or fading fast. The men and women you called your best friends, the ones who "had your back no matter what," all disappear.

We've seen it happen to others. No one wants to see it happen to them. The thought of it happening to you is so bad it drives hundreds to kill themselves rather than go through that kind of loss, humiliation, and emasculation.

When you admit to anyone other than the voices in your head that you're having troubles coping with the stress of the job, with your marriage, with your finances, with your health—your career's end is near. You're not allowed to treat your pain like a civilian, with the use of prescribed pain killers, or with anything any normal person can openly and freely admit to (like therapy or counseling). You're no longer a human being with a pain to be addressed. You're a departmental liability.

That's a key reason why in 2019, 228 American police officers died by suicide. That's almost twice the number (129) of officers who were killed in the line of duty the same year. News articles and books will tell you officers get up every day and strap on their vests and guns and wonder if they'll be killed in the line of duty. No one talks about the officers who get up and wonder, as I did, if today will be the day they kill themselves.

Suicide is the number one killer of police and military—both active and retired. According to a Pentagon medical statistical analysis journal, between 2004 and 2011, war was the leading cause of death in the military until suicides surpassed dying in battle.[4]

Between 2012 and 2013, suicide became the top means of dying for troops. According to an article in the *Military Times*, four times as many troops and vets have died by suicide than in combat.[5] in 2012 and 2013 suicide accounted for more deaths than war, cancer, heart disease, homicide, transportation accidents and other causes, making suicide responsible for three in 10 military deaths both years.

Per researchers' estimates, "30,177 Global War on Terror veterans have died by suicide, compared to 7,057 who have died while deployed in support of the Global War on Terror."[6]

According to Pentagon data, more than 6,800 troops have died in Iraq and Afghanistan since 9/11. More than 3,000 additional service members have taken their lives in that same time.[7]

In 2019, the suicide rate in the Active Component was 25.9 suicide deaths per 100,000 Service members. Across the Military Services, suicide rates ranged from 21.5 to 29.8 per 100,000 Active Component Service members. I don't have to tell you that there's something seriously wrong if the strongest, bravest, most focused men and women in the world are killing themselves at a greater rate than combat.

To be a man, or a hero, or a someone that society, family and friends expects to be forever strong, in control, and fearless without being able to admit you're scared, uncertain, tired, lonely, hurting, doubting or lost is a recipe for suicide. I had all the ingredients, but thankfully, never "baked the cake," never pulled the trigger.

The stresses that lead to suicide rarely hit you all at once. You don't wake up one day happy and the next day you're suicidal. The stresses and demands creep up on you and you don't see them coming until the last thing piles on and breaks that proverbial straw, and you snap.

Admitting you're struggling means admitting you can't cope, or you're "not worthy" in so many ways. So you learn to keep your mouth shut until you can't do it anymore. You smile. When, or if, someone notices and says, "You okay?" you nod and say, "I'm good brother. I'm good." I know that's how it happens because I said it myself.

The day was March 9, 2017, my wedding anniversary, or what would have been, should have been a day for celebration. Instead, it was only a painful reminder I was divorced. I hated being reminded I was single. I hated the day. It was hard, but being at work made it easier. At least it did until Brian, my Chief, my friend, mentor, and my partner brought it up.

"You know what day it is. If you can't work it I can comp you out," he said. And I told him, "No, I'm good brother. I'm good." No matter what I was really feeling, copping to the pain and taking the day off wasn't who I was. And maybe Brian knew that, or maybe he didn't. But he didn't push it. He was, "Okay. let me know." And then I went on shift, and he went home two hours later after that exact conversation and killed himself. I didn't get it. Yet, on March 17, only a couple of weeks later, I was about to follow in his footsteps.

I can't tell you why Brian asked me if I was okay. He knew it was my wedding anniversary and how painful my divorce was. But there was something more in his question, maybe a hope I'd open up, and he could open up, and we could have an honest conversation. Or maybe that's my pain and regret talking. I'll never know. Why?

Because, like me, like everyone else, Brian never shared his pain. I don't know why, but I think I do. In the midst of my pain I didn't recognize his pain. He saw something in me and asked me how I was out of genuine concern, but even with my best friend, I knew the drill. Even when people you trust ask if you're okay, you deny the pain. If you talk, you risk being put on the sidelines. That's how the game is played across the country in all kinds of departments. It's why so many officers, firefighters, and veterans are taking their lives. So I denied my best friend the biggest truth of my life, my pain, and we never got to have the difficult conversation that might have saved his life.

In hindsight I understand some of what happened to Brian, and a lot of what happened to me several weeks later. It wasn't one thing that tripped the depression. There were a lot of things. It was the perfect storm of feeling that I was alone, with no one to talk with, combined with my sense of failure from my divorce, from the job, and more.

It was my wife hitting the end of her tolerance of my being gone all the time because of my undercover work. I was rarely home. I was out saving the world—or so I thought at the time. How could she not support me being a hero? It was my failure to see her side of the marriage and understand what she was experiencing that led to our divorce. I was so caught up in saving everyone else I didn't stop to think about saving us, and our marriage. When the divorce was finally a reality it hit me like a battering ram to the chest.

I was depressed, but I was also angry about the fact that we weren't going to be married anymore. And, there I was, pouring my life into trying to save other people and all I could see was that she was down on me for not being home more often and that the community was down on me for not working more.

I thought I was protecting the community by being available to my job 24/7, and doing everything I could to protect those I loved. It never occurred to me that when I was headed home for date night, and got a call to go somewhere for the job that I was sending my wife the wrong message—the message she didn't matter as much as the job. When I sat down to dinner at a restaurant and laid out four cell phones and monitored them during dinner with my wife, I didn't think it was odd. You get the picture. I was really married to the job and what I thought I was doing to save my community. I didn't see where I was pushing my wife and family aside, but Kendra did.

I never saw what she needed. So I never imagined being divorced when that situation came to a head. That was the toughest thing. My wife and I were together for 15 years, we had four boys, and so I was angry about the situation we were in, and I was angry about the divorce, and I was angry at myself for misreading everything.

I believed I had a talent for communication, but the one place where communication mattered most, I was blind. Because I thought I was doing a good thing, I didn't see the bad thing coming. I take a lot of responsibility for the divorce because I felt I was doing something we were both behind and supporting. I learned I had the talent to be skilled in undercover work. I realized I could talk to everybody from a CEO to a janitor. I could connect with them and make them feel like they wanted to be around me. It's what growing up in the projects, in poverty, and then later in a privileged high school where I was surrounded by celebrities' kids, and CEO's kids did for me. It developed that gift and I kept it polished.

I was bi-lingual in that I grew up in both worlds, the world of gangs, the ghetto and elite private schools. I was beaten up by MS 13 in a gang initiation to "fit in." It wasn't pretend for me. It was my life. I lived it before I worked it.

Undercover life found me. So, it was destiny, a calling I thought. Fresh out of the police academy I was working patrol. I was newly released from my field training, when my sergeant and I made a traffic stop. He was talking to the driver when I noticed several half straws in a cup in the center console of the car.

I told my sergeant to have the driver get out of the car.

"Why?" he asked.

"Trust me," I said. What I knew from my upbringing at the private high school was that rich kids didn't carry cash. Because they didn't have a dollar or a hundred dollar bill to roll to use for their drugs they'd grab straws from McDonalds, or Burger King and shove them into the center console. When they need to bump a line of coke they'd cut the straw in half. My sergeant got the driver out of the car and we found he had a gram or two of coke on him. My sergeant was amazed and asked how I knew he had coke on him.

"It's how I grew up," I said. I told him the short version of my story and that one small incident made a big impact in my future. That sergeant helped me get into undercover work as a result of that stop. See? Destiny. I was born to go undercover.

Seriously though, the world of privilege and wealth isn't so different from a lot of what you see in a ghetto. It's just another, richer culture, different rules, names and faces, more expensive clothes and rides, but it's still a culture. My early life in the ghetto, and a later life among the rich and privileged served me well in police undercover work. I'd lived that gang life, that drug life and that privileged life. I was the real deal. I wasn't taught it in some police undercover classes. It was part of me from the inside out.

I could draw on my real life experience, language, body language, you name it when I went undercover. It came naturally.

There was the ghetto, and there was that "winning the educational/sports lottery" thing— a $65,000 a year lacrosse scholarship to Morristown-Beard, an independent, very upper class high school in northern New Jersey. Thanks to Finn Wentworth, the man who sponsored my scholarship, I went from living the ghetto life to living the rich kid's life and it all happened because in high school I happened to be good at sports, and particularly good at lacrosse. No wait, I happened to be really, really, really good at lacrosse.

Along with a handful of other really good scholarship lacrosse players I helped the school produce a much better lacrosse team. Lacrosse became my ticket to a life I would have never known otherwise.

My experiences and friendships at Morristown-Beard taught me how to live and survive in a world where money, power, prestige, and the right credentials mattered. I learned the power side of networking. I got to see, live, and experience the best and worst of both worlds, but even that didn't prepare me for the journey to midnight I would take towards the edge of life in 2017.

Looking back, I can see that, according to the Ruderman Family Foundation that Brian was one of 140 police officers who died by suicide in 2017, compared to 129 officers who died in the line-of-duty that year. [8] After what happened with Benny, I could have been number 141.

Benny

If only I'd gotten there faster. If only I'd responded quicker, done more, done something different. If only. If you've been in a similar situation, you know the drill. You ask every question, agonize over everything you did, said, thought, or could have done differently. And no matter how many times you replay it in your head, nothing changes. The victim is still dead. The pain remains.

It was Christmas Eve and I was working surveillance. I was driving along Hampshire Lane in Virginia Beach and I saw Dave, an old Navy buddy, outside in his front yard. I pulled over and said, "Man, how are you? It's been a long time." And he said, "I'm doing great, man. Hey, meet Brittany and Ben junior."

So, I spent about a half hour, 45 minutes with them reminiscing about the Navy, and catching up on what we'd been doing, and playing with Benny.

Then he said, "Hey, if you're working tomorrow, on Christmas, I've got family coming over, we've got a huge spread, a ton of food, come over and grab a plate."

I said, "Dave, I really appreciate that. That'd be awesome."

Christmas comes the next day and I'm in the same area over by Hampshire lane, an area called Lake Edwards. It was a division of Virginia Beach, in the third precinct. It's a low income section; a section eight housing area. After I finished there, I popped over to Dave and Brittany's and grabbed a plate of food. I met the family and Karen, Brittany's mom. I'd met Benny—Ben junior, the day before. So when I saw him in the kitchen, up on a little step stool he said, "Mr. Matt, you gotta look at my cookies."

I went over to him, gave him a hug and looked at the Christmas cookies he was decorating. I started talking to him. I told him about his dad and me in the Navy. He was only two and a half or three years old at the time so it was just a kid talk and hugs and cookies kind of bonding. We had a great time, and I had some food and said "Hi," to everybody. It was a nice way to take a break on Christmas Day. I ate, then went back on shift.

A week later, on New year's Eve, I drew the short straw again because I was one of the younger new guys, and I was working again. Same precinct, same area—literally just around the corner from Dave and his family, maybe 15, 20 seconds away from Hampshire lane.

I was sitting there writing plates. I remember thinking, "this really sucks." But at the same time, I was like, "whatever, I'll get done with this. I'll still have New Year's Eve to go out." I was still young and I wanted to go out and party a little.

About five-thirty, maybe six o'clock, the call came over the radio. I don't remember the exact time, but I remember the call like it was yesterday. The call was for units to respond to 767 Hampshire lane for a two-and-a-half year-old, code gray.

I remember sitting in the car and saying, "Wow, that's a shitty call for New Year's Eve." A code gray means that the person is unconscious and not breathing. And I remember thinking, "I've had nightmares about something like that happening," and saying to myself, "I'm so glad that that's not my call."

Thirty seconds goes by, 45 seconds go by. I'm still sitting there, listening to the responding officers and the radio traffic. All of a sudden the numbers just click in my head. Holy crap, 767 Hampshire Lane—that's Brittany and Dave's address! That code grey is Benny. I couldn't get moving fast enough. I sped over, pulled right up on the front lawn, almost took the mailbox out coming in, and went running inside before my car's engine stopped spinning. I was slow, but I was still the first one there.

I got inside and Brittany was screaming, just screaming at the top of her lungs. She was holding her six-month old baby at the time. She was just screaming. And as soon as she saw me, she started screaming, "Matt, Matt, Matt!"

"Where is he? Where is he?" She stopped screaming my name long enough to say, "In there."

I rushed into the room and Benny was just hanging there. Brittany had taken the baby into the shower and put on Willy Wonka's Chocolate Factory for Benny to watch. While she was in the shower Benny had climbed up on the window sill. He wanted to swing from the window onto the dresser. He used the blind chord and it caught him right around the neck. I took him down and started doing CPR. I remember him taking his last breath in my mouth. I don't remember anything else because, I'm like, "Okay. He's going to be okay." I got in my head he was going to be okay.

"He's got a breath, he's got a breath, he's got to pull out of it, like, he's going to be okay." He exhaled into my mouth, and then he didn't take another breath. That was Benny's last breath. I carry that breath with me everyday, and have never taken another one for granted.

The fire department showed up maybe 10 seconds after that. I was still doing CPR, so they took over, and I fell back. Brittany was still screaming. I looked up on the wall by the window and I saw the scratch marks where Benny was trying to get down and he couldn't get down. I thought about the panic he must have felt, the fear. Those scratch marks were the source of my nightmares for many years to come.

I remember just sitting there, numb. Then I was helping Brittany, I was helping the paramedics get them both up on the stretcher. And as we took them out of the house, Britney was still screaming. She's screaming for herself, for Benny, and for me because I can't scream even though I want to. I just met him, just hugged him the week before and we were talking about Christmas cookies. And now he's gone.

As the ambulance is loading up the stretcher two young Mormons on bikes came up. They ask, "Can we help? Can we pray for you?"

Brittany had just started to calm down, but she started screaming again at the boys' request, "Pray for my firecracker, pray for my firecracker, save my firecracker."

I didn't know what she meant until later, but then I found out

Benny was born on July 4th, so she always called him her "little fire-cracker." My heart broke again when I learned that, and then it shattered completely when Benny was pronounced dead on the way to the Virginia Beach General Hospital.

We got there, he was placed in a bed, and Brittany climbed up next to him. I went in the room and I was just kind of combing through his hair and holding Brittany's hand. She started singing to him, and then we were both singing to him and petting him, just running our fingers through his hair, trying to take it in that he was gone.

I just remember touching his cold little head and thinking, I can't believe this is happening. The homicide detective, an older, rough-and-tough-seen-it-all type I'd never met before, showed up and said, "You guys need to get outta here."

I said, "We're not leaving."

He looked at me and said, "Then you need to get the mother out of the room. That's a homicide."

I said, "I'm not doing that."

"Well, if you don't do it, I'm doing it."

"You mean, you're going to go through me first?" I stood straight up and stared at him, daring him to try.

He looked at the fact I was a good foot, maybe a foot and a half taller than he was, and that I had more muscle in my biceps than he had in his entire body, and he reconsidered his options.

"You don't know what you're doing," he said, backing away.

"I know exactly what I'm doing." I was letting this grieving mother lay beside her dead son, her two-and-half-year-old son, her first-born, and hold him one last time while she had him there, while his little body was still warm and pliable and as close to life as it would ever be.

After the detective backed off a Lieutenant came over and pulled me aside. It was his turn to take a crack at me.

"Griff, you gotta let this go. You gotta move to the side and let this go."

"I'm not letting this go. Mama just lost her two and a half year old son. Her husband is at sea and is on his way back. She's all alone. Just give her some time with her boy."

Why five minutes or an hour makes a difference in a case like this, I don't understand. Why the rush? It was clearly an accident. I wondered how they would have reacted had it been their son on the bed.

I held it all together, ever the strong cop, for Brittany and the detectives. But when I went home that night I just cried and cried. I remember I couldn't shake the feeling that something was terribly wrong if God would allow this to happen to a child. It didn't make any sense. I get that we live in a fallen world and I get faith and I get, you know, everything else. But, I was still asking, how is this possible? How am I going to believe in a God that does nothing and lets a two-and-a-half year old hang himself from a blind cord?

Dave was at sea. The Navy had to fly him in, so he wasn't able to get home until about two days later. Every day, for the next week or so, Brittany wanted me around her. The family put a lot on me during that initial week. They wanted me at the funeral home. They wanted me at the wake. They wanted me to be at the autopsy. They wanted me to help dress Benny for the funeral.

I was their friend, but in that situation I was the cop first. I was supposed to be their foundation, no cracks, no loss of emotional control, no screaming at God. I had to be the rock they clung to. They needed me and I made sure they had me.

I didn't mind being there, but I wondered every day how long it would take for me to crumble and lose it in public like they were.

Brittany just wanted to hold my hand. She just wanted to be heard and held. But it wasn't just Brittany. When Dave got there, he needed the same thing. They were both wrecks, like children themselves needing to be protected and consoled. And then there I was, a brave face for public moments, for consoling, for doing what needed to be done, but crying myself to sleep at night and needing emotional support myself. Only, there was no one for me at night when I was hurting. It was up to me to stuff all those emotions down and be strong for everyone else. I still knew and followed the chill drill.

Then, during the funeral service Benny's grandfather got up with a guitar and started singing.

He didn't have the best voice, kinda raspy, but it was just so powerful. The service was at night, so the song was the lullaby that he or Brittany would sing to Benny every night before Benny went to bed, the last thing he heard before sleeping.

The song is just ingrained in my head and always will be—*Tears in Heaven*. In case you're not familiar with the song, it's a ballad Eric Clapton and Will Jennings wrote about the pain Clapton felt following the death of *his* four-year-old son, Conor, who fell from a fifty-three story window of his mother's friend.

The flyer at Benny's funeral had a picture of Benny in his Spiderman costume. That photo would also be part of the nightmares I had for the next three to five years.

From Brittany screaming, "Save my firecracker!" and me not responding to the first initial call, to the scratch marks on the wall and Benny in his Spiderman costume, I was a wreck. What if I had gotten there 30 seconds or a minute earlier? Why were they looking to me for comfort when I might have saved Benny if I'd responded as soon as I heard the call? Why, why? The questions and the guilt and the second-guessing didn't stop.

I thought they were going to be mad at me, so furious with me because I didn't respond fast enough. But they weren't. If anyone was going to beat me up, it would be me.

It took me a long time to make peace with the decision I made not to respond immediately. I struggled with a lot of things during that time. I struggled with my decision, I struggled with Benny's death, and I struggled with my faith.

I took two weeks off from work. I never left the room I had in a house in Chesapeake, Virginia overlooking the golf course. My second bedroom was kind of like an office and I just sat there and I just lived out of the office. There was a lot of music and a lot of tears, but I decided at that moment that I wasn't going to go to church in the morning. I wasn't going to pray anymore. I wasn't going to do the Sunday thing anymore unless I believed in God, and at that moment, I didn't. And, I didn't know if I ever would again.

He'd given me a home run I prayed for so many years ago as a child, but He couldn't save Benny? That wasn't the kind of God I wanted anything to do with. Yet, some part of me kept questioning, "Is God real?" Some part of my heart knew something some part of my brain didn't, and it wouldn't let me walk away.

The way I go about things like asking, "Why would God allow this?" was to look at it objectively. I'm a cop, right? I'm a detective. I'm an investigator. So let's, let's investigate. I found this book called *More Than a Carpenter* by James McDonnell. It was only about a hundred pages long. I said, okay, this is it, right. I'm going to go on this journey and decide whether or not there's a guy named Jesus Christ and is he who he says he is? Because if there's not a God I'm not going to go to church and I'm not going to continue to be fake.

It was a really powerful time in my life because I was able to kind of make peace with the things that I saw on the job. And, and one of the things I say in my speeches to the police officers, military people, and paramedics is that you're going to see more trauma in one day than the average person is going to see in a lifetime. And the images from that trauma are going to be ingrained into your head, burned on your retinas. Like I said in my prologue, you can't unsee those things.

It happens to us all. Some of us are more resilient. Some of us can bury things deeper. Some can put it aside, not carry it home. But no matter what you do, the job will affect you. It's up to you to find a way to cope, to debrief, to unwind, to not let it eat you up. I rediscovered my boyhood faith in God. He gave me the peace I needed to believe that everything, even death, tragedy and trauma, happens for a reason. I may not know that reason on this side of heaven, but I trust I'll learn it on the other side whenever that happens.

I interviewed dozens of officers, male and female, for this book. When I was talking to Ramon Batista, a police chief from Arizona, about it, and we were talking about trauma, he said, "Matt, I still remember my first dead body." I said, "I know, we all do. You can smell it. You can taste it. And you can put yourself right back in the situation like it was yesterday."

I'm telling you right now, there's got to be an outlet for it, and for me that outlet is God. I feel bad for officers that don't have a personal belief or faith in God. How do you rationalize or justify what you're seeing and experiencing every day if you don't believe we're here by intelligent design and purpose? How do you rationalize that this world is so random? One minute you're watching Willie Wonka's Chocolate Factory, the next minute you're hanging from a blind cord with your mother screaming over your body.

One minute you're at work, texting your significant other that you're going to be home in 15 minutes for dinner. And in the next three minutes you're in a head on head collision and you're gone, dead.

How do you rationalize the randomness of life if you don't believe in God? How do you make sense of how quick and how short things can be? Because if you really start to think about it, if there isn't somebody there, if there isn't a higher power controlling all this, you'd go crazy. I would. I almost did.

If there is no God, no design, no reason or rhyme, then it's all random crap, and the next thing you know, you're six feet under the ground.

After I went through that painful line of thinking, I wanted more answers. Books weren't enough for me. And so I decided that I was going to attend Lancaster Bible College. I wasn't your typical Bible college student—already having faith in God and going to a Bible college to become more ingrained in my faith in God. I was a doubting Thomas—needing to see and experience proof God was real. Don't just tell me. Show me you're real, I told God. Let me put my hands in the hole in your side. It has to be real, not just BS.

I was that angry, confused kid in class that was constantly asking questions. I didn't blindly accept anything anyone told me.

"So you want me to believe such and such? Tell me why. Convince me." That was my somewhat hostile response to my professors.

The instructors were getting as upset with me as I was with them. I sat back and remembered Benny's breath in my mouth and Brittany screaming, and the scratches on the wall, and hitting the home run I prayed God to give me in the eighth grade.

I remembered sitting next to the body of a guy who just shot himself in the head in front of me as I lunged for his weapon. I remembered the blood splatters, the brains, the tears, the deaths, the ruined lives. It all came rushing back to me and I told my professors, "This is why we're learning, right? If you can't convince me, someone who is seeking God and wanting to believe what you're telling me, how do you believe it yourself?"

Finally, one of the instructors pulled me aside after one of these conversations in class and asked me, "Do you know what grace means Matt?"

"No."

"What's your definition of grace then?"

"I don't know. I never really thought about it."

He paused for a second and then he said, "Grace is undeserved acceptance."

I remember how powerful that was. Undeserved acceptance.

He said, "Two words, that's what grace is. You are a sinful person, I'm a sinful person. We're all sinners, right? We all make mistakes. You made a mistake with Benny."

In my head, I agreed. Even as he was saying that, I was thinking, "I made a mistake with Ben Jr."

He kept going.

"I've made a lot of mistakes in my life. That's what God's all about. Undeserved acceptance."

I think that was powerful for me to understand that it's okay to make mistakes, even mistakes where someone dies, even if that someone is only two-and-a-half-years old—an innocent. No matter what, God is okay with you. He's okay with your sins. He traded his "son's life" for your sins, for the undeserved acceptance we accept when we believe in Him.

That one conversation had a huge impact on my life. What my

professor did when he told me that is something called *apologetics*. Apologetics is arguing the case for your faith.

That's all it took. I became very passionate about apologetics. I became very passionate about building the case for Jesus Christ walking this earth. I became very passionate about my faith. The door had opened and a light shone through. I finally got it.

Even people that aren't faithful, aren't spiritual, aren't religious, but who are educated, understand that a real person named Jesus Christ walked this planet 2,000 years ago. Whether you believe he was the son of God or not there's overwhelming evidence for the case that Jesus walked the earth. It can be proven in a court of law.

After learning about undeserved acceptance, and what faith meant, school became awesome. God became real, and I was back on track. I was finally beginning to make sense of what happened with Ben Jr., finally beginning to forgive myself, and finally finding a reason to trust the process, to trust God.

After everything that had happened, police work became even more of my dream job. My life was just a fantastic, incredible journey —until my divorce from my wife of 15 years.

CHAPTER TWO

Till Death Do You Part

*"And so rock bottom became the solid
foundation on which I rebuilt my life."*
- JK Rowling

I loved her. I still love her. I'll always love her. She's the mother of my four sons and the woman I gave my heart to two decades ago. You don't lose that soul connection even if you lose the marriage.

From the first moment Kendra and I met in Jacksonville, Florida I knew she would be my wife and my life. I never guessed that the other love of my life—police work—would be the one to break up our marriage.

Kendra was wicked smart, funny, principled and a good woman. She was also way out of my league. Or so I thought.

Her two friends, Ann and Erin lived downstairs from me in what has been referred to now as just "Apt 300."

There were six of us in that apartment building and the shared memories will not be forgotten. Five of the six are still with us. We lost David Denotto to a drug overdose on Dec 6, 2017 (ironically the same day I retired from the Virginia Beach police dept). When

David and I moved into the apartment we immediately met Ann and Erin downstairs. They were UNF college students.

Ann and Erin's best friend was Kendra. Kendra wasn't in college and had her own apartment on the other side of town but frequently stayed at Ann and Erins apartment as we would all go out and get bbq and hang out after.

Kendra and I became really good friends. She had a fiery personality and wasn't afraid to call people out when she had a reason, and sometimes when she didn't. She was extremely intelligent and driven. I loved all that about her. She had a strength and personality to match my own. And, she worked full time at Blue Cross and Blue Shield in Florida. She cared about people like I did.

"Griff, let's go camping." I'm not sure whose idea it was, but I was all in. We packed up all our stuff and headed to a camp ground about an hour south of Jacksonville.

That was the night that things changed for me and Kendra.

It was late and we were the only two still up by the campfire. Kendra had to go to the bathroom and asked if I'd walk with her. As we were walking back to the campsite we kissed.

I remember it very well. I remember thinking there was no way she was interested in me, yet, she kissed me. I melted.

At first we snuck around and hid our relationship because of the dynamics between everyone in apartment 300, along with the fact that we were leaving on a six month deployment in a couple weeks. If I'm going to be honest I never thought I had a shot with her.

So we went on deployment and Kendra and I kept in contact the entire time. We emailed, wrote letters and had the occasional pay phone call (yep, no one had cell phones in 2001).

I came back from deployment and it was like no time had gone by. We picked right back up where we left off. We were two people motivated to take over the world. We moved in together shortly after and fell madly in love with each other. She had a way about her that I will never forget.

There was a quiet confidence and resilience in her that I respected and loved. Anything she did, she did well. It was like she was the perfect kind of perfectionist. Not OCD or obnoxious, but just able to do whatever she did better than anyone else. I think some of that comes from the way she grew up. She had a tough upbringing and overcame many battles and obstacles. I understood her and believed she understood me. We were both going to change the world.

We married on March 9, 2002 in Beaufort SC. It was a beautiful day. Our families were there. I'll never forget the night before our wedding my mother pulled Kendra aside (still within earshot of me) and said "I'm sorry Kendra....I did the best I could with him." I responded "wow mom, thanks."

For the next 15 years we would tackle life together—the ups and downs and everything in between. There was the birth of our four awesome sons, one with special needs we tackled and loved even stronger.

So many amazing memories, yet also so many sleepless nights. Some of my favorite memories include taking our children to Disney World, vacationing in the White Mountains and summer vacations in Florida. Life was good, but it wasn't easy. We lived paycheck to paycheck. And, we still needed help from credit cards. There is no good life or living high on the hog when you're a cop.

Only overtime shifts and tax returns brought in the extra money. Side hustles needed to be approved and even with that you were subject to be called in at any moment. Fifty-eight thousand a year doesn't do much for a family of six. To be honest, it barely puts food on the table.

That all changed when my undercover work came along. The money that was already so tight became even tighter with the lack of overtime pay and detail work. Yet, once I was working undercover the money, legit money from the cartels, was there. I'd say, "Let's go to the steakhouse," and Kendra would say, "We can't afford it," yet I had a roll of legal hundred dollar bills in my pocket. She didn't get me, and I didn't get her. We started drifting apart and things got tense, but I was apparently too blind and too focused on work to notice. If I sound like I'm publicly apologizing, I guess I am. I feel a lot of guilt and regret for our breaking up, and I can say that now, so I am.

I take a lot of responsibility for my divorce and have apologized for my actions, the actions I believe that led to it. I firmly believe my devotion to my undercover life took my marriage. The lack of consistency/support and the pressure and stress of leading multiple lives led me to chase the undercover life and try and make it more real than the one I had. I forgot to be a husband and father. I forgot to be compassionate and sensitive. All I knew was aggression and manipulation. The fighting intensified and on July 08, 2016 Kendra and I separated.

I will be absolutely clear about this. It was the *hardest* thing I've ever gone through in my life. I do not wish divorce on anyone, even my worst enemy. The heartache and sickness I felt in my stomach every day was overwhelming. The ding of my cell phone signalling an email which was possibly from her attorney left me frozen with fear. So, I ran into someone else's arms— which turned out to be a terrible mistake for me and my children.

I just thought I was doing something great as an undercover cop. Something no one else could do. I felt like my life had prepared me for this career, and yet Kendra wanted no part of it. She hated my beard, my tattoos, my lip ring....everything.

Whereas I loved it all. Every moment and every day was an adventure for me. My excitement around coming home and sharing the parts of my day I could share would quickly diminish as Kendra would say things like "I don't wanna hear it."

I missed what we had had. I wanted back what we had had. I held onto the thought and the belief we could get it back. I was in denial over everything, thinking I could talk my way, apologize my way out of it. Kendra saw right through it. And it about killed me.

So when we divorced on January 5th, 2017 and it finally became very obvious we weren't going to be married anymore, I was angry, and hurt and confused about that fact.

The divorce was just one of those eye-opening things for me. We had a lot of really happy times. We had loved each other for so long.

We had had four sons together. We had each other in many ways, but we no longer had a marriage and we would never have a marriage again. It was another death-of-a-passion blow that hit me hard.

The conversations in my head during that entire time went something like this, "Here I am pouring my life into trying to save other people and she can't be bothered." Looking back I can see that wasn't entirely true, but at the time I was convinced it was.

When we were separated and sharing custody of the boys her attorney froze my bank accounts, so I had $1.13 to my name. I was living in my Yukon until I found a temporary room. If you're immersed in a warrior mentality, that's emasculating, and depressing all by itself. For me, that was just the beginning of the slippery slope to suicide.

It was that room, and what happened there, that pushed me closer to the edge.

While I was the SRO (School Resource Officer) at my local high-school I also became the head lacrosse coach. I made a ton of life-long friendships from that time and memories, for better or for worse, that I will take with me my entire life. I also met another woman who would push me deeper into depression than any cop trauma had.

Karen, one of the players' mothers, became our team mom. She was extremely passionate about lacrosse, and sometimes a little crazy about helping the team and me. When Kendra and I separated, she offered me one small room in her house so I'd have someplace to sleep, and access to a shower and facilities.

At first everything was great. She was super supportive and always had a sympathetic, listening ear for me to talk or vent to. That didn't last long. It quickly became apparent that something was a little off with her. Her eccentric ways at times became obsessive ways. But, it was a room, not my car. I could have my kids with me, and it wasn't going to be forever.

The sleeping arrangements in my room were pretty tight when I had my kids with me. There was a blow up mattress, a futon, and a recliner in the room. I slept on the floor, Zach and Micah took the futon, Jonny claimed the blow up and Caleb had the recliner.

We woke up one morning around 6 am and four-year old Caleb said, "daddy, I peed my pants." Well, it wasn't just his pants. It was his "bed" (the recliner) he peed on too. The recliner was about 8,000 years old so I didn't think much of what was just one more accident it survived. But, I cleaned everything up as best I could. I left a note for Karen, explained what had happened and apologized. Kids.

That happened to be the Saturday I'd also received free tickets so I could take my kids to the Great Adventure theme park.

This was really exciting for me since I wasn't able to do much with my kids during my separation from Kendra. I had no money (bank accounts frozen), and was grateful for the time with my sons.

We had a beautiful day and my four boys loved every minute of it. Zachary, my second oldest, and I won a basketball shooting 3-pointers. Everything about the day was exactly what I needed, craved, and soaked up.

It was a memorable bonding day and it couldn't have been better. Then we got back to Karen's house, and my temporary room for the boys' second night with me.

We arrived home around 8 p.m that night from probably the best day I'd had in many weeks. I was feeling good, the boys were exhausted, but also in a good mood. It couldn't have gotten better, so I guess it had to get worse.

When we walked in, I immediately knew something was wrong. The music in the house was blaring and Karen was nowhere to be found. I walked my kids upstairs and began getting them ready for bed. I began to hear yelling and arguing downstairs so I walked down and asked Steve, Karen's husband, what was going on. He said "nothing, everything is fine."

Not thinking much of it, I went back upstairs and got my kids into bed. Again, I heard loud arguing and yelling and things crashing. I went back downstairs and as I got to the bottom of the stairs one of Karen's dogs (a very aggressive rescue dog) began coming towards me. Karen whipped a blanket off of a piece of furniture to block the dog and then began screaming. I could immediately tell she was drunk.

I remembered my note, and the recliner and began to suspect what the problem was. So I asked Steve again, "is everything ok?" Once again Steve said "yeah, no problem."

I asked "is she mad at me? Did I do something wrong?"

Steve said, "no it's just Karen being Karen."

I began to feel the stress I'd left behind for the day. My good feelings about the day were quickly disappearing.

"Steve, my kids have been through a lot, I don't know what's going on but please tell me if I need to take them and find another place to go tonight."

In my head I had no idea where another place would be since I had no money and nowhere to go. As I was saying this, I also asked Steve if Karen was mad at me. He looked sideways at me.

My heart sank. He didn't have to say anything. I knew. But I pushed him.

With a little more force, I said, "Steve, tell me now if she's mad at me because I need to get my kids out of here if she is. I can't have her yelling like this at my kids."

I asked, " is it because of the recliner?"

Steve said "yes."

"Steve, my son is four, cut him some slack."

"I know. It's just Karen being Karen."

That didn't matter. I wasn't going to let Karen being Karen hurt my kids. I grabbed my kids and their bags and headed for the door. I had nowhere to go so I made a desperate move. I drove to their mothers house at about 10 pm. I called her before we got there and said something happened at Karen's and I needed to bring the boys home. She graciously said ok.

When I got there, all four kids piled out of the car and moved towards the door where Kendra was standing. Once inside, I thanked her.

In a moment of despair, weakness, and self doubt I said " Hey, I have nowhere to go. I have no money. And I don't know who to call.

Can I just sleep on the couch for tonight? I'll get up and take the kids in the morning and go to church?" This is where her strong boundaries and the perfect OCD I loved so much kicked in and crushed my heart.

Kendra looked at me and after a couple seconds said "No, you're not welcome here anymore!"

That hurt. Bad. I knew we would never reconcile after that. I was devastated and lost, nowhere to go. So I headed to the only safe space I still had.

I drove to the police department and parked my car in the back parking lot and decided to sleep in my car. I was hungry. I was broke. I had no one. I walked into the police department and took a shower.

After my shower I walked by the break room and decided to see if anyone was in there hanging out. It was empty. I walked over to the fridge and opened it. There was someone else's sandwich, probably dinner or lunch for them. I looked over my shoulder to make sure no one was looking, and took the sandwich and ate it.

That was one of the lowest points of my life. I remember feeling like the biggest piece of shit in the world with each bite I choked down. That was the start of the suicidal thoughts—a stolen sandwich. Not a bad guy, a drug bust gone wrong, or police work. It was being forced to steal someone else's dinner because I'd screwed up. It was the straw that broke me. It was the start of my failures, or my not wanting my kids to see this person that I'd become. The shame washed over me in waves, and I felt like I couldn't climb back in the car and go to sleep, not now.

If you can imagine, the night actually got worse.

After an hour or so, I called my friend, Ben. Ben was the same friend that would save my life in the coming months as I sat in my Yukon getting ready to end my life. I broke down crying and said "Man, I have nowhere to go."

I asked if I could crash on his couch.

Without hesitation, without a "let me check with my wife," he immediately said, "get your ass over here."

I got over to his house with my tail between my knees. We began to talk for a bit and it was closing in on almost 11 or 12 pm when the doorbell at his house rang. We looked at each other puzzled and he went upstairs.

Several minutes later, he came down to the basement where we had been sitting and said, "there's a cop at the door."

Lt. Maxfield was there, and wanted to speak with me. Completely off guard I went upstairs and saw Shane.

"What's up?"

"Karen called the police department and told us you were drunk and driving your kids around."

I was dumbfounded. I was sure there couldn't possibly be a deeper low than how I felt eating someone else's sandwich but sure enough, there was, and I found it.

I explained the situation and what had happened at Karen's house earlier.

"Blood test, breathalyzer, check my eyes, smell my breath or whatever else you need to do," I said. "I'm not drinking and I'm sure not drunk."

"Griff, I can tell you're not drinking, and haven't been drinking."

My shame turned to anger.

"How is this fair? How can she call the police and make a blatantly false 'check the welfare complaint' when she's the one who's drunk? All this over a ratty recliner."

Once you're already feeling bad about yourself and your life, It doesn't take much to start chipping away chunks of your self-esteem. When you're already low, even an old woman who's drunk and angry about nothing can bring you to your knees.

Shane looked at the ground, then at me, and shook his head. He didn't have an answer, but at least he sympathized with me about how fucked up the situation was.

I couldn't imagine how many of my fellow cops heard the radio traffic and thought "wow, Griff is driving around town drunk with his kids in the car."

What if the neighboring agencies heard the call (as my friend's house was in a neighboring town) or if the State Police were monitoring the call? In my head I was sure they all had heard it and now knew I was exactly how I secretly felt—that I was an utter failure and a complete piece of shit.

Just when you think you're already lower than whale shit, somehow something else will come along to make you feel even lower and that's how my night went. That day was the highest high with my sons, and the night was the lowest low with one failure after another. There is no limit to how bad you can feel about yourself when nothing is going right.

If I could have punched a button and disappeared off the face of the earth, I would have. The shame was like nothing I'd ever faced.

What looked to me like the end of my life and all my friendships, and work, was just God's plans in action. Looking back at this time, what I learned about God is that He is not rushed, even if we're desperate and at the edge of a cliff and begging for a miracle, He hears us. Someone once explained that the things and events we experience aren't miraculous in themselves. What makes them miraculous is the timing of the event. Ben's inviting me over to crash on his couch, and later calling to check on me the night I planned to kill myself—it was all in the timing.

There is no such thing as too soon, or too late with God. He exists outside of time, so He's always exactly on time no matter how we feel about what seems like His delays. I would later question God's timing in my life. No matter where I turned things fell apart. Why? The more I thought about "God's timing," the more humbled I became. I thought about Job and how he lost everything, children, livestock, homes, and still believed God had a plan for his life. Then God restored everything Job had lost.

I wanted to know how Job kept it together—losing all his sons and daughters and livestock in a day, then living with head-to-toe boils for a year. Yet, he never doubted God.

I wanted to know how Abraham felt when God told him to climb a mountain and sacrifice his own son on an altar He asked Abraham to build. Abraham listened and obeyed. He didn't argue, plead, or object. He went with it. I don't think for a New York second he wanted to do it. But he trusted God. I thought of my four sons. Could I have done the same with one of them?

It wasn't until Abraham raised his knife to plunge it into his son's chest that an angel stopped his hand. Seconds away, God stopped him, and stayed the killing blow. Was it too soon? Too late? What matters is, he stopped Abraham from killing his son. I'm sure Abraham would have preferred it didn't happen at all, but whether it was two hours or two seconds, the fact was, God stopped him at the precise second He needed to. It's one of God's mysteries—His perfect timing. He knew where I was on the path to ending it all, and He knew exactly when to intervene. I wish I'd known that at the time. Like they say, "Hindsight is 20-20."

At that time I'd hit my limit of losing. I look back now and can see that it was a long string of failures, a loss of the love and support I had, and a lot of little things piling on and piling on. Someone pointed out that snowflakes don't weigh much by themselves, but when they pile up on tree branches during a bad storm, the weight of these weightless flakes can break an oak tree, and bring it crashing to the ground. I got it. There weren't any huge things, but a lot of little to medium things, and a few big things, that brought me crashing to the ground. If there had been a bell to ring to quit, I'd have rung it. After that day, a day that should have been a defining and glorious chance to bond with my sons, and prove I wasn't a loser and a failure, I was done. After one miserable thing after another I was counting down the hours and minutes I had left on earth when Ben's phone call came for me.

The flash of light that illuminated the inside of the Yukon that night came from my phone, not my gun. "Hey bro, are you doing okay? Why don't you come over?"

My decision to end my life could have happened weeks, months, years sooner, but it didn't. It happened within God's perfect timing. It happened when Ben was moved to call. It happened as it was meant to. That timing kicked in, right down to the very seconds before midnight, and an angel stayed the hand, my hand, from an unnecessary sacrifice.

I don't know what God had planned, other than to get my attention. He certainly got that. And over the next hours, weeks, months, and years He would guide me towards His purpose for me.

CHAPTER THREE

The Long Road to Midnight

"I was a reluctant pariah:
Two roads diverged in a forest,
I took the one less traveled."

S ay what you want, but after all that happened, and continues to happen to me, I guarantee you that God's perfect timing is a beautiful and consistent thing. We rarely see His hand at the moment He's acting on our behalf. But if you look back at your life, as I'm doing here, it all begins to make sense. What looked like random crime scene clues began to fall into place and I could see so clearly what happened and why it had to happen as it had.

I get chills thinking about all the things that aligned to take me where I am right now. Don't get me wrong. A lot, maybe most of the events in my life weren't pleasant or fun, but they were necessary for me to have the voice, the passion, and the experiences I have had. It was necessary for me to do what I do now. All those seemingly sense-less drills I went through in lacrosse and SAR school, made sense the second I needed the skill that drill provided. Intelligent design? I think so.

This book is not in your hands by chance. You aren't who you are, or where you are by chance. You're here, reading this book because of that same intelligent design. This book is not just my memoir. It's part message, part urgent plea for people to wake up and find God; but it's also about my passion—helping other LEO, veterans, and first responders with suicidal thoughts, mental illness and substance abuse.

It's about God and the faith I found along the way. It's a way to reach people who might not otherwise pick up a book. So if it seems part educational, part testimonial, part Bible thumping evangelism, that's by design. If getting this book into the hands of just one person who stops and backs away from suicide, it's done its job. If it's not for you, it's for someone. So please share it.

My editor tells me that memoirs are about creating a narrative and telling a story, communicating what happened to you, what you learned from it, and how you emerged a better person because of it. It's about making sense of your story so that others can relate and get something out of reading about your experience.

So, apparently writing a memoir is like having a beer in a bar and "remembering when," with a bunch of friends, only on paper.

They tell a story and it reminds you of a story, which reminds them of a story, and so it goes until the beer is gone and the memories all run together. In a memoir you have a theme, and tell a story or reveal some insight that can be passed along outside of choir practice, to others who might benefit from your mistakes.

Looking back at the evening and the stories and memories, you think it was all random, but it makes sense in an odd way. I believe my story, this book, my "journey to midnight," is not as random as it seems. I'm not a psychologist and I don't claim to be.

I'm a born again believer, a Christian. What worked for me, what brought me back to life was God. I'm not shy about saying that or encouraging you to at least explore the possibility there's a creator who loves you and has a plan for you too.

When I started this book I wanted to tell my story of course, and share my testimony and how I went from almost the bottom of the abyss to the life I think God had planned for me. I wanted to focus on the mental health of police officers, and my attempt at suicide and my own pain, and the salvation, hope and grace I found in returning to God. But writing isn't always that clean and easy, cut and dried, or black and white.

When I started writing about my suicidal thoughts and plans, and what led to them, Benny and Brian and everything else pinged me back to my divorce, and that memory threw me into SAR training, high school, drug rehab, and then on to all the other things that came together to bring me to writing this book—the Navy, being a cop, being undercover, seeing good people at their worst, and bad people being even worse.

How I remember life leading up to my divorce, and all the events in my career aren't a crafted documentary and I didn't have a videotape to draw from. Some memories are fuzzy, and other things are crystal clear, like they just happened 10 minutes, not 10 years ago.

Ask Kendra why we got divorced and she'll say I didn't pay any attention to her. I abandoned her to focus on "the job." Looking back, yeah, I did abandon her, but it was because I was eaten up with protecting our community, and her and the boys.

She didn't see it that way. She saw the undercover me. She didn't like the fact I had cornrows and tattoos and a lip ring. She didn't like us going to dinner and watching me pull four cell phones out of my pockets and put them on the table, ready to jump and run if I got a call. She would be on pins and needles wondering if I was going to be home when I said I would be, or if I'd get a call and turn around to go save something or someone and leave her stranded or stood up once again.

I'd changed, she said. Had I? I thought I was saving people, saving the community I loved with all my efforts. I thought wrong. So did others.

During that time I remember being in a bar having a beer and a burger on a Friday, and a guy walking in and looking at me. It had been a long week—a successful week. We had served a couple search warrants and so Friday was a paperwork day. I was tired but I decided to head into town for a burger and a beer. I just wanted to be left alone, get something to eat, and unwind from the stress of a busy week. I was sitting in the corner of my local bar by myself, with my meal, when I noticed someone walk in. He noticed me too, and redirected his course towards me.

I watched him and thought, "Do I know him?" It's a cop thing to think like that. You meet so many people, arrest so many more. "Good guy or bad guy?" I'm asking myself so I'm ready for whatever comes next.

He stopped. He walked past me, looking at me again. Immediately I'm on alert on the inside, calm on the outside. He's looking at me and I'm wondering what's going on, then he says to me, "Matt Griffin right? You're that undercover cop right?"

"Yes." I put my burger down so my hands were free. I'm still waiting for the punch line and it doesn't take him long to get right to it.

"What the fuck are you doing?"

"Excuse me?" I'm not sure whether I heard him right or If I was buying time to figure out if this was gonna escalate to a fight.

"What the fuck are you doing sitting in a bar on a Friday night? Maybe if you were out doing your job my kid wouldn't have died from a drug overdose last night."

I didn't know what to say. Was he right? I wasn't gonna fight a father that just lost his kid the night before.

So I said, "You know what, you're right." I asked for my check and got up and left the bar. Maybe he was right. Why was I sitting in a bar having a burger and a beer when drug dealers were putting poison into our kids' bodies? Why was I enjoying a beer when the pain of losing a child was happening every day? I must not be doing my job.

Over 150 people a day fatally overdose from an opioid, and here was the father of one of them and here I am sitting in a bar trying to eat a hamburger and enjoy 20 minutes of downtime. Maybe he was right, I was to blame for not clearing the streets of every drug dealer in town instead of just the ones I could. I was doing everything I could, but I couldn't win. Was I responsible for his kid overdosing?

No, but it felt like it. He was in pain, so it wasn't personal, but he made it personal and I took the bait.

His kid wasn't the first, or the last to overdose. Tragic, but true. Years after that I met Deanna, another parent I met who lost a child to drugs. I met Deanna at one of my speaking events where she was describing her 21-year-old daughter, Morgan, overdosing on fentanyl.

Deanna was angry at the cops too—but for a different reason. As the rescue squad was wheeling her daughter's body out to the ambulance there were some officers off to one side laughing, drinking coffee, and talking about something—probably not related to Morgan or the case. But, it didn't feel that way to Deanna. She felt they were laughing at her, at her daughter, at the untimely death, at the whole scene. They weren't, of course, but when your pain is that fresh, that raw, anything can feel callous and wrong. Her anger, like the guy in the bar, was directed at all things cops.

I'm putting Deanna's story in here because it goes to the heart of how a lot of cops, and a lot of people in general, feel about addicts.

First of all, I don't believe anyone wakes up one day and says, "You know what, I think I'd like to become addicted to drugs and screw up my life for the next ten years. I'd like to maybe overdose a few times before it kills me and destroys my family and ruins my parents." No. That's not a thing anyone consciously plans for.

Morgan certainly didn't wake up one morning and decide to do drugs. No matter how much people who heard about her suicide think and assume she did just that, I assure you, she didn't.

I tell this to the recruits I speak to. When you look at somebody suffering from mental health issues, think. Don't judge them. Try to come from a place of not thinking or saying "What the hell is wrong with you?" but "My gosh, what happened to you? What made you this way?" If you can do that it changes your whole perspective on the person and how you interact with them. When I heard Deanna's story and how Morgan spiraled down the path to death, my heart goes out to addicts.

Cops aren't immune to alcohol and drug addiction either. In fact, they're more likely to use and abuse than the public they protect. We all have to deal with pain one way or the other. Pain and unresolved problems are going to come up and out one way or the other. You can beat the pain down with drugs, alcohol, sex, gambling, or violence, or you can get help, or you can take yourself out.

I do know this, the mechanism that triggers suicide is emotional pain. It's feeling overwhelmed with no place to go, no one to talk to, and a feeling like no one is on your side or cares about you.

People say, "I wish he'd felt like he could talk to me." I say, "When you suspect something, don't wait to be asked. Step up and make a point of checking on them." Chances are very, very good they're not going to ask for help. It's just one more thing that they believe makes them a burden to people who they think have already given up on them.

Therapists are there, and they can help, but few people turn to them because they're part of the culture that certifies something is wrong with you if you can't control your own emotions, fears, nightmares and sleeplessness. You're caught between a rock and a hard place. You need help to save yourself and your job, but the thing that can save you will also take away the thing you love.

I say that because I know that if getting help is going to cost you your job and your reputation, therapy is going to be at the bottom of that resources list you create. Drugs and alcohol, the self-medication of choice for most of us, is going to be at the top of how we handle things. It's okay for cops to get drunk. That's acceptable. Most officers will look the other way if a cop gets angry, aggressive, or abusive with his spouse. But they won't tolerate someone crying or saying they need help. Go figure.

While the research on the topic varies, one study found that substance abuse among police officers is **around 20-30%.** By comparison, the prevalence of drug use disorders and alcohol dependence for the general population of adults in the United States is estimated to be 9.9% and 5.8%.[1] Yeah. Surprised me too, but not much.

So I ask you, knowing what officers deal with every day, and how they cope with trauma, can you step back and look at mental illness, whether it's PTSD, or schizophrenia, or ADHD, or dementia a little differently, and with more compassion? That could be you one day after too many traffic accidents, too many bodies, too much trauma, grief, shame, or loss.

Like Deanna told me, "People don't bring you casseroles when you lose your child to addiction. You know if it was cancer or something like that you know the whole neighborhood is going to come in and help you through the grief. They're feeding you and they're doing all these things and there's a month rotation and everybody you know is there for you. It's different when you lose a child to addiction. No one comes calling, or shows up with sympathy or a casserole in hand."

People don't know that at 17, Morgan's boyfriend, Brendan, committed suicide with a shotgun while he was on the phone with her.

She heard the threat he made that he was going to do it, then heard the shotgun, then the screaming of kids who were there behind him who saw him shoot himself.

Brendan was her first boyfriend, and like Morgan, he had also been diagnosed with ADHD. (By the way, the propensity for kids with ADHD to become addicted is nearly 80%.)[2] Deanna suspected, but didn't know much about Morgan or Brendan's drug addiction and its impact until after their deaths. Again, too late. What if?

"I just knew he was gonna wrap his car around a tree one day or he's gonna drink and drive or he's gonna do something," Deanna said. "But he was like Morgan. He was so funny and likeable you didn't focus on that. But he made me so nervous because I could tell he also had ADHD and they related in the fact that they couldn't really control their thoughts and everything so that impulse control that she didn't have, he also didn't have."

Deanna now speaks to police officers and tells them Morgan's history, and her story. She tells them that Morgan was ADHD, that Brendan talked her into trying drugs, that she got off of them after Brendan died and then she discovered she was pregnant, but then got back on them via prescription to calm her down after his death.

There's a story behind every suicide, and Morgan, Brendan, and Deanna's story is heartbreaking.

So, the deaths and tragedy kept on coming. This wasn't just one guy in a bar calling me out. Or one mother sharing her story about her daughter's suicide that piled higher and deeper on me. It wasn't the guy who threatened to shoot himself in the head in front of me, and then did before I could grab the gun. It wasn't that I had to sit next to his body for hours afterwards waiting for investigators. It was all that and more—one more thing on top of one more thing.

It wasn't just Benny. Those were a few of the tragedies. But my successes couldn't drown them out. All the guns, drugs, and dealers I stopped or arrested weren't enough. What does it matter if you have a table full of drugs, money, and guns you've seized if you still have to respond to death calls, or hold a dying toddler in your arms? Sure, we're getting drugs and dealers off of the streets, but not as fast as they're getting on the streets.

After a lifetime of success after success, failure was suddenly blanketing everything I did, and didn't do. I couldn't do enough good. I couldn't win enough awards, or shine like I wanted. All my hard work felt invisible. The idea of suicide became more than a passing thought. It fluttered out of the sky like some large dark bird and perched on my shoulder and wouldn't let go.

I could feel the claws gripping my shoulder, piercing my heart. The idea of killing myself took on a kind of peaceful glow. It wasn't an escape. It was an answer, an honorable way out of the pain and the shame that overwhelmed me. I began to feel good about my decision—something I now know is a precursor to a successful suicide—the person has made a decision and will likely follow through.

I didn't look at suicide as a suicide. I looked at it as a sacrifice. I was going to sacrifice my life for the betterment of my kids because that's how depression was tricking my brain. I want people to know that suicidal ideas don't come from a place of mental health or mental weakness. They come from a place of a person trying to find answers to what seems like problems without a solution.

It's an answer, but it's a permanent solution to a temporary problem. It's not a weak thing, it's not a strong thing. It's just mental illness. It's a trick of the mind. It's the whisper of depression promising some kind of rest and warmth from whatever is overwhelming you.

Sometimes resisting the voice is just a minute by minute and sometimes it's an hour by hour thing. Sometimes you give up and make a deal and an appointment with the voice rather than choose to fight it. I made my deal, peace, then picked midnight on March 17, 2017 at 00:00 for my appointment.

Then I stood death up. My permanent solution was waylaid when my buddy Ben called me out of the blue and said, "You know there's light at the end of the tunnel, and I'm here to go through it with you. Come on over here and have a beer with me." I told him I had "something to do," without saying what, and then I declined his invitation. But he persisted.

Finally, I said to myself, "you know what, If today is a good day to die, so is tomorrow." And with that, I put off shooting myself until "tomorrow." And then a day became a week, and a week became a month as I kept putting it off. It's not like the sun burst through the clouds, and everything fell in place for me after that. I'm not going to blow smoke and say the angels sang and miracles happened, because they didn't. They continued to be hard. I just had a different perspective—one where I convinced myself I could eventually change things if I stayed here and stuck with it.

Things are still hard. I still have issues, challenges, and problems. I have to deal with my kids. Life is still hard. There are amazing, wonderful, fantastic days, but there are almost just as many lows. That's life. So, I cheated death, but I didn't escape the hard times. I got through the bad times because I found someone to help me through them.

God doesn't rescue us from things. He accompanies us through them. If you're a parent, you get this. You don't protect your kids from things they can handle. You teach them to handle challenges, to walk through trouble, to figure things out. The big stuff, the stuff they can't handle, you handle for them until they can do it on their own. God is a father. That's how He deals with us. He's there for the things we can't handle, and helping teach us the things we need to know to handle ourselves.

We can't learn patience until we're put into situations where we have to have patience. We can't learn empathy or compassion until we experience events and the compassion and empathy of others towards us. I learned God was there, and I just needed to trust Him.

Things didn't get any easier for me for probably the next 6-7 months, but I had someone who cared—God. It's like a 12-step program. You do life one hour, one day at a time. Then one day you wake up with a year's sobriety under your belt. That doesn't mean everything is all roses and rainbows. Life is challenging, and you deal with it. But you keep waking up and you keep trusting God. I kept waking up. I kept trusting God. If He could create the universe in seven days He could show me how to fix the problems I had. Choosing to stay, and not to give up and die, was the biggest accomplishment of my life to date. Once I made that decision I started changing how I looked at things.

I told myself, I'm not *losing* my job at the Police Department but I am *leaving* the Police Department. I reframed things. I'd hit rock bottom having $1.13 in my checking account and nowhere to live, eating someone else's lunch, and sleeping in my car for several days. What would it hurt to find another way to frame that? I could always circle back and beat myself up, but what if I focused on the things that were going right? What if I tried being grateful for what I had? So I tried it.

I prayed. I used the mental tactics I'd learned in SARS. I picked one thing to accomplish and I ground on that until I finished it. Then I picked another thing.

I couldn't get much lower, or feel much worse about myself, but I hung on, day by day. I said, "I believe in myself and I know Brian believes in me and it's time for me to do something that I'm passionate about. I'm going to wake up every day and I'm going to do the things that I care about." And I did.

Before I launch into what else I did, I think it'll help to string things together if I sort of start at the beginning. Let me tell you how I got to the point where my good friend Brian's suicide was still fresh, that he wasn't a month in his grave, and I was sitting in my Yukon thinking that blowing my brains out was a noble thing that would make everyone's life, including mine, so much easier. So, here goes.

I was born in 1978, in Northern New Jersey, the third son to my parents Neal, an accountant, and Margo, a nurse. We weren't rich. We lived in a neighborhood where I was raised with Latinos, Blacks, and every race but White. I know it pisses off people to hear me say, "I don't see color," but I don't. I see character. So, I come from "the hood," and I probably would have grown up in the hood except for my ability to play sports of any kind, and to play them well.

As I've said, I also happened to be a very good lacrosse player. So, one thing led to another and a very wealthy benefactor found me, and I got a scholarship to a very exclusive, $65,000 a year high school. It was where all the cool kids went. Kids whose parents were CEOs, celebrities, actors, politicians, the kind of school where you learn networking, appearance, and the very real truth that *who* you know is more important than *what* you know. It's the kind of school you go to if you want to be rich and connected and powerful when you grow up.

To the cool (rich) kids I was the poor kid, the scholarship kid, the kid who didn't belong — except when it came to sports, and only then if we were winning. Looking back I can see how the scholarship kids were shorted in a lot of ways by the school. The school may have had a lot of rich, successful donors and board members, and professors, but they didn't know how to deal with, teach, relate to, or coach "scholarship" (poor) kids. I'm guessing they've changed since I attended. I sure hope so.

The rich kids had their culture, the scholarship kids had theirs. They didn't always mesh. In fact, they rarely saw eye-to-eye, let alone bonded. The stereotypes about rich kids and poor kids, and rich folks and poor folks don't change simply because they're true. I know it. You know it. My dad knew it.

My poor dad liked to buddy up with the rich dads. The rich dads *let him* buddy up with them even though he wasn't wearing designer clothes, or shoes, or driving a car that cost the same as a small house. They let him buddy up because his kid, me, was the best player on the field. They didn't particularly like him, but they liked winning and his kid was winning for them.

Dad lived vicariously through me. He also used the leverage I provided as a star athlete to pump up his ego. He was as impressed with the rich dads as I was with their rich kids. What happened to him in the stands during a lacrosse game was a microcosm of what happened to me in my classes. I can't blame him for wanting to soak up some of the "love." I get it.

When I scored a game-winning goal to take us to the finals my junior year, it was both a blessing and a curse. It would set the stage for what would become a defining year of my life. If you think people are going to welcome you with open arms and warm fuzzies because you're the best at what you do, think again. They embrace you for what you can do for them, and drop or ghost you when you have nothing left they want, or you can no longer help them.

I'm not jaded, or bitter. It's how the world works. It was a hard lesson for me to learn, but Rob C., the Alpha male of the football team, was more than willing to teach me the rules in a way he thought I'd remember—by literally beating my ass.

Remember this. The seat at the head of the table, or the number one spot in any organization or business often has very little to do with your competence or performance and more to do with politics, pecking order, and "pull." I learned early it was better to be liked than to be the best, although I went back and forth between the two as I learned to balance them. I'm not saying "all" businesses or companies—just most of them.

At the time, I had none of the social skills, or personality and pull and rich kid street smarts and Rob C. had them all. I had the performance, the speed, the hustle and muscle, but I had a lot to learn about having the "pull" and how and when to rise in the pecking order to avoid pissing anyone off. No worries. Like I said, Rob C. was there to teach me what I needed to learn.

It was the Wednesday before our first Friday night football game. I couldn't have been more excited. I was a freshman and had just learned I was getting the starting spot at Free Safety. A freshman! No one gave it to me. I earned it. I worked hard for it. I'd trained all summer, lifted weights, ate right—I grabbed that spot based solely on ability and skill and busting my ass.

Remember, I'm a kid. I'm coming out of the ghetto to the 'Mo-Beard' campus. Mo-Beard wasn't an ordinary high school, but more of a southern plantation with beautiful buildings and sparkling lawns that oozed wealth, privilege, and prestige.

And, by the luck of the draw, or the grace of God, I was part of it. I stepped on campus that first day and was in awe of what I was seeing. By Wednesday the mystique had been replaced with motivation—motivation to win our first varsity football game. It was opening day and time for the "Friday night lights." I began to walk from the locker room area to the gymnasium for gym class. It was about a ¼ mile walk to the boys locker room and change up for gym class.

It was bright and sunny and clean and manicured and spectacular outside and I was happy. I was starting Friday night and I was gonna show everyone what I could do. I was about to reap the benefits of all my hard work and it felt good.

I got down to the locker room about five minutes later. As I walked in I noticed everyone circled up. I'm no dummy. I was from the hood and I immediately knew exactly what was going down. I knew that the circle was a fight that was getting ready to happen and my being inside said circle didn't bode well for me.

I couldn't imagine anything I'd done or said to make me part of the fight, but like I said, Rob C was about to school me in a major way. As I rounded the corner, Rob C came over to me, leaned in and put the rim of his hat on my forehead.

"You think you're taking my starting spot Friday night?" he said.

Me being the smart ass I was, and not afraid of some rich tight ass kid, even though he had me in size and age (he was a senior) I responded "I'm pretty sure I already did!"

With that remark, the fight was on. I got a couple licks in but for the most part Rob C, got the best of me.

Our fight was broken up and we were both escorted to Principal Garrity's office for discipline.

"Matt, you know fighting isn't allowed on school grounds." Principal Garrity said.

I nodded. I almost shed a tear from the stress and tension building inside me.

But I kept it all inside while I pled my case.

"I'm a freshman, he's a senior! And HE started it."

Lesson one, you can't win a *political* argument based on facts or on what's fair or right. There are times when *who* you know matters more than *what* you know. What Principal Garrity knew, that I didn't, was that what was happening wasn't about football. It was about Rob C and his father's position and status at the school. I was arguing right and wrong, morals, ethics, and fairness. Principal Garrity was telling me, in an appropriately veiled way, that Rob C wasn't going to lose his starting position and Mr. C was going to continue to donate to the school because I was expendable.

"It doesn't matter who started it Matt." (it did to me)

"You can't fight here."

Then he gave me "the talk." You know, the one that comes before the bad news, the talk about how you're supposed to rise above all the temptation, to walk away, to not defend yourself. I hated most knowing that what he was telling me was a lie and nothing I said to him mattered. His mind was made up. I felt what was coming and then bam. I remember Mr. Garrity said the thing I was afraid of the most.

"Matt, you're suspended." He handed down a three day out of school suspension—meaning I would miss opening night and my starting spot.

I learned later that day that Rob received a Saturday detention and kept his starting spot (taking my rightly earned spot) at Free Safety even after starting a fight and kicking my ass. I kept saying "it wasn't fair," to anyone who would listen. For all my complaining nothing changed. People nodded, but did nothing. It was all on me. I wallowed in my anger and the knowledge he'd stolen something from me in a way I couldn't get back. It wouldn't be the last time I experienced that feeling.

I kept complaining my detention wasn't fair, as if the more I complained, the more likely things would change. I had a lot to learn. The fact is, life isn't fair.

Life isn't fair on a high school campus, or in the hood, or if you're rich or poor, black or white, or if you work hard or not. It's not fair on the streets or off of the streets. Even if you do everything right, follow all the rules, and bust your ass, it's not fair.

What I eventually learned is that life isn't about being fair. It's about pull, pecking order, and power. You can't fight it, but you can choose to respond to it on your terms and take back your power. It's a game, sometimes a ruthless, hard hitting game where people get hurt.

I'm not saying quit being moral, or don't play fair yourself. I'm saying, "Be fair, play fair, do the right thing even when no one else is." Why? Because you'll be doing four things, (1) building your character (2) building resilience, and (3) preparing yourself to survive anything haters can throw at you. (4) Most of all you'll be doing what God created you do—represent to the world what justice, fairness, and love is truly all about. Not playing fair is the slippery slope to becoming who and what Rob C and his father were all about, money and power and political gain—not people. Not Godliness.

The fight was a set-up to give Rob C the thing he and his father wanted, the thing he thought he deserved, and to put me "in my place." It didn't matter if I 'earned' the spot, that I was a better player, and a better choice for the position. For the most part, and certainly in certain arenas, that's not how decisions are made in life. It was a very hard lesson to learn. Thank God my brother was there to teach me the real lesson in it all.

After all my complaining my brother pulled me aside and said "Use it Matty. Use it as fire, use it as passion, use it every time someone says you can't do something. Every time someone stacks the deck against you, you rise up and be better, do better."

"If they throw you to the wolves, you return leading the fucking pack!" he said.

With that timely inspiration and pep talk I was on fire again. Rob C's bank account and status in school would prove to be no match for my renewed heart and drive. After that one humiliating detention I started every single football game for the next four years. Like Toby Keith's country music song asks, "How do you like me now!?"[3]

You *can* win by playing fair, working hard, and doing the right thing. But there are times when knowing how the other side plays is critical. Like the Bible says, *"Be as wise as serpents and as innocent as doves."* Matthew 10:16.

Shrewdness, and the ability to discern people's motives and act with character, not deceit, is a strength. I like Al Capone's take on kindness—which is part of character. He said:

"Don't mistake my kindness for weakness. I am kind to everyone, but when someone is unkind to me, weak is not what you are going to remember about me."

Rob C. and his father and Mo-Beard and Principal Garity mistook my innocence, naivete, and understanding (or lack of it) for weakness. Bad mistake.

The suspension was both a low and a high point in my education, but the timing, again, was perfect. I learned an incredibly powerful lesson at the beginning of my time at Mo-Beard. I learned, it's not enough to just be the best, and do the right thing. You have to understand the game and how it's played. You have to know who and what you're up against and draw on the resources, skills, and character you have. I had the physical skills, but even more importantly, I was learning the mental and social skills to play with as well.

What I didn't know at the time was that this locker room fight didn't just mark my transition into a different culture. It marked my transition into a skill set that would serve me very well as an adult.

I had three very long days to think about that fight and what had happened to me. I focused even more on what I realized was just as important as time in the gym and on the weights. I learned how to bond and befriend everyone, athletes and honor students, rich and poor, book smart and street smart. I learned how to blend, how to fit in, how to read people, how to work with people. I learned character and that doing what's right might not be the best course of action in life, but that it would be the honorable one—the one that would allow me to stand before God when I die, not ashamed of being a fraud.

I didn't have the status of a big bank account but what I had was better. I had character and ethics. People lose riches, but no one could take my character, or those hard earned social and moral skills away from me. They were mine, and they were golden. I was on my way to a very successful career in undercover work, but all I knew at the time was I had to keep learning this stuff to survive. So I did.

I was 14-years-old and thriving in my first undercover operation — fitting in with the rich kids, being someone I was not, and doing it very convincingly. At the same time I was learning how to talk, walk, what to wear, drink, and smoke, I was trying to fit in with the other "scholarship kids" like me because they were outcast, multiculturally poor, and struggling too. Not only did I learn to fit in with the kids from both sides of the track, I reached the top of the ladder in that culture by being voted to take the reins as Senior Class President.

In less than five years I'd gone from being suspended for a fight I didn't start by a rich kid who got the starting position because of the pull of his parents and money and influence, to a school leader. Like I said, I'd been thrown to the wolves and came back leading the pack.

What I learned during my informal high school career was that rich kids don't carry cash, and they don't do poor man's drugs. They do designer drugs, not street drugs. They didn't smoke weed, they didn't drink Natty Lite (Natural Light) or Bud light beer. Everything from the food they ate, to the cars they drove screamed elite. Everything had to be what other people couldn't afford. It was BMWs, Audis, Porsche and cars that cost as much as a house.

The clothing was all Gucci, Klein, and Tommy. It was a very different culture and way of life than what I went home to when I went home. It taught me things I'm still learning about as an adult. I learned that most of the time who you know matters more than what you know. I learned that combining what you know with who you know will accelerate your path to success, but that things, like loyalty, respect, trust, and power can change on a dime. And that was a much harder lesson to recover from than a few punches in the mouth. I didn't waltz into my senior year as the King of Hot Shit. Well, I started to, until I hit another roadblock.

What I am about to tell you is something that I've held deep down and have not spoken about to anyone in many many years. I don't even know if I told my boy's mother about this in the 17 years we were together. This is a very difficult thing for me to put in this book but it's important, it shaped, molded, created and blessed my life in unmeasurable ways.

My mother traveled every week for work so I essentially raised myself in my high school years as my father worked long hours in New York City.

One day my parents discovered about a half ounce of weed in my bedroom. Half an ounce. Based on the way they reacted you'd have thought I was one step away from shooting heroin and starting a meth lab in the bathroom, or earning myself a spot on the FBI's "top ten most wanted" list.

Thank God for paranoid, over reactive parents.

"Ma! It's just a little weed." Not to them. My mother said "You choose your drugs or your family."

Of course I chose my family. So, in my senior year my mother entered me into a 30 day drug inpatient treatment program for my "addiction." At the time I was embarrassed, horrified, and ashamed. In retrospect, I met the very people and mentors who would change my life. Looking back, it wasn't about the drugs, it was about the lessons, the timing, the wisdom God brought into my orbit.

God uses the unexpected to teach us and get our attention. I wouldn't have picked rehab, but hey. You end up where you need to be, even if you don't want to be there, and you learn the things that ultimately lead you to your destiny.

Rehab. I guess it brings up images of dirty brick buildings and crack heads and misery for some. But it was different for me. The drive to the rehab clinic at Clearview in Western PA was surreal and not what I expected. I wish I could have been a fly on the wall hearing my parents decide where to send me. They didn't pick a dingy brick prison looking facility in the city. This rehab was in a rural area of Pennsylvania. I remember noticing the houses, manufacturing plants and overall difference in cultures. It mirrored what was happening in my head— that I was a good kid on my way to something I didn't deserve.

I couldn't believe my circumstances. I was the damn Senior class president, a varsity football and lacrosse player, an honors student and the pride of Morristown-Beard. I was well known, well respected, and now I was on my way to rehab for smoking the same weed most of the kids at school smoked. I kept saying in my head "what in the hell is happening?"

Then we were there. Intake. Addicts. Woods. Weird people. I was overwhelmed and exhausted. I sat down in the cafeteria with the intake counselor and she began to speak about guidelines, procedures, protocols, and rules, etc. At the end of the conversation, she asked me what drugs I used. She asked it in a plain no nonsense way like she was asking me, "what did you have for dinner?" I was taken aback and didn't respond. She noticed the hesitation on my face and said "I really don't care what you use. I just want to see whether or not you're going to have to detox."

"Detox?" I muttered.

"Ya, like withdrawals....?" She looked at me, waiting indifferently for my answer.

Embarrassed I was even in a place where someone was asking me that question was humiliating. I was able to respond that I wouldn't have to detox. What had I done by going along with my parent's insistence on rehab?

My saving grace that day was when the counselor led me into the enormous gymnasium and I saw a bunch of kids playing basketball. Sports have always been my thing. There's one great equalizer for me in this world— a basketball court, a lacrosse or football field. For that brief hour I felt like I might get through this without going nuts.

I quickly began to shoot on the other side of the court hoping that someone would recognize I could play and invite me to join in their game. I wasn't being coy, waiting to be invited to the dance. I was doing what I did well, sizing people up, checking out the pecking order, the competition, seeing who was a leader, who was not, who could play, who could not. I knew more about those kids' basketball and athletic abilities in an hour than they'd learn about mine in a month.

I sized up every person on and off the court and I quickly saw I was a better athlete than any of them. Arrogance? No. I just knew that to survive new environments I had to take inventory and see where I stood in the pecking order.

I know. It's kind of weird that the only thing I worried about at this moment was the basketball talents of a bunch of drug addicts at a rehab facility. But that was the hustle, the opening, the place I would be able to meet people who would hopefully help me navigate and survive this place.

Collecting and using a network of friends in the facility would ensure I succeeded there—whatever success in rehab was. I needed to succeed. I needed to shine. I needed to be respected. I needed to blend and to win the hearts of the other kids at the center. A therapist would have a field day with those confessions, but it was true. I wanted desperately to fit in, to belong, to be a part of whatever was there to belong to.

I would hone that networking skill over the next 20 years and love the Navy, love being a Search and Rescue Swimmer (SAR) and love being an undercover cop.

I already had a knack and an ability to find common ground with anyone from an addict, janitor, or CEO. I was confident I knew all I needed to know. I had no idea I didn't know shit, but was about to learn what I most needed to learn.

Our first group session started shortly after I walked into the gym. This old rugged cuss walked in shortly after I did. I'd heard the rumblings about this guy, Joe C. No one knew how old he was but rumors were that he'd spent many years in prison after killing someone.

Apparently we weren't supposed to mess with Joe C. He stood there with a cigarette dangling from his mouth and I was immediately intimidated. He only stood about 5'8, 150 lbs but there wasn't a lick of fat on him. He had that no nonsense look about him that I'd later learn to spot in a heartbeat in the Navy.

There are people who are given power and positions, or hired into them. And there are natural leaders who just assume, and everyone else assumes, are the true power in the organization. With or without a title they're the natural leaders, the born leaders. They rarely have to prove anything to anyone. Their confidence just radiates from them. You immediately know you do not mess with them if you want to survive in their presence. Joe C was a natural leader and then some.

As brash and confident as I was at the time, even I thought to myself, this was not the time to be the loudest person in the room. Group began, led by Joe. As the discussion began to take off, Joe looked at a hispanic kid in the group who I hadn't met yet. He quietly called him out.

"Louis, why are you so quiet?"

Louis was at the end of his time at Clearview. He was what you called a trustee. I believe he was going home at the end of the week.

Joe started in on Louis about his lack of participation.

"Louis, what's going on man?"

Louis just sat there, looking down at the floor. I felt a pang of sympathy for him.

"If you don't open up, you know you'll find your way back here after you get out."

No response.

"Correction. I mean, if you're lucky you'll find yourself back here."

Joe continued to hone in on Louis, ragging on him. He peppered him with questions. I sat there and watched the exchange, emotionally projecting myself into Louis's place. Always looking for an angle or a way to make a friend I chimed in on the onslaught.

"Give him a break" I blurted out.

"That's gonna leave a mark," I thought proudly. Louis looked up to see who had come to his defense and I gave him a little head nod and a tight smile. "I got your back," I was saying. Apparently he knew something I didn't because he didn't respond.

An awkward moment went by and Joe turned his head and stared at me. He had these icy blue eyes. I remember thinking "those eyes have killed someone, I probably should shut the fuck up."

Joe looked at me and said, "WHO THE FUCK ARE YOU?"

We were sitting in a circle and Joe stood up and began walking towards me. It's a good thing I packed extra underwear cause I was about to need a new pair. We were sitting cross legged, Indian style in a circle. Joe circled behind me. To my shock and surprise, he grabbed my shirt and lifted me off the ground with ease. He spun me around and said "Don't ever interrupt me again." The sternness and clarity of his voice and the fire in his piercing blue eyes told me to stay quiet. I didn't need to be told twice. He looked at both of my eyes several times.

"What's your name?"

"Matt," I said. He nodded his head ever so slightly and then looked around the group and sarcastically said.

"Apparently Matt wants to lead group today. Apparently, Matt (as he looked me up and down) knows more about drugs and recovery than I do." With that, he let go of my shirt and walked back to his position in the circle and we both sat down.

There was complete silence. If anyone had my back, including Louis, there was no way in hell they were going to do anything to let on to Joe C, at least not then and there.

I just learned my first lesson. Don't mess with Joe C. Over the next month I learned to fear him, but I also learned to respect him. A couple days later, we druggies were in our rooms (four of us in a room). One of my roommates (Kevin) was having a rough time for whatever reason. He was a golden glove boxer and thought he was an all around badass.

I've learned in my life that if you have to convince someone you're tough, you're probably not. Kevin was not. He wanted to be, and for him, ploughing through me, chewing me up, beating me up, was his fastest way of showing everyone there how tough he was.

We were all in rehab for a reason, and he had his reasons. His reasons turned into issues, and then his issues turned into acting out.

For whatever reason, Kevin began freaking out breaking chairs and anything else he could get his hands on. I was one of the things he wanted to get his hands on.

"C'mon Griff, you're tough. C'mon out and let's see who's tougher!"

There was a common area with hallways that led to our quads at Clearview. Kevin kept screaming at me and security was called in to intervene. But for some reason, even with the guards there restraining him, he kept screaming for me to come out and fight him. I had nothing to prove to Kevin, but a lot to prove to myself and to Joe C., so that was a decision that was easy enough to make. I didn't fight him.

That night was the last time I saw Kevin. After he was removed, Joe C pulled me out of my room "to talk." I had only been there long enough to know not to mess with Joe C, and to keep doing what I do best, blend, make friends, and avoid fights. Thanks Mr. Garrity. You taught me that much at least.

Joe C and I walked outside. It was so dark but the moonlight gave us enough light to get a little glimpse of what was ahead. We walked and Joe and I talked for about an hour about my attitude at Clearview, and about life. I'll honor his request and not repeat some of the things he told me about his past but I can tell you the rumors I heard barely scratched the surface. It was one of the many "Come to Jesus" moments I would have—and by that, I don't necessarily mean anything spiritual.

Religious contexts aside, "a *come to Jesus*" meeting, moment, or conversation is where you undergo a "difficult but positive and powerful realization or change in character or behavior."

It can be a foot planted up your ass, or an honest confrontation about how you're screwing up and how it's going to get worse if you don't change. With Joe, it was both, and he had a big foot and excellent aim.

Joe told me I had two choices.

"Start being the leader you're destined to be OR LEAVE." His voice and tone wasn't "Joe the counselor" talking to "Griff the kid." He was talking to me man-to-man, brother-to-brother. There was no bull-shit, no cajoling, no sugar coating. It didn't get any more real. He meant every word he said.

I was quiet, listening, thinking, wondering where he was going with his talk.

"That's right, leave. You're 18. Walk away. There's the road. Take a hike. Let life punch you in the face like it's done me."

I stood there looking at the forest, considering his "offer."

"Leave," he paused, "Or stay here and be the leader I know you are. Every person here looks up to you. Every person here wants to know you, hear you and be around you."

We stood in the darkness together, silent while I thought about what he was saying.

"But I'm not an addict, Joe. I got caught with a little weed and everyone thinks I'm some kind of druggie. Hell, there are guys here addicted to coke and heroin. Man, I'm embarrassed to be in group with some of these guys because I smoked a little weed, and they're hardcore."

I could feel my anger and resentment at the whole situation beginning to heat up. It was like the detention I got when Rob C kicked my ass and I was punished for something I never started. It wasn't fair. It just wasn't fair and I was going to go down making sure he knew that and everyone around me knew that. I wasn't expecting what he said next.

What he said is something that I've carried with me my whole life.

"Griff, it's not about being an addict. It's not about you smoking weed, or someone else smoking meth. It's about learning how to deal with your problems—big problems, little problems, personal problems, work problems, whatever. Here's a secret. Everyone is an addict. Everyone has something they do too much of. Hell, coffee, working out, work, sex, porn, eating, and drugs are addictive."

I think, even in the dark, he could see the surprise on my face. I said nothing and kept listening. He kept going.

"This place isn't about being an addict, it's about learning how to deal with your problems. Take your problem, feel it from your head to your toes. Make a decision on how you're going to resolve it and take the first step in that direction. To get through it... you MUST go through it. "Go through it Griff, get through it....be the man I know you can be."

I don't think it was just the words that cut through the wall I'd built up. It was his tone of voice, his belief in me, his obvious caring about what happened to me even though he said nothing about that. I had a lot to think about after our talk, and even more to think about the end of that week—especially when the weekend was over.

Remember Louis? He left rehab on Friday. The following Monday we were told he passed away from a suspected drug overdose. Joe was right. God's perfect timing.

I didn't leave. I chose to stay and I chose to learn. I chose to quit complaining about how unfair it was that I was there, and instead to look for how I would respond to *where* I was. I would stop being a victim and start taking control of my life and accepting the consequences for my actions. It was a huge shift.

When we take responsibility for ourselves, for our actions, and decisions, and for how we're going to respond and act when life, people and the world are unfair, we get back our power. When we act like victims and blame others, or circumstances for what's going on with us, we have no power. The people and circumstances have all the power as long as we keep giving it to them. When I'm complaining about how "unfair" something is, I'm really expecting someone else to "fix it." I don't believe I have the power to fix it myself.

When we say, "This crap happened to me. I can't control that, but I can control what I'm going to do about it," our world turns upside down—in the best of ways. If "they" are to blame, then "they" hold all the power. If "they" do X and I choose to do Y, I act based on what I have determined is in my best interest. I act without waiting for someone else to "be fair." When I do that, then I hold onto my power. I would forget that, and need to be reminded of it, throughout my life, but eventually, it would sink in.

Later that week, as my time there was almost over, the other kids decided I should be the trustee leader, essentially the liaison between staff and patients. For the next two weeks, I worked through so many emotions, both internal and external as I took Joe C's words, and Louis' death, to heart. I was helping other kids and helping myself learn what true problems looked like.

There was Melissa, for instance. Melissa's problem wasn't heroin, although she was in Clearview for using heroin. Heroin was the symptom. I learned that her drug was how she coped when I listened to her explain how she was mentally and physically abused for years by a family member.

She turned to heroin to self medicate so she could deal with the trauma the abuse caused.

Joe C was right. Clearview wasn't about addiction. It was about the problems that drove us to our addiction. Whether it was sexual abuse, crappy parents, poverty, not fitting in, all the trauma and drama a teenager can have, or create, drugs weren't the problem. They were a symptom. Not knowing how to face and deal with our problems, was the problem.

It's funny, not funny ha-ha, but funny strange how true Joe C was about addiction. Since my time at Clearview I read a study about rats who were given the choice of cocaine or community. Researchers proved that when rats were placed in a cage, all alone, with no other community of rats, and they were offered two water bottles—one filled with water and the other with heroin or cocaine —the rats would drink from the drug-laced bottles until they all overdosed and died. They were relentless in their addiction. They drank the cocaine laced water until their bodies and brains were overcome with the effects of the drug, and they died.

Before Joe C ever shared that tip about drug use being a way to avoid dealing with my problems, a psychologist, Dr Bruce Alexander, wondered whether the setting, or the drug, drove the rat's addiction to cocaine. He had this little glimmer of a suspicion that addiction is about far more than any drug. So he created "rat parks." These parks were very rat centric, social environments, like sports bars without alcohol, just for rats.

The rats could have sex, run around, play, meet other rats, and just chill and hang out and be rat buddies. After all the rats were settled into rat heaven and having a chill time, he offered them the choice of plain water or cocaine laced water. They avoided the drugged water, drank the plain water, and continued to connect with their buddies.

What Dr. Alexander learned, and what Joe C knew, was that humans, not just rats, need to be part of a community—a community that encourages us to relate to, seek out and find and experience the support of others. Joe knew that community and facing your problems is far more appealing than any drug.

This "truth" about community and connection doesn't get any easier to understand, or implement. Remember it. Rehab was about my learning how to connect, to seek support, to find an authentic community where I could be who I was, and not just where I could blend in. It wasn't about my using weed at all.

Given that weed is a "gateway" drug—meaning it reinforces the belief that we can self-medicate to solve our pain (not that it guarantees we'll use other drugs) I was lucky to go into rehab early, before finding harder drugs to cope with.

When pot isn't enough to solve the pain, then we look for something stronger. It's like, "Oh this aspirin is doing nothing for my broken arm, I think I'll try some oxycontin." What my parents, and Clearview knew was that the drugs were the symptom. I don't think if you asked them at the time that they could have articulated that. Joe C could. My parents just knew "something was wrong with Matt," and I needed to be fixed.

I wouldn't have ended up in rehab if my drug of choice was socially accepted drugs—like alcohol, food, shopping, sex, porn, or seeking high risk activity. Those "addictions" would have gone unchallenged. But weed had been my drug of choice. Again, God's perfect timing. I wouldn't have been sent to rehab for too much time in the gym, or too much time spent practicing or doing sports drills. But pot? Yeah. That got my parent's attention without a lot of trauma to me physically. Anyway...

The issue was still how I dealt with my problems. How did I connect? Did I connect? At Clearview I learned connection with others, facing my problems and dealing with them would give me the strength, direction, and tools I needed going forward. That wasn't just a lesson or lecture they gave. Clearview was about being hands on and practicing the talk, walking the walk, not just hearing it.

So, I listened to Melissa's problems, and to the problems of the other kids there, and in listening I learned to listen. I learned to look at my feelings, and share them too. Clearview taught me how to love, how to listen, how to care. Clearview taught me how to connect with other hurting people. In other words, Clearview taught me Empathy. Many times in my life, I have been called an "Empath." I would cry and get emotional at commercials, (to this day I can't watch an ESPN 30 for 30 without tissues).

I would feel the pain of other people's problems as if they were my own. I used to think it was a curse but I know it now to be one of my best attributes.

Clearview was aptly named. It gave me something I'd been missing for a long time—a "clear view." Rehab wasn't something you did in order to stop using drugs. Rehab was a group of friends only interested in helping each other. We didn't care where you came from, what drugs you were addicted to, how much was in your bank account or what type of upbringing you had. We only cared about the person.

It was as far away from the "blending in" game I was playing at school as I could get. It was a lifetime from my childhood "in the hood," and essentially raising myself. It was a portal where I entered into another world, another way of being, living, seeing, acting and loving.

I always say that time stood still in Clearview. For the first time in my life, I focused on my head and my feelings. And it was okay to have feelings, and okay to express them. My emotions were understood and people empathized with me. Before Clearview I needed to suck it up and play the game. At Clearview I learned how to feel my problems, face my problems, and solve my problems.

It's easy to push off problems. It's easy to say "I'll deal with that tomorrow or I'll blame someone else for the problem at hand." Or, my favorite, "It's not my fault. It's not fair. I didn't do anything to deserve this." That's victim talk.

I learned to face problems head on. There's a saying when you're in a hole and trying frantically to get out of the hole— "First, stop digging."

It means, "Don't compound the problems you already have by making more bad decisions (digging)." The lessons I learned at Clearview would pay me dividends for many years to come.

Finally graduation day from Clearview had come. Joe C asked me to address the contingent of kids and parents.

"Take five minutes and tell everyone about your experience, Griff. No big deal."

I remember the nerves lighting me up, coursing through my body. I had no idea what I was going to say or how I was going to say it. I'd never given a speech before.

I looked around the audience in the same gymnasium I'd entered four weeks prior. One month, yet it felt like a year.

I felt so different, so clear. Joe called me to the stage and what happened next shocked everyone; I began speaking about what I learned. What I learned about the staff, the counselors, my new family but most importantly what I learned about myself. I talked about choices to the new kids. I told them they had a choice—a choice to listen, learn and love or end up like Louis. It was real talk and it was from my heart. I finished by saying my story isn't finished and neither is yours.

"They can throw us to the wolves but we WILL return leading the pack," I said.

Driving home from Clearview, I cried. In fact, I cried for most of the day. I can't even tell you why I was crying. Maybe it was emotions, maybe it was what I knew that laid ahead. Clearview was safe. We, the counselors and kids, were on the same path more or less. We were focused on learning to deal with our problems, face our demons, and take action. But high school? Life? The friends, the judgment, the decisions? What would happen once I was back in my old environment, "blending in," and being the Griff I worked four years to perfect?

I don't know what it was but that was the longest I'd ever cried until years later when Benny took his last breath in my mouth.

Monday morning came and the trepidation I felt going back to school was overwhelming. Everything had changed. Matt Griffin the Senior Class president and captain of the Football/lacrosse team was gone. In his place and in everyone's view was Matt Griffin the junky. I remember the looks, the whispers. Even the teachers treated me like I had a disease.

I'd smoked a little weed and knew that many of the classmates around me, judging me, had done far harder drugs, and for much longer. The difference between us, I thought, beyond getting caught, was that I had learned addiction was a symptom, and dealing with life head on was the solution. I was privy to secrets about life that even with all their money, prestige, and status, they didn't have. I'd run the gauntlet, survived my first crucible, and come back knowing I was in an environment of facades—from the teachers, to my classmates.

I felt alone. I felt abandoned. But I had new tools, tools Clearview had given me, and a three step solution I would turn to for the next decade: "Feel the problem, deal with the problem and take the first step towards the resolution."

"Fast" Eddie Franz, head varsity basketball coach and one of the best history teachers and leaders of men I'd ever met, called me into his office. We sat there for a minute and just looked at each other. He knew me well. He had grown up in a similar fashion as I had. He understood the struggles of being born with a plastic spoon, not a silver one in your mouth.

"So Griff, you okay?"

I nodded.

"I'm proud of you," he said. He watched my reaction.

"Things are going to be different from here out," he assured me.

Then it got real. We talked through the struggles I was going to face by being labeled by my peers and friends' and their families. The old song I used to play, the "It's not fair, it's not my fault," pop song was fading fast. Thanks to Joe C and Clearview, I almost couldn't remember the words of that song. A new song was playing in my head, one whose chorus was, "I got this. I'm in control. Gotta go through it to get through it."

What I learned from Clearview was already paying its dividends. We talked about how to move through others' perceptions and just be me, just do me.

No one else defines who I am but me. For the first time my life was mine and in MY control. Others could stare, whisper or make fun of me all they wanted, but it was my choice to allow it to affect me or to be the man Joe C and Eddie Franz knew I could be. "Gotta go through it to get through it," I kept saying to myself.

The amazing thing I learned during this time is that people will eventually see us as we see ourselves. They will reinforce the image we project. If you project leadership, strength, confidence, and control, that's what they will see. If you project fear, weakness, victimhood, that's what they will see and they will help you reinforce whatever it is you project.

It takes some people longer than others to notice we've changed. And, those who for whatever reason never want to see us as strong, will fade from our lives and go in search of those who welcome their judgment and criticism. It's an odd lesson, but a critical one, one that has a lot to do with addiction, PTSD, depression, mental illness and self-image.

Your son or daughter, husband or wife, partner, or colleague may be struggling with addiction. You may be struggling with addiction. What I want to say to you is keep going, you can get through it. Keep grinding, there's light at the end of the tunnel.

When you feel like giving up, remember what you're fighting for. Think about what your life was like before your addiction. And remember, your addiction may be to sex, porn, eating, alcohol, drugs, shopping, rage (yes, you can be addicted to anger and violence), working insane hours, whatever.

Hobbies, work, sex, food, going to the gym, playing video games, whatever are healthy activities until they turn negative. What I learned at Clearview, and since then, is that the line between activity and *addiction* is where that "fun" activity begins to control you.

Are you carving out more time for it than you used to, planned to, or want to for your new addiction? Are you pushing aside family, friends, and work to engage in it? How important is it to you? Does doing it or not doing it create or lessen your sense of self-esteem? For most police officers it can be uncomfortable to wake up and realize, as I later did, that police work (undercover work for me), was my addiction. The more of it I did, the better I felt—even when it negatively impacted my marriage. The thought of losing my identity, my badge, my "power" as a law enforcement officer terrified me.

Just like an addict who thinks, "How will I survive without my drugs/sex/porn/money/shopping habit/alcohol or whatever," we panic with the idea of "the man" coming to take away our badge, our gun, our identify and our life as an officer. Like any addict, many of us would choose to die (suicide) rather than face life without that identity. It's scary as hell to contemplate our mental health. I challenge you to do it.

Live the life you were destined to have. Give God a chance to take the pain away. Give God a chance to give you the life He planned for you. Many officers who do seek help, who do go into therapy do leave police work. But many of them stay. Others, like myself, and Byron, turn their police experience into a business where we call the shots and we can prioritize our mental health and still do what we love to do, help others.

What helped me the most the past decade was God. At Clearview we were taught about "higher powers" and how to use them.

"During your life struggles—whether it's addiction or whatever, use those struggles as an opportunity to show your higher power how blessed you are," the counselor said.

"Essentially be grateful for the struggles. On the other side of your struggle is happiness. When we say, 'This too shall pass,' isn't just about the bad times, it's about the good times as well. In time, good or bad, it will all pass. Be grateful for all of it."

When I came home from Clearview I was in for another shock. I'd hoped people would be supportive and happy for me. A few were, but most of the people around me wanted to see me fail. They had created this negative, drug addict, worthless loser image of me, and they wanted to see me be this person they created in their head. By seeing me lose, they somehow figured that would make them stronger or better, without them having to change their life.

There's something about other people doing better than them that makes people want to pull them down. It's like crabs in a bucket. If you put a bunch of crabs in a bucket they will pull down any crab who is about to escape the bucket. It's as if they would rather they all die, than have some or most escape. Rather than grab hold of another crab who is getting out of the bucket and escaping with them, they pull everyone down all while trying to escape themselves.

It's why coming out of rehab addicts are told not to associate with old friends in the lifestyle they had. They don't want to see someone who used to be an addict like them getting clean. They will do anything they can, consciously or not, to cause that person to lapse back into old behaviors.

When I didn't allow them to affect me and I rose above their judgements they saw their image of me wasn't about me. It was a reflection of their own insecurities and fears projected onto me. Things changed. I was their kid, and most importantly I was OK. You will be too! I promise.

Your story isn't over, feel each problem from your head to your toes. Take some time to pray about the resolution. Then make a decision and take the first step towards it. Minute by minute, hour by hour, day by day...you go through it and before you know it.....You got through it and found the light.

Looking back I can attest to the fact that nothing you learn is ever wasted. God has a reason and a plan for all the skill sets you develop in life. And I promise you this. Life will kick your butt before handing you the prize. SAR, (Search and Rescue school), was one of those things—ups and downs of like, you know, star school. Rehab was another school where I learned life lessons. Marriage was another, undercover was another. Everything is an education. If you start realizing that now, and see the challenges you face, and how you face them, as a test, as a lesson, you'll go farther, faster, and with less stress than if you fight it all and protest, "It isn't fair."

That's why, after four years of passing as a rich kid, and fresh from all the wisdom I picked up in rehab, I decided I didn't want to do the college thing. I didn't want to pretend to be something and someone I wasn't for four more years. I could have.

I was a really good athlete, an all state lacrosse/football player. It wouldn't have been much of a stretch to get another scholarship and get into a top university and keep playing the fame and celebrity game. I just didn't want to do that anymore. I had lived that life for four years and I was done with it. I wanted to make my own journey and find out who I really was. I watched a commercial about the US Navy and at the end they said "LET THE JOURNEY BEGIN." And so I did. I joined the Navy, and I went off to boot camp in Illinois and then on to California.

The Navy was definitely not all Armani and designer clothes, cutting edge haircuts, or high priced cars. We all wore the same thing. I was judged on who I was, what I could do, how dependable I was, and not the size of my bank account. I still had to fit in. I still had challenges. I had people who hated and envied me, and others who became my brothers for life.

Everyone in the Navy came from a different background, so there was learning to negotiate that, but it was nothing like high school had been. I put my ability to blend in with any culture and my newfound listening skills, to good use.

After boot camp, I was stationed in San Diego for the next 18 months learning how to become a Sonar Technician. I can still taste the flavor of a California burrito. If you've never had one, put it on your bucket list—you'll thank me later. My 18 months in San Diego was surreal. I was on my own. Making my own money but still just a baby.

I remember getting my first paycheck of $315 for a week or two of work. It was directly deposited into an account I had set up while in boot camp. I had the freedom to choose what I wanted to do each night, where I wanted to go and who I wanted to be with. No one cared about anything other than who I was. I thrived.

The next 18 months were everything I hoped it would be. I was able to live. I went to Tijuana, Los Angeles, and Las Vegas. I saw and experienced so many different cultures and lifestyles—not all of them things I'd repeat here.

I learned something new too. I learned that the bond you share with your brothers and sisters in uniform is unlike anything I've ever experienced. After A school, I was sent to Mayport Florida to the

USS Dewert. Once I received my orders, I was given the date I was going to meet up with my ship.

The base shuttle took me and another sailor—Dave Shulthies—to the airport. I learned that he had orders for the same ship and that we were going to fly to Amsterdam where the *USS Dewert* was docked for the next two weeks. On the flight we became instant friends. To this day, Dave is one of my closest friends on the planet. After Amsterdam I was stationed in Mayport, Florida for the next four years where once my enlistment was up I would join the Virginia Beach Police Department and begin my career working narcotics. It was in Mayport onboard the *USS Dewert* where my life once again took a drastic turn. After about a year on the *USS Dewert*, Adam Goss and I were working out in the ship's makeshift gym located in one of the helo hangers.

The Ops LT walks in and we both pop tall with salutes. He looks Adam and I up and down and says "you guys are in pretty good shape."

We responded "thank you sir."

"Can you both swim?" He asks.

Adam was one of the best surfers I'd ever seen and I grew up in the water so we both responded yes.

Ops continued "Look guys, we're in a pinch...I need two SAR swimmers for the upcoming deployment. Are you two interested in going to SAR school?"

In my head I was trying to figure out what the hell SAR was. I learned it stood for Search and Rescue Swimmer.

Adam and I both responded with shrugs and "Sure." One week later I had entered what would be the toughest test of my life. Five weeks of absolute living hell. Five weeks of instructors trying to kill me—and I mean literally trying to kill me. I had no idea what I was getting myself into. Looking back, maybe that was a good thing. If I'd have known what lay ahead I might have politely declined the invitation.

What I learned during that three months of SAR training would be the foundation of my resilience and strength for the rest of my life.

Day 1, we all lined up on the brickyard. There were over 100 of us. We began with stretching and some light push ups/sit ups, etc. as these badass intimidating instructors circled us, not saying a word, just looking menacing. They moved in and around us like sharks who have not been fed in months scoping out their first meal. It got real during the first run.

"Ok line up!" they screamed..

Once we all lined up the lead instructor lulled us into thinking this was going to be just another exercise. He began by saying "Gentlemen...we have a three mile run in front of you, here is the route..."

After the route was laid out, he dropped the bomb. "We have a motto in SAR and it goes far beyond us....DON'T BE LAST."

With that, we started the first run of the day. Thankfully, I've always been a good runner. Lacrosse is a stamina sport and speed and endurance was something I always had. I began fast out of the gate and was holding about a 6:30/7:00 minute mile. There was a group of about 10 of us that were holding that pace pretty solid.

I looked back and found a couple more pockets of groups holding their own pace as well. As we moved to finish the three mile course the pack leaders all glided through the finish line. What happened next still makes me shudder.

The last group of about 20 people came across the finish line. They looked slow, out of breath and for the most part not ready for SAR. As they came across the finish line, the sharks began to feed. They grabbed each one as they crossed the finish line and physically yanked the shit out of them. (Similar process to walling someone). It's a shocking gesture not meant to injure but to catch you off guard and rattle you. After they grabbed each person, they put them in the pushup position and began screaming at them about how they were the weakest link, they were last.

"You were told, 'don't be last,'" they screamed, "but you didn't listen, did you?" Then the firehose came out. They were all still in the push-up position, arms trembling and still trying to catch their breaths from the run. There's some crazy person screaming in their ears and spitting in their face when they're suddenly hit with cold water from a high pressure hose. I watched as one after another they got up and rang the bell. Every. Single. One.

I remember thinking "you've done it this time Griffin. You're in waaay over your head."

By the end of day one, that class of about 100 was down to 72. By week's end we had 40 still standing. Thankfully Adam and I were still upright. We had each other. Constant sideways glances at each other, and almost unnoticeable shakes of the head between us kept us going. Those little glances said "Don't fucking leave me Griff." My glance back said "I got you brother, we are here to the end!"

Without Adam next to me for the next five weeks, I would never have made it. SAR school is rated the 3rd hardest training curriculum in the world behind only SEAL Training and EOD training. US Navy Search and Rescue swimmers are the elite of the Naval Aviation Community. Sailors must complete some of the most rigorous training pipelines in the course of their goals. US Coast Guard SAR swimmers were made famous with the 2006 motion picture "The Guardian" with Ashton Kutcher and Kevin Costner. One super interesting and awesome fact is that the Coast Guard and Navy are the only two branches that allow women to serve as SAR swimmers.

"Don't be last..." I heard it over and over again and as the rank and file were ruthlessly trimmed down. My ability to blend in became increasingly harder. Week Two, I learned another valuable lesson. As the three mile run was coming to a close, the group of runners I was running with began pushing it in order to be first. Now it wasn't about being last, it was about being the first to cross the finish line. I was content in the middle but somehow without paying attention I fell into the last 5-10 people running. With about ¼ mile left, an all out sprint began. I looked around and knew I didn't want to be last and feel the wrath of the always hungry sharks. So I began sprinting with the back of the packers. I gave everything I had and crossed the finish before about 7 or 8 others. I was gassed.

Those last couple of runners were pulled out to receive their reward for being last as the rest of us lined up.

The head instructor looked at us all and said "Did we say three miles??"

"We meant six miles.....GO!"

Crap, I thought. I got nothing in the tank. Adam grabbed my arm and said "C'mon Griff, not today bro...not today." I learned a lot about myself that day. I learned when I think I have nothing left in the tank...I have an entire spare tank waiting to be called upon. Your brain will trick your body into thinking you can't do something, when in actuality you can and you will. It wasn't a choice. It was will power. It was my brother next to me who I would rather die before disappointing. The lesson of week two—If you think you can't go any longer, keep grinding because you have more in the tank than you can ever imagine.

Week three started with disappointment. Adam and I had become close with another guy in class and on Monday morning we looked around and couldn't find him at morning muster. He dropped over the weekend. And then there were 19 left. Adam and I came up with a strategy that I would use the rest of my life. I talk about this later on in this book.

Essentially, get through everything minute by minute...hour by hour, day by day. On Mondays, we decided we wouldn't look at the next several weeks or even the entire week—all we would say to each other is let's get to Wednesday. On Wednesdays— "Hump day"— the base bar would stay open until midnight. No matter what time we got done with training on Wednesday we would go to the base bar and split a pitcher of Budweiser.

The two of us doing that would eventually grow to five of us and then to 10 of us. There were two females in the group, and it was that community of brotherhood and sisterhood that got us through it all.

The nods and silent glances that started between Adam and I became glances and nods from nine others if it was "your day." What I mean by "your day," is if that day you were singled out by staff, it was your day to be broken. The staff worked tirelessly trying to break you and get you to quit. We never did. We used the power of community and faith to shut out the noise and harassment. We knew that no matter what they did to us, today or tomorrow, Wednesday WOULD come. The minutes would tick on no matter what they threw at us. Just hang in there. Your brothers and sisters are pulling for you, and they've got your back. All you had to do was glance around to see the wall of support for you.

One of the biggest challenges we all faced was the mental aspect of swimming with a snorkel. Every week we had timed swims. Swims with snorkels and fins in this Olympic sized pool that was 500m or 1000m long.

The swim was timed and if you didn't make the time you were out. On face value this doesn't seem too difficult right? Well, what the average person doesn't understand is that with a snorkel in your mouth breathing is very difficult. Instead of breathing normally, you're pulling oxygen through this narrow snorkel tube. When you become gassed or over exerted, your brain tells you to rip the snorkel out of your mouth and take a huge breath.

Imagine the end of an all out sprint. You're doubled over with your hands on your knees gasping for air. Now imagine having a snorkel in your mouth and having to pull the oxygen down through it. Unknown to us, there were divers under the water as we conducted these timed swims. As we were coming to the last 50 or 100m's they would swim underneath us and pull us under water. This filled our snorkels and mouths with water. If you ripped your mask off you were automatically DQ'd or disqualified. (two disqualifications and you were sent home).

The toughest thing I ever had to do was get dunked as I'm hauling ass to finish my timed swim. Every fiber of your body and mind tells you to rip the mask off and get oxygen. NO, you had to fight your instincts and your brain, you had to calm yourself mentally and exhale as hard as you could to clear your snorkel. The mental aspect of this exercise paid me many dividends the rest of my life.

The lesson for week three—In the face of danger/desperation

remain calm and assess the situation, then act and move through it. Essentially, think before you act.

Week four and then Week five were about tactics and critical thinking. These two weeks shaped my ability to navigate through crisis incidents in a way most police or military members would never imagine. When a crisis hits (man overboard/shooting/combat/traffic accident etc..) you have the ability to switch on, critically think and finally act.

There is nothing routine about a plane/helo crash, shooting, or whatever the incident is. You have to be able to breath, assess and act. This was reinforced every morning as we lined up on the pool's edge awaiting inspection.

If something was off, your mask was ripped from your head and tossed into a 12 foot deep pool. You had to immediately dive in the water, retrieve your mask while sitting on the bottom of the pool, put your mask on, press the top of the mask while pushing oxygen out of your nose to clear the water from your mask. Once this process was completed—you gave a thumbs up to the diver staring at you.

Only when he gave you the returned thumbs up sign were you allowed to swim to the surface. When lives are at stake, your split second decisions are the difference between someone going home to their families or the family getting the life changing knock on the door. I've been present for that life changing knock on the door. The pain, confusion and hurt of the family on the other side is something I will never forget, but that I would often repeat as a police officer responding to suicides, accidents, and trauma. More lessons to learn. God's timing, teaching, and training was right on track and I didn't have a clue.

Adam and I both graduated from SAR school. Five grueling weeks of hell, but the plaque still hangs on my wall. "So others may live." That's the motto of SAR swimmers and a theme in this memoir. "So others may live," isn't just a motto and theme and a plaque on the wall. It's a way of life. It's a calling to protect and serve. To be that sheepdog protecting the sheep from the wolves that prey on their innocence was my goal. I became that sheepdog on June 22nd, 2001 as I crossed the stage after completing the US Navy Search and Rescue school.

My assumption I'd spend a fairly uneventful career in the Navy was over. If anything I was even more passionate and committed to a Naval Career after SARs, until I was waitlisted for the Seaman to Admiral (STA) fast track I'd applied for. My enlistment was six months from coming to an end. I had more decisions to make and to make fast or I was going to be without a job.

CHAPTER FOUR

Learning the Trade

"Throw me to the wolves
and I'll return leading the pack."
- Author unknown

With only six months to figure out whether to stay in the Navy, work to get accepted into the Navy's Seaman to Admiral program (which I was waitlisted for), or find yet another career path, I had to figure out where I wanted my paychecks to come from—the Navy, or something else.

After explaining my limited options to him, my older brother encouraged me to apply for the Virginia Beach Police Department's (VBPD) police officer position as a backup, a plan B in case I wasn't selected for the STA program. It sounded like a decent option. I'd never wanted to be a cop, but it was a job I could do. I visited him, and after the next few weeks, my reenlistment papers went unsigned, and I swapped my Navy whites for Police blues and began working for the VBPD right after my enlistment was over.

My life had taken some radical twists and turns to get me into police work, but I'd need everyone of those twists and turns, every failure, every success, every miserable minute in hell I survived, and everything I learned along the way to get to the point where I made the smartest decision of my life—to not pull that trigger and check out.

A lot of recruits join the police department and think their police career is starting with day one of the academy. They mistakenly believe that showing up in whatever uniform they're given, being a recruit, and being gung-ho is where learning their trade (police work) begins. It doesn't.

It begins when you're a kid and you're learning about character, and caring, and good and bad, and what it means to be a man (or woman), and how to survive and how to thrive, wherever you end up. It begins every time you learn a new skill, take a new job, meet a new person. Nothing that happens to you is ever wasted unless you choose to ignore the lesson.

Like I said, I started learning the trade I call "blending" at age 14 when I went from the ghetto to a rich private elite highschool, literally overnight. I learned the trade as a teenager in a rehab program where the most I'd done is smoke pot, but was surrounded by hardcore drug and alcohol addictions. Before I was old enough to drive I knew the drug trade from all sides, and was hobnobbing with the kids of celebrities, and learning to handle my own fame and accomplishments. It all became a part of who I was, and where I ended up, and how I handled things on the job, and after the job.

When I interviewed the officers I did for this book, I learned that everything we do, everything that happens to us, or around us, becomes a part of us. And by "becoming a part of us," I mean it's more than a "lesson" we learn.

Our experiences shape our character. It becomes part of our knowledge bank, which controls how we see life, and how we choose to respond to the challenges life throws at us.

I've talked to a lot of officers who lost family members, partners, and parents to suicide. Suicide is more common than you'd think, and it profoundly impacts those left behind to deal with the aftermath and fallout.

Recognizing 'tells' and signs of drug dealing, using and activity was something I learned in high school. Learning how to chase down a bad guy, or understand how he thought—and be better and smarter than the dealer thought, came from my high school years, running the streets with a gang, not from the police academy or SAR training.

The academy prepares you for working the tip of the iceberg, but the real lessons are underwater, out of sight, and are bigger and go deeper than you can ever imagine. The dangerous part of the iceberg is what you can't see, and don't know. It's the part you learn to look for when you graduate from the academy and hit the street with your Field Training Officer (FTO).

Ask anyone who hasn't been to rehab what you learn there, and they're likely to focus on the "stop doing drugs" angle. That's not what I learned. Okay, I mean I learned how smoking weed was going to hurt my chances to do a lot of the things I might want to do one day, but I learned more about myself.

I think it's because of my upbringing, and the mentors in rehab, the supervisors on the police force, and my time in the Navy that gave me the advantage I had. Those, and my Type A personality and drive to outperform resulted in a career with a nickname I learned to love—"The Dark Cloud."

The name had nothing to do with evil or depression, but with the outcome of every traffic stop I made. As a fellow officer said, "Every time Griff makes a traffic stop it's bad news for the bad guys—he's just a dark cloud over their heads."

I was working at Virginia Beach's 3rd Precinct when I got the nickname. The 1st Precinct was the upper crust and courts of VA Beach. The 2nd Precinct was the beach beat, mostly tourists, students, and out-of-towners. The 3rd Precinct was mine—the "ghetto." And, the 4th Precinct, where Dave and Brittany lived, was a residential, middle-class area.

Rudy's advice to me when it came time to choose a precinct, was to go for the 3rd Precinct because of my experience, and influence from my upbringing, drug knowledge, and what I learned about blending in from high school. It was there, he said, and I agreed, that my skills would serve me best. I was about to learn more in a position where I thought I was already an expert.

As I said, originally I planned to be career Navy. I loved what I did, where I was, and everything about the sea and being on board a ship. I loved every moment of being in the Navy, but when I was coming to the end of my enlistment I decided I wanted to be a Naval Officer. I wanted to lead. So I applied to what was called the Seaman to Admiral program (STA). It was basically a fancy inspiring name which essentially meant that I would go to college and the Navy would pay for that college. Once finished with my bachelor degree, I would be an enlisted officer. I was really excited for the opportunity.

I went through the application process to go into the program. I did the PT test and did well. I had this captain on my ship—the USS Dewert. His name was Captain TK Shannon. He was just an amazing man and a great person. He's the one that really believed in me and walked me through the entire application process.

I remember him coming to me on a Thursday afternoon. He said "Griff, I need you to take the SAT's."

I looked at him and said "Captain, I'm a 23 year old man...I can't take the SATs."

He said "Yes you can. You need to take these as part of the STA application process."

You don't argue with a Captain. So, on a Saturday morning I went down to this place on base where I sat in line waiting to take the SATs. It brought back a memory from my time in HS. At Morristown beard I played football and after a Friday night football game a bunch of us went into NYC for the night.

I think we went to see 311 in concert or something. I got home around 3 a.m. and found a sticky note on my bedroom door, reminding me I needed to be at the high school at 8 a.m to take the SATs. I remember getting over there at about 8:30 a.m., tired, bleary-eyed and half asleep after barely getting any sleep the night before. I took the SATs with one eye open. I think I just kind of circled and filled in blanks everywhere I needed just to try and get through the day without passing out.

Out of 1600 possible points I got a 940 which really isn't good. All of the coaches that were recruiting me to play lacrosse and football in college saw my scores and said I needed to get my scores up to be admitted. They were nice about it, but I think they were also silently asking themselves why they were recruiting a dumbass. I tried to explain that I hadn't prepared for this, that I had had about two hours of notice.

My blame game, "it's not my fault," came back full force. I'm not sure whether I wanted someone to feel sorry for me and give me another shot, or just ignore my scores and focus on my physical abilities. Either way, nobody really wanted to hear my excuses, so I wound up taking the Kaplan S80 course and working really hard over the next several months.

When the time came to take them again, I got a good night's sleep and felt prepared. When the score came back I got a 1510 on my SATs and was so pumped and proud of myself. I was like " I did it."

I remember screaming to the high rooftops about getting a 1510 on my SATs like I knew I could do it. About two weeks later I got a note from the state SATs board exam review saying they believed I cheated and they were going to nullify my 1510 on the SATs. You've got to be kidding me.

To say I was pissed was an understatement. They said essentially there's no way someone can go from a 940 to a 1510 score without cheating. They needed me to take the test again. Once again, the feeling of unfairness rippled through my body. But that was my life. I had to work twice as hard for half as much.

"It wasn't fair," I heard myself saying. As hard as I worked, as much as I did, I could not seem to shake the "unfairness" I encountered at every turn in my life. Would it ever end?

I went back a month later and knocked the SATs out of the park and received a 1520. So here I am, sitting there on a Saturday morning and I'm like I cannot believe that this is happening all over again. Almost ten years later and everything revolves around the scores I get on these SATs. Why does this matter so much? How do SAT scores translate to whether or not I would be a good naval officer?

I started down the road of, "It's not fair," but stopped shy of playing the victim and took the SATs once again. This time I got a 1270 with zero preparation with zero study time. I was like "OK... alright.... I can do this!" I was beginning to believe I was going to be accepted for STA and kept going through the evaluation process.

Then, Captain TK Shannon got promoted to Admiral and left the ship. A new captain, Captain Berube, came in. He doesn't know me from Adam and essentially could care less whether not I made it to STA or not.

So, I got waitlisted. It was the first time I'd ever applied to something and not been immediately accepted. I still remember the feeling of getting waitlisted and the first time I ever ever felt the pang of rejection. It wasn't a full rejection, but it might as well have been.

I sat there for about half a day thinking about the lessons Joe C had taught me. Thinking about my problem (getting into STA) and how I was going to deal with it. Full speed ahead. If it's meant to be it'll be. That weekend I was going up to Chesapeake, Virginia to see my older brother. I had about six months left in my enlistment with the Navy. I told him about my concerns, and the STA program wait-listing.

He said "Matt, Virginia Beach police are hiring ...why don't you use that as a backup?"

I said OK, that's not a bad idea. That Sunday the department had a PT test as the first part of the application process to enter the Police Academy. I showed up at 8:00 AM to the Virginia Beach Police Department on Birdneck Ave., rested and ready to roll. I remember driving down there like at 7:00 o'clock in the morning thinking to myself "what am I doing??"

· · ·

I was never one of those people that grew up always wanting to be a cop. I was never that person. At the end of the day I needed a job and being a police officer seemed like a good thing to be. It met my need for adrenaline, for something different to look forward to every day, and a way to help others and be with members of a tribe. I'd grown accustomed to the deep bonding I had with other military men and women, and thought I'd find the same camaraderie in police work.

I was really hoping that the STA thing was going to come through. If it didn't, at the end of the day I'd probably just reenlist in the Navy and be a 20 year Navy guy if the police thing didn't work out. I assumed I'd just walk in and walk out with the job. How much competition could there be? How many people wanted to be cops? I had no idea.

On my way down to the Police academy, I was on Rt 64 just before you get off the exit onto Birdneck Ave. You can see the police Academy's back facility from there. I looked down and I saw tons and tons of people standing around there. I couldn't believe all these people were here for the police PT test.

Sure enough I get there and there's probably 2,000 people vying for 30 spots. I remember saying to myself there's no way I'm going to get a spot. I began talking to one of the volunteers and he said yeah this is just one of two or three dates for passing the basics. What, 5,000 people were applying for 30 spots? What am I doing here?

I was paired up with a guy named Matt Muzzy who to this day is still one of my best friends. Muzz and I paired up and we became PT buddies. He had to count my sit-ups/pushups and I counted his. Then we all lined up to do this timed obstacle course. We both smoked the obstacle course, and didn't do badly on the sit-ups and push-ups.

Once we finished the PT test we were rated on our scores. If you made it past that aspect of it you were invited back to take the written test. We both made it past the obstacle course/PT test and were invited back that afternoon for the written test. The crowd of

2000 applicants had been narrowed down to about 700 people, all crammed into this auditorium for the written test.

We finished the written test and we're all standing out in the auditorium hallway. Someone starts calling people out by their last names. They passed through the Gs and Ms and Muzzy looked at me and asked, "Did we really fail the written test?"

No worries. The names they called were for the people who *failed* the test. They walked those folks out. Everyone who was left, including Muzzy and I, were the applicants who passed the first and second phases. Now they're down to about 200 people out of 2,000 and they said "Congratulations. You guys have passed both the physical portion and the written test portion of the application process to the Virginia Beach Police Academy."

Muzz and I shook hands and both of us kind of looked at each other.

"Good meeting you bro," I said.

"You too," he said.

"You know what, we'll probably never see each other again but you know, good luck in the rest of your life," I said.

Next came the background checks, and our initial oral boards. I get through all that and I get to the final interview with the Chief of Police. As I'm walking in I see Matthew Muzzy walking out.

I grinned and waved. I knew we were both going to be in the Academy together. Day one we sat next to each other and we've been best friends ever since.

Matt moved on from Virginia Beach and became a Federal Air Marshal. I stayed in Virginia Beach.

At the end of the Academy they rank everything that you do. They rank your PT tests (Pushups in 60 seconds, sit ups in 60 seconds and 1.5m run) they rank your firearm proficiency along with every score from every written test. Five thousand people and I finished number one. One of the things I held onto for a long time was finishing the VBPD academy as the number one overall recruit. It fed everything I ever believed in—that hard work would get me what I wanted. This wasn't about who I knew, but what I knew and how well I performed. I took it.

Muzz would always look at me and say things like "Is there anything you're NOT good at?" I'd respond back and say "I'm a jack of all trades but master of none."

On our exit PT test, Muzz and I squared off to run the mile and a half. We lined up on the Virginia Beach Boardwalk. Muzz looked at me and said "You know I'm gonna smoke you right?" I laughed.

Someone yelled "Go!" and we took off.. We had a blistering pace somewhere around a 5 minute mile. We crossed the one mile mark and Muzz was getting stronger. He looked over at me and said "bye buddy!" He beat me on that exit PT test and to this day doesn't let me live it down. Muzz finished his 1.5m at 7:48 and I came in 7 seconds later at 7:55. If you're going to lose at something, try to lose to someone you respect.

After graduation I was assigned to duty in Virginia Beach, where I would learn to love narcotics and undercover work, meet and marry Kendra, lose Benny, and become the "Dark Cloud," for hundreds of unsuspecting drug dealers, and criminals.

Then, after four years of being "the dark cloud" in the third precinct, I moved to New Hampshire to a small town called Keene. I immediately got right back into narcotic work. I went undercover in 2014. Thoughts of a Naval career faded fast. I discovered police and undercover work was everything I'd ever wanted to do.

I loved everything about it — from the tattoos, to the lip ring and cornrows. It was another side of me. I got to explore another life of "blending" that paid great dividends as I made more arrests, busted more drug dealers and, in my mind, was well on the way to saving my small community from hard drugs and deaths by overdose.

Kendra and I had four sons, and life was great, until it wasn't, and I started planning my permanent exit from a life I thought I had screwed up beyond fixing.

CHAPTER FIVE

Suicide, Drugs, Police and Cultures

"Because this is how it's always been done...."
Well I think it's time for a change!

For two decades, practically since the invention of the Internet there has been more information, more books, more videos, more talk about suicide than ever before. Yet suicide has been on the rise for two decades. From 1999 to 2016, suicide rates rose significantly in 44 states, with 25 states experiencing increases of more than 30 percent.1 Why? I believe culture has a lot to do with it.

I also think the pressure on officers from social media, videos, the hatred of police from the way the media covers crime, and the constant pressure to never make a mistake has a lot to do with it too. What civilian could stand wearing a camera and audio device every day, all day, with every decision they make—good or bad, right or wrong—a matter of public record?

Police, military veterans, emergency services, and firefighters have a culture, like any group or job, gang, drug scene, sport, or way of life. It's a closed, secret culture, a warrior culture fed by the things we see, experience, and deal with on a day-to-day basis.

For police officers and first responders it's the culture of brotherhood, of the thin blue line, of silence even when silence kills. Every workplace has its culture. Quoting Jace Valcore, PhD, NLC Houston, "Broadly defined, culture refers to the shared norms, values, and beliefs of a group of people. Culture is how police officers, and any other group, make sense of their world and their role in it."

Making sense of our world, a world that is changing every day, with every video, every shooting, every call to defund police, or to limit their powers, just ratchets up the stress.

One of the things that's changing is how police and first responders are having to make sense of their world. In a world where, for decades cops were respected and obeyed, now they're ambushed, hunted, and hated. Even when they're doing their job and doing it well, the suits and supervisors are throwing them under the bus, the media and the left are calling for defunding rather than increasing funding, and character is laughed at, not sought out, respected, or honored.

That's not every department. But it's a lot of them. It makes it very hard to embrace your job of protecting the community when the media tells you no one wants you protecting them. I know the percentage of people who want the police on their streets, and want increased funding is greater than those who want to defund the police, but it's demoralizing to see anyone calling for less training, fewer boots on the ground, and social workers replacing officers.

Like the military, police culture is about how you see your job, how you do your job, and how you interact with your peers and supervisors in the job. It affects how you respond to, view, and rate the suicides of friends. It's a culture LEOs learn after they leave the police academy, and a culture most embrace until they retire, or run up against the suicide of a buddy, or partner while on the force — or worse — when they consider taking their own life.

All the things that make up how you live, engage in, and move among the other members of this culture are just as real and can be learned or taught, including how we view suicide, getting help, and turning our lives around.

Police culture is not the culture of the average citizen and they refuse to try to understand it. Police culture seems unnecessarily physical, even violent. They haven't had the training, seen the streets, or confronted evil. Of course they hate it. They don't understand it.

What constitutes success or failure, how you relate, and what matters to the other members of that culture is created by the people in that culture. If you're a cop or a first responder, you get it. But no amount of explaining can convince others that how you live, and what you live for, is what's keeping them safe while putting you at risk for ambush, murder, assault, and even suicide.

As I've looked at my own past, and begun to speak to groups and individuals about suicide, either a family member's suicide, or a partner's suicide, or even just suicide in general, I've begun to recognize the warrior culture that allow suicides to increase.

The LEO and first responder culture has its own language, buzz words, emotions, reactions, and stories—and almost all of them have to do with avoiding the stigma of mental health, no matter what your profession, race, ethnicity, or age.

What I think it's important to tell you is that not everyone commits suicide just because they're depressed. You can't just look at someone and say, "They seem depressed. They may be a suicide risk," and approach them from that perspective. Lots of depressed people never commit suicide.

Culture plays a huge role behind why people commit suicide. Psychologists are just now, late 2017 and 2018, learning that there are cultural factors that may increase—or decrease—racial and ethnic minorities' vulnerability to suicide. Native Indians have the country's highest rate of suicide. Why? Is it related to generations of human rights abuses and trauma or a different culture around mental health issues?

Rebecca Clay looks at the culture and suicide in an artcie in the American Psychological Association writing "A Korean-American man dies by suicide. Was it because he lost his job and felt intense shame over the loss of his breadwinner role in a patriarchal culture?

A Latina teenager attempts suicide. Was she upset because her immigrant parents restricted her movements and intruded on her decisions and relationships?"

What is so fascinating to me are the stories behind the suicides I've learned about. The one consistent factor in all suicides, regardless of culture, is that the people who kill themselves are in pain. That pain may be from feeling shame, or grief, or loss, but it's pain— unrelenting, unescapable pain. The culture may give the pain a context, but it comes down to pain.

Retired Vegas Metro police officer Joe Pannullo and I met several years ago when he became an instructor for PLET. We immediately gravitated towards each other and built a friendship that has lasted through ups and downs.

One night Joe and I were having dinner and he began telling me about the infamous Las Vegas concert shooting which he responded to. His level of courage in the face of grave danger overwhelms me to this day.

With less than a month to go before his retirement of 20 years with the LVMPD Joe was at a friend's house with his wife. They were talking about life after the police department and making plans when his pager went off. Joe was part of the Vegas Metro Swat team and was their primary hostage negotiator. He quickly turned the radio on and heard every cop's worst nightmare. "Active shooter, shots fired...shots fired.."

The radio traffic was ramping up as he listened. What he, and the world, would later learn was that 64 year old Stephen Paddock had opened fire on the thousands of people gathered at the Route 91 Harvest Music festival. Before the shots were silenced, Paddock would kill 61 and wound another 411.

At the time all Joe knew was he was needed. He "kitted up" (the process of donning swat gear) and began to head out of his friend's house and directly into the fire fight. With less than 30 days to retirement his wife grabbed his arm and said "Joe...you don't have to go, you're retiring in a month..." Joe said "I have to go baby, this is what I do; they need me."

As Joe was driving away he drove past the friend's porch to see his wife Carly standing on it crying, mouthing the words "don't go joe..."

I tell you this because as Joe spoke about the incident, I asked him about being a hostage negotiator. I asked what it was like and how it had impacted his career, why he'd gotten into it.

"My mother committed suicide when I was young." Joe said. He had tears beginning to form in his eyes.

"I didn't become a hostage negotiator because I thought it was interesting or cool, I became a hostage negotiator because I didn't want anyone else to have to go through the loss of a loved one like I did."

Joe's calm demeanor and genuine humble way about himself are why he is loved by so many. There isn't a mean bone in his body. I learned a valuable lesson that night. Don't ever judge someone's journey, you never know what they've gone through.

Masculinity Culture

If you have grown up male, in almost any culture, you know the rules of the masculinity culture whether you follow them, revere or hate them, or embrace them. The traditional masculine gender roles emphasize self-reliance, invulnerability, and stoicism.

Negative emotions are perceived as a sign of weakness. Bottom line? "Don't share your feelings." Sound familiar? So what happens when we feel overwhelmed? Where do we turn? How do we cope? Sex, drugs, alcohol, and suicide. I get it. So do you. You're as steeped in it as I am. There's nothing wrong with that.

I love the masculinity culture. I grew up in it. From sports to the military, SARS, and undercover work, you can't get more masculine culture than I was immersed in. But there's one drawback, the thing I hate most about it, is it doesn't allow for healthy sharing of our emotions.

I'm no longer on the job so I'm free to talk about emotions, to cry, to openly care. I have four boys and I assure you we talk about emotions, feelings, all the things the masculinity culture says we're not supposed to avoid. We call it real talk time in my household. My boys are encouraged to feel emotions. They're encouraged to cry if they need to, and are praised when they talk about how they feel.

How Male Culture Promotes Suicides

When your culture, your peers, and everyone around you is silently pressuring you to keep your mouth shut, to not cry, to not express emotions so you won't appear weak, you have two stressors —the emotions themselves, and the pressure to hide them at all costs.

My writing this book, or getting up in front of an audience and telling you this part of the culture has to change, is not going to change male culture. Old habits and old cultures die hard. Many of the officers coming on the force today have a military background like I do, like many of you do. That culture is even more warrior focused. We have to ask ourselves is that feeling of "being a man" at all costs worth dying for? What if we become better, stronger, more capable men by being able to discuss our emotions, our struggles, our doubts and fears instead of hiding them?

The only model society has for expressing feelings is the female culture. Even when society tries to make it okay for men to feel and express their emotions, they turn men into caricatures of women, to do so. The fashion industry dresses men in skirts and makeup, and makes gender reassignment or emasculation of a man necessary the permission for a man to feel emotions. Men don't have to give up being men to feel, or to care, or to be supportive. I believe by transitioning away from the warrior culture into a "guardian culture," where we are protectors of our communities, rather than combatants with them, is a first step. Changing society's deeply held belief that "warriors aren't allowed to weep," is going to be hard. Adrienne Rich, a poet and award winning essayist, writes:

"That's why I want to speak to you now.

To say: no person, trying to take responsibility for her or his identity, should have to be so alone. There must be those among whom we can sit down and weep, and still be counted as warriors. (I make up this strange, angry packet for you, threaded with love.)

I think you thought there was no such place for you, and perhaps there was none then, and perhaps there is none now; but we will have to make it, we who want an end to suffering, who want to change the laws of history, if we are not to give ourselves away."2

But what if there's a way to make something natural, our emotions, a part of us, a part of our culture? We have lots of ways of expressing positive emotions—from chest bumps, high fives, and physical expressions that most women don't use. What if we found a way to express the negative ones? What if it was okay for men to cry?

And before anyone accuses me of being sexist, let me point out that women have a warrior culture too. From Amazons, to Queens, to mothers who fought alongside their sons in wars throughout history, women have been warriors as long as men have—and may have been even more fierce and brutal. Some women have bought into the "don't cry," culture.

Female officers also commit suicide, just not in as high numbers as males, mostly because there are not only fewer female officers, but because they're more likely to ask for help, and more likely not to be judged if they do seek counseling.

When Chicago Police Officer Ruby Falcon put a gun to her head in 2016, she was surrounded by police officers, and even used another officer's gun to kill herself. According to the Chicago Sun-Times, she was suffering the same kinds of losses as male officers do—including a personal relationship, and financial issues. The bank was about to seize her house. She'd been taking antidepressants, and she had made suicidal comments—classic suicidal behaviors. The Sun Times also reported that according to the U.S. Justice Department, Falcon's death added to a suicide rate in the CPD that is 60 percent higher than other departments across the nation.3

In 2019, 67.1 percent of full-time civilian law enforcement employees in the United States were female. But only 12.8 percent of full-time law enforcement officers, boots on the street, were female, while 87.2 percent of law enforcement officers were male.4

There are exceptions of course. Madison, Wisconsin's police force is 30 percent female and they have a female SWAT team captain.

When's the last time you remember seeing a female police officer in a situation like any of the police shootings we've seen this last decade? Has there been one? I couldn't find it.

Female officers, according to researchers, are:
 • Less likely to face allegations of excessive force
 • Less likely to use force
 • More likely to reduce the use of force among other officers in the department
 • Tend to communicate better and use words, not physical confrontation, to make a point
 • They reduce citizen complaints overall
 • They have more empathy and are better at handling sexual assaults and domestic violence calls
 • They don't have the same cultural or societal stigma against asking for help

I can't think of any female officer I've worked with that I wouldn't trust my life with, or that I have less than 100 percent confidence to have my back. They bring skills to the table I wish more men could —especially when it comes to feelings. In all my research about female suicides, I couldn't find much. Women officers do kill themselves and they do develop PTSD, just like their male counterparts.

However, women experience PTSD differently. Unlike men, who have a male bonding thing, women, especially if they're the only woman in their agency, tend to experience stress from PTSD differently from male officers. In one of the few studies I could find about female officers and stress, I learned they suffer from "a lack of support from colleagues, gender discrimination, sexual harassment, interpersonal conflict, and lack of confidentiality. And, the better they are at something, the less support they get from their colleagues."5

1 . Stone DM, Simon TR, Fowler KA, et al. (2018). Vital Signs: Trends in state suicide rates - United States, 1999-2016 and circumstances contributing to suicide - 27 states, 2015. Morbidity and Mortality Weekly Report, 67(22), 617-624. doi: 10.15585/mmwr.mm6722a1

2 . Leonard Cohen Files. 2009. "What Kinds of Times Are These?" LeonarCohenFiles.com. https://www.leonardcohenforum.com/viewtopic.php?t=31754.

3 . Chicago Sun Times, Matthew Hendrickson, Jon Seidel, and Sam Charles. 2017. "A Chicago Police officer's suicide — in a house full of cops." Chicago Sun-Times. https://chicago.suntimes.com/2017/8/7/18319386/a-chicago-police-officer-s-suicide-in-a-house-full-of-cops.

4 . Statista.com and Erin Duffin. 2020. "Gender distribution of full-time law enforcement employees in the United States in 2019." Law enforcement. https://www.statista.com/statistics/195324/gender-distribution-of-full-time-law-enforcement-employees-in-the-us/.

5 . Rousseau, Danielle. 2020. "Environmental Stress and PTSD for Women Police." sites.bu.edu. https://sites.bu.edu/daniellerousseau/2020/06/26/environmental-stress-and-ptsd-for-women-police/.

CHAPTER SIX

Mental Health and Having "The Talk"

*"What mental health needs is more
sunlight, more candor, and more
unashamed conversation."*
~ Glenn Close

Trauma. It happens to all of us eventually. It happened to Byron Boston, the owner of Professional Law Enforcement Training (PLET), five years ago. Twelve police officers, and two civilians were shot in an ambush in Dallas, Texas. Five of the officers died. The shooting happened on July 7, 2016, near the end of what had been a peaceful protest against police violence. The shooter, Micah Xavier Johnson, was killed in an explosion.

The ambush is now known simply as the 7/7 shooting. Byron was one of the dozens of officers that ran toward the sounds of gunfire that night.

After the 7/7 shooting, he was having nightmares but he didn't say anything to anybody. He believed, as most LEOs do, that admitting he was having problems would make him seem weak. Fortunately for him, he didn't need to ask for help. The department had a mandatory checkup for all the officers involved in the event. This included going to speak with a psychologist. Byron's interview was at noon. Afterwards, he said, the guys were all going out. So they're texting him like, "Hey, Byron, you coming?" And he's texting back, "Yeah, man, I just gotta do my final interview with the psychologist. I should be out in like 30 minutes, man. I'll meet you guys there at one o'clock."

But Byron wouldn't make it to the party. He went into the psychologist's office, thinking he would be in and out in 30 minutes. The psychologist said to him, "How are you sleeping?" That's all it took. He just broke down. He told her, "I'm not sleeping. I'm having these nightmares..."

He told me as soon as she asked that, he just started crying.

"The next thing, you know, she's got me for like three hours," he said.

"But Griff, when I left there, I just felt like a million dollars. I never expected it, but because I wasn't the one asking for help, but help was brought to me, you know? And and so I don't know, and I'm back and forth on that. And I read a lot about therapy, and I ask a lot of cops, right. It works."

Byron is like most of us. We know getting help will probably work, but the stigma, the fear of appearing weak, or broken is stronger than the will to seek help.

Like I said earlier, "Suicide is a permanent solution to a temporary problem." I didn't see that at the time I was well on my way to a permanent solution, but I do now.

When you're in pain, and you're in that space where nothing you do is working, and everything you do just makes things worse, hell yeah, suicide *seems* like the best option. Let me stress that again, it SEEMS like the best option.

Suicide, no matter how messed up you, or your life, or your situation is, is never the option. Walk away. Get some distance. Wait. Look at things from a different day. I promise, no wait, I *guarantee* things will change. They did for me. Time will help you if you give time a chance.

After Ben called and I went over for a beer and to chill, I told myself, "If tonight was a good night to die, then so is tomorrow." I postponed my dying. I postponed my suicide. I postponed my "date with destiny and death."

That's the secret. Put some time between you and the gun, razor, or rope, or the pills. Get some distance. If your friend wants to "die now," sit with them. Listen to them. Distract them. Play catch, watch a movie, talk, work out, do whatever, but put some time between them and their plan to give them that healing time they need to change their mind.

Getting drunk, or getting your friend drunk, will make things worse and loosen your inhibitions and theirs, making suicide more likely, not less. Drinking or drugging is not a way to put distance between yourself and your pain. No matter how tempting, don't self-medicate, or don't let your friend self-medicate.

When the military formally became a "Don't ask, don't tell" culture there wasn't much of a stretch among members to understand what it meant. Most warrior cultures, i.e. the military and law enforcement, first responders, already understand that you don't talk, you don't confront the things that make you uncomfortable, like feelings, fear, doubts, questions, and mental health.

But if you want to live, you have to talk. It's basic. It's hard. And it's not generally accepted if you want to keep your career. But what's more important—your life or your badge? As I've learned, for hundreds of us, it's the badge. Silence rules, until you permanently silence yourself.

As Ramon Batista, former Chief of Police for Mesa, Arizona, with 34 plus years of policing experience, said, "I hate it, but it's true in so many departments. If you talk about the mental health issues you're having, you *can* lose the thing that's most important to you—your career, and your identity as a police officer."

Those of you reading this who aren't LEO may not understand that attachment or the incredible bond with your identity as a police officer. It's hard to explain, but anyone who has been or is an officer knows to their core what's at risk—being taken offline (off of patrol) and losing not just your career, but your very identity.

Most of us have wanted to be police officers more than anything else in our lives for most of our lives. Some people see it as just another job, but most of us embrace it to our core. When that, (gun, badge, ID and job) essentially our identity, is pulled from us because we're "having mental health issues," it can be devastating.

It destroys us because we lose who we are, what we stood for, and what we worked so hard for. We lose the power, status, and prestige of being an officer. That loss can push us over the edge. If you were only thinking about suicide before, now you begin to think you really "have a reason" to act on those thoughts now since your "life" as a cop is over.

Getting help or not getting help puts you between a rock and a hard place. If you don't get help, you're negatively impacted. If you do get help you're definitely impacted. How do you cope? What do you do? Ramon had two answers for me:

"If you're a young or new officer reading this, think 'building resiliency,' going forward.

"You've got to learn to deal with the streets, but more importantly, you've got to be resilient to the administrative bureaucracy and the BS that comes from the criminal justice system, and with some of the people that we deal with in the community." Ramon said.

"My advice," Ramon told me, is, "Stay focused on the things that matter.' So as the chief, I would tell my guys, 'Make sure you love somebody.' It may sound kind of corny, but I swear, I thought that that was so important. To make sure that there was somebody and something in your life, something that you really cared about other than your job. I believe having something that is just as important to you as your job needs to be there for you if you lose the job for any reason. Those outside activities, your family, your loved one(s)—whatever. Just make sure that those things also play a prominent role in your life so that you don't just have all your eggs in one basket," he said. I agree.

Looking back I can see how I had "other interests," I had a wife, four boys, and my family and friends, but I didn't put as much of myself into them as I did my job. I thought by pouring my efforts into the job I was helping them the best way I could. I got it backward.

It's hard to admit you need help when you're struggling if you haven't put that time and effort into your support system all along. We're most likely to insist that we don't need help long past the time that help could make a difference, if we've neglected those relationships.

The preferred position is silence—"Don't say anything, and hope it goes away." We don't need more silence. We don't need to keep ignoring the issue of mental health. We need to talk about it. We need leaders who are willing to admit caring for their people's mental health as well as their physical health is the sign of a confident leader.

I know the rank and file are quick to believe their supervisors don't want to hear about feelings, and mental illness. It's more paperwork, more responsibility, more worrying about whether or not to pull the guy off of the street, or out of undercover. But that's not true.

Ramon, who also worked for the Tucson PD, is a strong believer in mental health for his officers because of the things he saw and experienced throughout his decades in police and undercover work. He said he made the mental health of his guys a priority.

"The things that I went through and the things that I saw close friends go through (as a cop) made it so that when I finally became an Assistant Police Chief, and then, a Chief, I started to pay really close attention to my officer's mental and physical wellness. I was very focused on the fact that, "Hey, if we are doing so much work to try and meet the needs of the community with respect to mental illness and trauma informed care then we need to make sure that we're doing at least the same amount of work for our personnel, for our officers, because our demands of them are sky high. We want them to be on the money, and don't want them to make a mistake.

"The profession tells our officers, 'Don't show emotion, carry a body-worn camera that's recording your every movement and recording your voice and actions under high stress situations.' Then we expect them to not have any stress over that stuff. Heaven forbid if you introduce any kind of addiction, gambling, drugs, alcohol sex, extramarital affairs into that scenario. I mean, that is just a recipe for huge issues and disaster, because that job of being a police officer, never lets up because, oh, hey, you're having a rough week, or a rough month. Maybe, the calls will be a little bit less hard this week. You know what I mean?

"You're still responding to other people's problems, domestic violence, violence or the victims of robbery, or murder on top of your personal bad day. If you're doing anything involving children, where the parents are complete morons, and you're trying to help a kid through a situation that is impossible it's stressful because you didn't go to school for that.

"You're not a trained psychologist. No one teaches you how to deal with all the psychological issues for the people you interact with. All you have is your innate, compassionate, human way of trying to fix things and make that better for a child.

"So, the officer will have all these demands on them from the job, and their own stuff, and other issues, yet everyone expects them to make it right, to fix it, to create a 'happily-ever-after ending' for everyone involved without failing, without making a mistake, day after day, week after week, year after year. No stress there, right?

"We're making choices that are harmful to our physical and mental health and we're doing it day after day, year after year. An officer's personal life challenges just adds to the enormous stress they're already under at work.

"So, when I finally got to a point where I had the ability to make a difference in this arena I made sure that we put a lot of resources and energy and effort into trying to make that help doable. I wanted officers who were at a breaking point, or approaching a breaking point to look at something like that and say, 'okay, I'll take the help.'

"One of the things that we did when I was in Mesa was create a dedicated unit. It had two officers to begin with, but they had no home. They were the wellness unit, but they had no Sergeant. They kind of fell under human resources and they operated out of the main station. And although we had a robust peer support program with employees that were pure support members all throughout the organization, these two, the ones who were heading the program, didn't have a supervisor and it didn't have a dedicated mission, but they did have this special training.

"What I did was create a sergeant's position and then move them from the main station over to the training academy with the idea that they would meet every new officer coming through the department. They would have dedicated time through basic training where they would introduce themselves and introduce the programs."

Ramon wasn't working with only a handful of officers. The Mesa Police Department is the primary law enforcement agency in Mesa, Arizona, and employs about 1,200 law enforcement officers. Statistically there are going to be officers with mental health issues and Ramon confirmed that.

"We had a handful of cases when I was at Mesa, officers that were beginning to show signs and symptoms of something we needed to focus on right from the onset. I never hesitated in making sure that if somebody was either showing signs of stress, or expressing some issues, that we were going to go out of our way to make sure we had somebody talking to them.

"I had a lot of support from the city manager's office to be able to put these guys on some type of a light duty status. If I didn't think it was going to work on a shift, I would do the best thing for them.

"We would take them offline and they were still getting paid. They were getting a kind of a breather, and the help and support they needed in order to get well. The administration wouldn't say this, but their peers would say, 'Hey, you know, we have a specialist with, you know, sleep disorders or addiction or whatever.'

"We had built a contract system with local providers that had a specific clientele in public safety. That was their specialty. And, and you know, I'm fortunate that during the time period that I was a police chief, I never lost one officer, either from a suicide or from an encounter on the street. I'm very happy about that because you can prepare all you want and, you know, the day that it happens, it's just a really difficult deal."

Ramon isn't alone among police chiefs in acknowledging that something needs to be done to help officers deal with what they're going through. Like others, he prefers issues to be addressed before they reach crisis levels where the officer needs to be taken offline for their, and the community's own safety. It's not an easy decision for any supervisor or chief to make, to decide to pull someone off the line.

What's the solution? Acknowledging something is going on with your officers is the first step. You don't wait until a drug dealer has taken over a whole section of town and is selling millions of dollars of drugs before you start enforcing the drug laws. Hopefully you start working on a solution to stop the crime before it overwhelms an area. You don't wait until you're forced to tackle something that's grown into a monster. You tackle it when it's a manageable size. The same is true with personnel issues.

You make mental health counseling after certain kinds of incidents mandatory. This stops the stigma of anyone "seeking help," and it slows the rumors down too because everyone has to see a professional, not just a select few.

This is where I hate Hollywood. They always show officers in a therapist's office as strong, tough, and hating to talk about 'the incident,' whether it's a shooting, or whatever because "they're fine." It's not accurate.

When an officer is forced into counseling as a precaution they're actually craving the help, but they're worried that the therapist is going to think they're unfit for duty if they're honest with them. The therapist literally holds their future in their hands. What if they don't believe them? What if they think they're not capable of getting back on the streets? If a therapist finds them "mentally ill," they may lose their right to even own a gun.[1] Then what? They worry about whether the therapist is reporting back on their sessions, or acting on the agency's behalf or theirs. Hollywood pounds those images home. So what do you do?

We need, as I say in my talks, "To have the mental health talk." You need to know what your options are, as well as what the consequences of that option are going to be *before* being in the situation where you have to decide while under stress. You need to weigh your options while you're in a good place mentally.

Experts advise people not to make any big decisions after the loss of a spouse, or after a traumatic injury, or when under financial duress. They stress, "Get a clear head," and make those decisions to quit, move, get a divorce, or whatever from a place of clearheadedness and strength, not from a place of fear and panic.

Most, if not all of us, get the "official" talk in the academy about what to do if you're stressed, or showing signs of PTSD, or of feeling overwhelmed. We're told what we can expect to hear or experience from the department after a shooting, or traumatic event, or during a debriefing. Then all that changes radically when you get on the street.

There are the official rules, and the unofficial rules. Leave your camera on, turn your camera off, talk to your supervisor or buddy, don't talk. There are a lot of in the moment decisions you're going to have to make in a few seconds, and those few seconds will determine what happens next. You can be making a decision that may end your career, pause it, or save it. The time to think about all that is now, before you have to.

First off, there are the academy rules, and then there are the street rules. We hear about mental health, stress, how to recognize the symptoms, and so on in the academy and then hear nothing after —only crickets.

The message you get in the academy is not reinforced outside the academy. It becomes one more thing we can forget, ignore and do without until we suddenly need it—and then it's too late.

You hit the streets with your training officer, and other veterans and you learn that most of what you learned in the academy isn't how the world of law enforcement actually works. There's the official, take it to court "legal" approach, then there's the day-to-day survival rules. One will protect you during a lawsuit, the other may protect you better in the moment, on the streets. Which way do you go? How do you choose?

It's not just that your environment changes after the academy. You do too. You start to realize everyone, even innocent people and other officers, will and do lie to you. You begin to trust fewer and fewer people every day. You develop a tough skin. You see what's out there in terms of criminals and bad guys, and not-so-bad guys, and you develop a different mindset. It becomes you against them. You do whatever you need to do to protect yourself and your coworkers.

You may learn, as I did, that the public begins to come second. Rather than thinking of your community as something you want to protect and serve, you see it as an enemy. We become warriors, not guardians. Small wonder we're so stressed.

Agencies and officers need to start focusing as much or more on the mental aspect of policing, including before, during and after events—as much as we do on crime. We need to quit fearing the feelings of our peers. We need to stop stigmatizing the word "suicide" and start realizing you don't have to be a psychologist or therapist to save someone's life. You need to listen, to let them know you care, and to tell them they can get through it. You need to be there for them. When my buddy told me he "loved me," and that there was light at the end of the tunnel, it wasn't profound, but it was powerful and more importantly, it was exactly what I needed to hear.

The Mental Process You Go Through Before Entering a Situation

"I can't wait. If the situation comes where someone's got to go down (be shot), I want to be that guy. I'm in."

Those are the words of the new recruits who watch too much television and see way too many movies. They have no idea of the impact a shooting, or taking someone's life—even a bad guy's life, will have on them. We're warned about it in the academy. We're told that even while it was a righteous shooting, and it was clearly justified to save our life or our partner's life, or a victim's life, that we're not going to feel so righteous about it—at least once what just happened really sinks in.

How do you deal with that? How do you deal with the reality that your status as an officer is elevated if you do commit a legitimate shooting, and do save someone's life at the expense of taking another? How do you deal with the body in the street? Are you really ready for the things that come after? The questions, the investigation, the social media storm, the doubts, the "what if's" from all the Monday morning quarterbacks? How do you face that?

"No comment" and referring the person to the department spokesperson may get them off of your back, but the pressure and their questions are still there. Then comes the day it all appears in print or on the web and no one has your back. Then what?

We train for those moments, but we're not really prepared for them the first time we encounter them. You don't really know how you'll feel when someone is shooting at you until someone shoots at you.

You don't know how you'll react to your first dead body, your first murder scene, decapitation, suicide, accident, or natural passing, until you see it. There's only so much trauma we can prepare for, and it's never really what we're taught in the academy it will be.

As if we didn't get enough training, let's add more—but let's add the important stuff, like the mental process you should go through before entering a situation. That's right. Mental health is also about preparing your mind to be successful, preparing your mind to handle the hard things, and practicing those skills before you need them.

Why not teach officers how to work in a positive way on their mental health rather than let them develop detrimental mental health issues? An hour lecture during a three, six, or even nine month long academy won't cut it. It's got to be ongoing.

Why not teach officers to recognize stress and anger and depression in other officers and learn to reach out, not to be their therapist, but to say, "It's okay. There's a light at the end of the tunnel. You are valued for who you are. You don't have to be a hero every day. You can be human. There's a time for everything and that includes taking time to protect your mental health."

As I learned from Joe C, "If you can go through it, you can get through it." It only takes one person to reach out and say, "I love you man." It's not weak. It's not gay, it's not stupid. It's important. So, how do you know when someone is experiencing suicidal thoughts, and what should you do?

Signs of Suicide in General

This is not a cram course in psychology. You do not have to be a therapist to make a difference in someone's life. You just have to pay attention and care. The life you impact may be a co-worker, supervisor, or family member, friend or even yourself. Know the signs of risk factors—conditions that increase the likelihood of a suicide attempt. Learning these signs can help you on the job when family members of a teenager, or suicidal person result in a call to 911. You are the person the caller is depending on to help. A person with these signs may be more at risk for suicide:

- Mental disorders, particularly mood disorders, PTSD, schizophrenia, anxiety disorders, and certain personality disorders
- Recent traumatic incident on the job or outside of the job (traffic, suicide, domestic violence, rape)
- Increasing alcohol or drug use
- Withdrawing from family and friends
- Feeling like there's no reason to live
- Engaging in risky activities without thinking
- Feeling or expressing hopelessness
- Impulsive and/or aggressive tendencies on or off the job

- Expressing rage over simple matters
- Difficulty sleeping—sleeping too much or too little
- Talking about wanting to die or to kill themselves
- Looking for a way to kill themselves, like searching online
- Talking about feeling hopeless or having no reason to live
- Talking about feeling trapped or in unbearable pain
- Talking about being a burden to others
- Acting anxious or agitated; behaving recklessly
- Showing rage or talking about seeking revenge
- Extreme mood swings
- History of trauma or abuse
- Major physical illnesses—including COVID-19
- Previous suicide attempt(s)
- Family history of suicide
- Job or financial loss
- Loss of relationship(s) (divorce, etc.)
- Easy access to lethal means (gun, drugs)
- Local clusters of suicide
- Lack of social support and sense of isolation
- Stigma associated with asking for help (warrior culture)
- Lack of healthcare, especially mental health and substance abuse treatment
- Cultural and religious beliefs, such as the belief that suicide is a sacrifice or a noble resolution of a personal dilemma
- Exposure to others who have died by suicide (in real life or via the media and Internet)
- Posting on social media that, "There's no way out of this," or other thoughts that indicate a feeling of being trapped

Any of these signs may be an indication the person may be thinking about suicide. You probably got all this in the academy. I did. But at the time it didn't mean anything really because I was more focused on doing a great job, being an awesome cop, and being invincible. If you're thinking the same things, let me tell you, you're not a supercop. You're human. So are your colleagues. And if you care about them, one day, one (or more) of them are going to need you to know about these signs.

What to Say

Trust your gut. Say something. It doesn't have to be brilliant, insightful, or therapy talk. It just has to be real. Ben knew something was off, but he wasn't sure what. He reached out and made a difference without knowing he was directly intervening in my suicide attempt. For that, I am eternally grateful. If you suspect something, say something. Ask the most important question of all to ask: "Are you thinking of killing yourself?" You can start with an, "Are you okay bro?" but if you believe something is wrong, head towards that hard question —"Are you thinking about killing yourself?"

Contrary to popular belief that question is not going to put the idea into someone's head. In fact, it's most likely to do the opposite —to get them to open up about their plans, their fears, their feelings.

To a person considering suicide the question will come as a relief. It tells them it's okay for them to talk about their feelings. Most people don't really want to die. They just want the pain to stop. It's important to know how to ask them. Some of the ways to ask *the* question are:

• "Are you thinking of killing yourself?"
• "Are you thinking of suicide?"
• "Have you had thoughts about taking your own life?"
When asking that question, remember:
• DO ask the question seriously and don't be dissuaded by a joking reply
• DO ask the question if you've identified warning signs or symptoms
• DO ask the question in such a way that is natural and flows with the conversation
• DO NOT ask the question as though you are looking for a

"no" answer ("You're not really thinking of killing yourself, are you?")
• DO NOT wait to ask the question until he or she is halfway out the door. It may be extremely hard to ask, but if you don't and they do kill themselves, the pain of asking "What if I had said something..." will hurt far longer and deeper than just asking them the question.
• DO NOT keep their suicidal behavior a secret
• DO NOT leave him or her alone
• Try to get the person to seek immediate help from his or her doctor or the nearest hospital or emergency room, OR
• Call 911

As you listen, let him/her do the talking. Don't butt in with, "You should do this," or try to talk them out of it. Listen. Be compassionate. You'll probably feel uncomfortable, or awkward. That's normal. Stay with them. Your discomfort is nothing as intense or scary as what they're feeling right then. Listen to what the person has to say, and take it seriously. Just talking to someone who really cares can make a big difference in someone who is considering suicide. It did me. Other ways you can make a difference:

• Be supportive and encouraging
• Acknowledge their pain
• Tell them they matter, to you, to their family
• Talk openly about suicide – Be willing to listen and allow them to express his or her feelings
• Recognize the situation is serious
• Do not pass judgement
• Don't be patronizing, like saying, "It could be worse."
• Reassure them that help is available and you'll help them get it
• Be sensitive, but ask direct questions, such as:
• How are you coping with what's been happening in your life?

- Do you ever feel like just giving up?
- Are you thinking about dying?
- Are you thinking about hurting yourself?
- Are you thinking about suicide?
- Have you ever thought about suicide before, or tried to harm yourself before?
- Have you thought about how or when you'd do it?
- Do you have access to weapons or things that can be used as weapons to harm yourself?

If someone has attempted suicide and not succumbed, don't leave the person alone.

- Call 911 or your local emergency number right away. Or, if you think you can do so safely, take the person to the nearest hospital emergency room yourself.
- Try to find out if he or she is under the influence of alcohol or drugs or may have taken an overdose.
- Tell a family member or friend right away what's going on.
- Get help from someone who knows what to do—a doctor, emergency room, or therapist.

Get help from a trained mental health professional as quickly as possible.

You're not a therapist or psychologist (unless of course you are). Fixing their suicidal thoughts is not in your wheelhouse. They need a professional. You're the person on scene calling for, and waiting for a medical transport. You can do that. Do it with respect and humility —you may be on the other end of that scenario one day and will need someone to make that call for you.

The person may need to be hospitalized until the suicidal crisis has passed. But, don't worry about that, or the possibility you're straining your relationship with someone by asking if they're suicidal. If you don't ask, you may not have a relationship if they act and you said nothing. You're NOT responsible for anyone elses suicide or decisions, but your intervention could save their life. If you try and fail, that's better than not trying at all.

Signs of Suicide in Military, in and Out of Service

Chances are you've seen or heard some suicide warning signs in yourself, or a buddy. Chances are you felt something was "off," but didn't want to say anything or ask a question. In hindsight many of the people I've talked to about a friend, family member, or co-worker all recognized the warning signs.

They even thought that the sign was serious, but failed to act, not wanting to believe suicide was a possibility until it was too late, and the person was dead. They didn't say anything because they didn't want to offend the person, ruin the friendship, or make their friend angry. They didn't want to "butt in" into something that wasn't their business. Don't be that guy/gal. Ask. If you value their friendship you'll ask.

All warning signs require attention, and some require immediate action. Some people will make jokes about suicide when they are having serious suicidal thoughts. It's an effort to reach out to someone without admitting they're on the edge. Not everyone who makes a suicide attempt shows warning signs. However, warning signs of suicide should always be taken seriously, even if the person seems to be joking.

You may notice other people who have been depressed or anxious may suddenly appear calmer or happier than usual. That may be because they have decided to attempt suicide and they finally feel relief at making a decision and not wondering if they should take action or not.

A Spouse's Role in Getting Help

Spouses, more than anyone else except maybe a duty partner, are going to be the first to notice a change in behavior. Maybe your spouse is moodier than normal, or more quiet. Maybe they've been depressed for weeks or months and suddenly seem happy and at peace (often this is a sign they've made the decision to take their life). Maybe you've been arguing for weeks and months and all of a sudden they stop fighting with you and just go silent.

If you're in a healthy, or close relationship with your spouse, they can be the support and listening ear you need. If you're not, I'm sorry.

According to the Suicide Prevention Center, "Automatic spousal attitudes—quick emotional associations with one's husband or wife —can predict suicidal thoughts in married couples. Automatic spousal attitudes are a more reliable predictor of suicidal thoughts than self-reported marital satisfaction or automatic attitudes toward oneself.

"Researchers conducted three longitudinal studies with newly married heterosexual couples. In two of the studies, participants were shown a photo of their spouse and were then asked to categorize a series of positive and negative words. Participants who could more quickly classify positive words after viewing a photo of their spouse were identified as having positive automatic spousal attitudes. Participants also completed baseline surveys on overall marital satisfaction and suicidal thoughts. One year later, participants reported on their suicidal thoughts again. Participants who demonstrated more positive automatic spousal attitudes were less likely to report suicidal thoughts one year later."[2]

If you're married to, or living with a police officer, you can be the first person to recognize a difference in them. Don't be afraid to bring up your concerns. Here are some of the top myths people have about suicide:

Don't Believe the Myths

In spite of all the information on the Internet about suicide, some people still believe the myths. Don't. Educate yourself. Research shows people who are having thoughts of suicide feel relief when someone asks after them in a caring way. Here are the top myths I hear from people who are worried about suicide in a friend, or even themselves:

Myth 1: People who attempt suicide are cowards.

This myth blames the victim. By attributing a behavior (suicide) to a negative and derogatory personality trait, they avoid responsibility for not noticing the person's distress or cries for help. In fact, people who commit suicide are not cowards, but people who are suffering. They may even see their actions as heroic, something that will leave those they love in peace. I know I did, and I believe my best friend Brian, who did succeed in killing himself, thought the same, that he was sacrificing himself for his family.

Myth 2: People who want to kill themselves will deny they want to die.

This is a deadly myth because it makes people think it's okay to ignore, or not take seriously people who express their suicidal ideas or threaten to commit suicide. I hear, "They're just wanting attention. Ignore them." Duh. Yes they want attention and help. Do not ignore them. Take them seriously. They are crying for help. If you saw someone drowning in a lake or swimming pool would you say, "They're just wanting attention, ignore them."? No. In studies around people who committed suicide, a total of 9 out of 10 people who committed suicide clearly expressed their purposes to those around them. It is likely 10 in 10 people who commit suicide will have hinted at their intention to put an end to their life.

Myth 3: People who say they will kill themselves, will not actually do it.

I'm not sure why there are so many callous people in the world, but they seem to like this myth. This myth leads to suicide threats not taken seriously because they are taken as blackmail, manipulation, bluff, etc. Many people, especially those who have never experienced loss, trauma, or depression may not understand the seriousness of someone experiencing this level of depression.

In fact, every person who commits suicide announces their intention with words, threats, gestures or changes of behavior what is about to happen.

Myth 4: Truly suicidal people, those who do commit suicide, don't give any hints about what he or she is up to.

As I said in Myth 2, every person who commits suicide announces their intent with words, threats, gestures or changes of behavior what is about to happen. People rarely want to commit suicide. They want the pain to stop, not their lives. Right up until they commit the act, they will give hints of their intention. Sadly, most people ignore the hints — in denial about what they're hearing. Or, they hope it's "just talk." If you hear anything that raises a flag or concern from someone, even said jokingly, confront them. Tell them you're worried, that you care, that you're there for them.

Myth 5: Those who attempt suicide are courageous people.

This myth tries to attribute suicidal behavior to a positive personality trait. This criterion hinders suicide prevention because it portrays suicidal behavior as justified, as it is considered synonymous to bravery, an asset that everybody would like to possess. I believed I was being courageous and making a sacrifice, but that's how a mental illness twists your brain. You aren't thinking correctly.

Those who attempt to commit suicide are neither brave people nor cowards, as bravery and cowardice are personality traits that cannot be quantified or measured by the number of times you attempt to kill yourself or decide to give yourself another chance.

Myth 6: Asking a person at risk if they have thought of committing suicide could actually push or motivate them to do it.

This myth instills a fear of speaking about the topic of suicide with people who are at risk of committing it. It often eliminates any chance of that person getting the help they want and need.

It has been proven over and over again that talking about suicide with a person at risk of suicide does not encourage or push the person into the act. Instead talking about their feelings and desires to kill themselves helps reduce the likelihood they will commit suicide. In fact, it might be the only possibility they have of getting help to look at their self-destructive reasoning.

Sometimes it takes someone "in charge," like a supervisor, Chief, or HR to force officers to undergo an evaluation or series of appointments after an event. Making a number of hours mandatory for every officer involved, even if they were only a witness, after a shooting, a public event, or riot—like the Washington DC Capital riots, can bring help to those, like Byron, who would not otherwise seek it out.

CHAPTER SEVEN

**Not Everything is Black and White,
Life Happens in the Gray**

*"There is a multitude of gray that occurs between a shooting scenario and
some of the critical incidents that unfold without warning, or even with
warning, on an officer. Afterwards, I'm sure they're thinking back and saying
to themselves. If I'd have just waited a second longer, if I'd have just backed
up, if I'd have just waited for my backup, if I had taken cover, or taken better
cover, or different cover we could have dealt with that guy differently, you
know?"*
— Police Chief Ramon Batista

M aking split second decisions about when to act, how to
act, what to do or say is insanely difficult when you've
had enough sleep, had your coffee, and you're relaxed,
yet alert. You have the experience and the training, and have
prepared for that moment your entire career.

But what about when you're sitting in your car having lunch, or a
cup of coffee, or finishing up some paperwork and the unexpected

happens. What if you roll up on a kid, and they whip out what looks like a real gun, and they point it at you? What happens if you're about to wrap up what's been a peaceful protest and go home when suddenly someone opens fire on you and kills the man next to you?

What happens if a terrorist pulls up in a truck bomb, or becomes an active shooter in the school where your kids go? What if you're in the middle of a divorce or separation, or you just learned your wife has cancer, or your 16-year daughter's pregnant, or you haven't been sleeping because you rolled up on a particularly bloody murder suicide the day before and you haven't processed that yet.

Yes, you have the training, and yes you know what to do, but no matter what you decide to do in the next three seconds, some journalist who's never even held a gun, or had someone shooting at them is going to become both judge and jury. That's right. Someone who has never faced someone hell bent on killing them in cold blood, is going to spend the next year finding multiple reasons to explain to their readers why your pulling a gun on a man charging you with an 18-inch Bowie knife and threatening to kill you was not a justified shooting and why you are a murdering, racist, privileged piece of shit for shooting him. And the public is going to listen to them, and to the dead man's parents telling the world that their son was a "good man." The public is not going to listen to you, They're not going to listen to the Community Affairs officer, or to your wife, or friends. People seem to prefer to believe the worst about someone, not the truth.

When you have nightmares because this criminal or mentally ill person got close enough to cut your shirt and arm, that same journalist, or their "followers," is going to pile on and say you deserved to be cut. Gray areas. Stress. PTSD. It happens.

There's definitely a reason departments pull officers offline. Some of the reasons, like a shooting or use of force, are justified. You need some time off to decompress even if you don't think you do. You may feel okay the day of the shooting, but it's the days and weeks that follow when issues begin. But there are other reasons to pull someone off of the street other than a shooting or traumatic call.

When an officer admits to suicidal ideations for any reason, even just family stuff, the tendency for most agencies is to pull them off the streets. They want to get them away from things that might trigger a poor decision, a shooting, or get them or a member of the public killed. Their gun and weapons are taken away from them, and they're put somewhere safe where they can be "watched," and not get into much trouble. If you're not that officer being scrutinized, it makes sense. Your first duty is to protect everyone, or as many people as possible. I get that.

My editor, who was also a police officer for a brief time, describes going to a Colorado courthouse in 1974 to pay a $10 fine for not having an emissions sticker on her vehicle. She was 20 years old at the time, and had just moved to the state and didn't know about the stickers. She stopped two officers she saw in the courthouse hallway, explained what happened, showed them her citation, and asked where she could pay her fine.

Without any warning or question, one officer grabbed her by the front of the shirt, slammed her into a wall and started screaming at her, "Who the FUCK do you think you are to not have an emissions sticker!" She was flabbergasted, but didn't resist.

"Griff, it was an emission's sticker I didn't have, not a capital warrant I'd skipped out on." She said she didn't know what she had done to make him physically assault her over a fine she was trying to pay, but she wasn't going to make him more angry by struggling or arguing.

The other officer apologized profusely, and pulled his partner off of her. He literally dragged him down the hallway, still screaming and cursing at her.

Is that the hair-trigger officer with a loaded gun and two speed loaders on his belt that you want on your force? She never found out what his problem was, and when she told the clerk at the office where she paid her fine what happened, he advised her to "just forget about it."

You're responsible for the public, for your other officers, for the officer who is struggling. But what are you doing *to* him, as well as *for* him?

Now, think about this. You've (justifiably) taken away the one thing they have going for them, their skills, their identity, the thing/job they're proud of, and their position as a member of the street force. You've taken away their reputation, their gun, their badge, their camaraderie with their colleagues, and their partner. You've signaled to the entire department that they're "not stable," or that they are "having issues," or have "done something wrong," since they're now riding a desk. You can't talk about what's going on. Their privacy and whatever investigation that's happening legally requires you not talk.

They're either feeling too humiliated to talk about what's going on, or they are aggressively demanding you talk to them. Where is this scenario going? No where good I assure you. Gray areas. It's a tough call, but departments make them every day. Do they pull someone offline for an inappropriate Facebook post or a YouTube video that satirizes an event? Or do they simply discipline them? What happens if something else happens because of that post — maybe it was sexist, racist, or insensitive and now they've gone and made another bonehead move. Now you're under scrutiny for not "doing enough" the first time they screwed up.

Just for an example, some cities have a "one bite" rule for dogs. A dog bites someone, for any reason—even if the animal was provoked —and the law says the dog has to be euthanized because it's "obviously" dangerous to people. Some cities give dogs two bites before being euthanized, and some dog loving cities never euthanize the dog—they just fine the heck out of the owners each time their dog bites someone—right up until that dog mauls a kid to death, then they get tough.

Police chiefs and supervisors face the same dilemma. Are they going to be "one bite" (incident) departments and get rid of an officer for one mistake? Or are they going to give them second, third and more choices? Or are they going to keep them on, but discipline them indefinitely, or quietly move them along to another department?

What happens when your officer makes the same mistake in another incident and that results in an innocent person's death or wounding? You knew they had issues, and yet let them off. Officers will understand, but the public and the media, and the lawyers who sue on behalf of police victims won't.

Do you ruin an officer's career for a single Tweet or a photo or video they post on Facebook or Instagram? What if what they posted wouldn't have caused anyone else to bat an eye? We're living and working in a society where even eye rolls are seen as offensive, and if it's an officer doing the eye rolling, it's 1,000 times worse.

I'm reminded of the Prager University video where a student calls campus security for "fear mongering" and for "terrorizing" students by asking them questions. The two responding officers seriously and carefully explain to the student that unless the journalist was physically threatening or detaining him against his will, that he had a right to his opinions, even if they differed from his own. "You simply agree to disagree," they tell him. "That's free speech," they said. "It's totally legal." The student was outraged that the officers wouldn't arrest the journalist for offending him for having a different opinion.[1]

So, that's what we're up against. The public demands firing, or at least strong discipline for the most minor, and often perfectly legal, actions. We live in a society that is offended by everything a police officer says or does, no matter how appropriate or legal. Knowing that one officer's actions reflect on all officer's actions, what do you do?

Police officers who make bad decisions, let alone tragic, life ending ones, aren't the only ones who suffer the consequences for those decisions. Their actions, good or bad, reflect on every other officer in the country.

When Derek Chauvin knelt on George Floyd's neck/shoulder blade, the public didn't wait to see *all* the video evidence, or wait for the facts and police body cam video to come in. They immediately and viscerally reacted to a Black man dying under the knee of a White cop. Society isn't used to seeing someone die in front of them. Officers are. But the public's rage didn't end there.

Over the next months and years after George Floyd's death, many citizens, Black and White, ambushed, shot and killed police officers in other states for the perceived actions of Derek Chauvin. As Ramon told me, "You've got to have leadership step up and say, "look guys you're ready to crucify this officer, but please let us get the details first before you're ready to react just on face value, or a cell phone video from one angle or person. Right now, in my initial interviews, there's more to this story that I'm going to release at a later date."

"If the leader doesn't get out there and begin the process of explaining, of comforting both the public and the officers, of being out there and being the voice of reason, then what that incident, justified or not, does for a part of the population who is always going to be angry no matter what—is not good.

"They are going to take advantage of the situation to use that negative energy, all that rage and hate, in their next encounter with a police officer. It takes one incident, and a snowball effect beginning with that incident, to make the lives of a bunch of other officers who had nothing to do with the original incident, really bad," Ramon said.

I agree. Look no further than Rodney King or George Floyd to see how the actions of those officers made the lives of officers across the country miserable, or even deadly. There are many good officers that are out there trying to do the right thing every day and they're suffering from the actions of a handful of officers who made traumatic decisions in a matter of seconds.

How all that social media, viral video and rumor translates to the boots on the street, and every officer who sees what happens adds to their stress, to their PTSD, to their depression. Older officers are looking at what's happening and calculating whether to stay long enough to get their pension and risk being killed or injured, or get out early.

I feel deeply for the younger officers who worked so hard for their position, only to find themselves wondering what they've gotten into.

Officers are saying, "I did what I knew was right. And nobody has my back on this." They're left swinging in the wind. That creates this culture where it's essentially police versus society. And they're stuck with deciding whether to risk that career by seeking counseling, versus sucking it up, putting it aside, and hoping they survive for the next 15 or 20 plus years.

And that's what I really want to change—how all that contributes to drug and alcohol abuse and suicide. Society's response to law enforcement has changed for the worse because of the lack of transparency and the lack of leadership in many areas. The stress it's having on officers of all ranks and experience is driving up the suicide rates, and the drug and alcohol abuse rates, and the domestic violence rates.

For supervisors, leadership isn't so clear cut anymore. They find themselves juggling character and ethics with politics and agenda from higher up. Outside influences from citizen groups to protestors, police unions, and school boards, or boards of supervisors have an influence they shouldn't. I'd love to have known what drove my Chief, Brian, to suicide.

I ask you, especially if you're an officer, veteran, or first responder, or fireman, "How do you face your peers, friends and loved ones, or family after a traumatic incident? Are they supportive? Do you have people in your life who support you and understand your job? When there isn't a clear cut answer or decision you need to have someone or something to turn to. While it's not likely one incident, or even a handful, will drive you to suicide, it's not impossible. I hope it drives you to change careers before it drives you to drink, drug, or develop depression and consider self-harm.

Good or bad, heroic or illegal, society is going to continue to call out an officer's actions—and that's their right. It's part of the 'checks and balances' we enjoy in this country. And police work is going to continue to put body-worn cameras on cops to record their entire day to show the entire story of any given incident. (I often wonder how many other professions could tolerate having a camera record them every day as they go about their day, and as they make decisions.) So far, body cameras benefit police, and I'm not saying that as an Axion representative.

In a March 2021 research paper released by the University of Chicago Crime Lab and the Council on Criminal Justice's Task Force on Policing, findings show the key benefit of body-worn cameras is the reduced use of police force.

For example, among the police departments studied, complaints against police dropped by 17% and the use of force by police, during fatal and non-fatal encounters, fell by nearly 10%.[2]

As cops and former cops, we look at those viral videos and have compassion for the officer because we've been there, we've done it. We understand what could have happened during that situation that led him or her to make the decisions they did.

But society doesn't understand their decisions because they've never been in that situation. They've never received that training, or understand the threat to an officer, or what even a small knife can do. They see something and on face value say, "holy crap, I can't believe that that officer just made that decision at that time, right there with what I've seen."

Imagine how that would play out in an emergency room, or any other situation where a professional is making life and death decisions based on their training and experience and someone sees a video and says, "Holy crap, I can't believe that doctor/nurse/medic just made that decision based on what I've seen watching reality television and know (or think I know) about medicine."

I think it's incumbent upon leadership to be more progressive as far as standing up for their officers, taking a stand not to jump to conclusions until all the facts are in, and supporting their officers through the process. It's not that you're going to combat society's response to a viral event but, but you're going to have a response and have a voice of reason when it comes down to one of your officers. There is nothing wrong with saying, "a video went viral, we're looking into it." Just because the social media circus demands answers immediately doesn't mean you have to be their clown. Leaders protect their own. I don't mean "cover up" for them. I mean treat them the way they would like to be treated if they were in their shoes—with dignity, respect, and support until all the facts are in. Prosecute the guilty, defend the innocent.

CHAPTER EIGHT

Resilience and Alternatives

"Courage isn't having the strength to
go on—it's going on when you
don't have the strength."

"I wouldn't put my brother's suicide in the same category as what you're looking for," Sharlene Jones told me. He walked through the processing plant where he worked and shot people he was in conflict with. He was reloading to take his own life as the police approached. He was a third striker who I'm sure didn't want to return to prison. He lived for a couple of days on life support and then died. It's probably more compelling to reflect on why we had very different life paths despite our shared experience growing up.

I had a partner commit suicide a few years ago. He was kind and decent and was always willing to help with anything you needed. I will never forget our time working patrol together. I could never have imagined his life would end by his own hand. I still ask myself if there's something I could have done to save him. Suicide, depression, coping — these are topics that are easier to speak freely about once you get some distance from your LE career — if you're fortunate enough to make it out.

"When I got the news about my brother, I went to a psychologist for the first time simply because although I'm not an emotional person, when I got the news, I cried. Me, a woman who has been accused of not having tear ducts—crying. Those tears rattled me. I had no idea where they were coming from.

"I called a psychologist I had worked with before during an investigation and just asked to meet about a personal circumstance this time. I basically told him my entire life from, from A to Z and when I finished, he was in tears.

I remember looking at him and interpreting from HIS tears, that I must be at MY breaking point—you know, that point they tell you about in the academy where your life stressors outweigh your capacity to cope. A police academy instructor gave us this sheet that listed a bunch of life events. We were supposed to tick which ones we experienced and then tally them up to get a score meant to indicate a risk level. I find it funny now - to think anyone would suggest that trauma and adversity could be so neatly calculated.

"Anyway, when I looked at the psychologist's face and into his eyes, I thought back to the sheet and I remember assuming I must have been getting close to the danger zone. But I didn't feel like I was getting close. I felt like I was just fine. As I was sitting there trying to reconcile my internal assessment with his outward reaction, he told me, "You know, Sharlene, I really shouldn't put it like this, but I feel like I know you well enough to tell you, I don't understand why you haven't committed suicide. Like how are you still here right now?"

"His question took the wind out of me. It was like hearing I had terminal cancer that should have killed me years prior, despite currently feeling as healthy as ever. I started to wonder myself why I never considered suicide but not in a way that made me start to consider it. Despite popular belief, you can't push a person, who wasn't already thinking about it, to that point . Instead, it became my question, one I needed to find an answer to—what was it about me that had gotten me through so much?"

At that point Sharlene and I turned to talking about our favorite topic—resilience. Sharlene is one of the officers I've met who has found out the secret to avoiding the funnel that leads *toward* suicide — that's her personal and professional resilience. She lives it, breathes it, teaches it, embodies it. She is immersed in it from the time she gets up to the time she goes to bed.

Resilience is the ability to "bounce back," or recover from bad things and people that happen to you. After a life of bouncing back, resilience is in her DNA. I thought I was resilient, but she has me beat.

I don't think she could do anything but bounce back no matter what happens. Her resilience is like super body armor, only it's what she's made of—like an exoskeleton of resilience. I was like that until I lost everything, all within a short time—including my wife, marriage, job and everything that mattered to me. That makes me wonder if the key to preventing suicide is a combination of community, support, and resilience.

It also made me reconsider what Ramon was telling me, "don't put all your eggs into one basket, and make sure there's someone outside police work who loves you, and something that you love as well." Wise advice. But what if you're single and don't have anything but police or fire, or rescue work? Find something, or see a professional.

For those of you reading this thinking, "No way I'm seeing a shrink, or therapist, or getting help and risking my career," I hear you. Millions of people experience profound levels of trauma and never kill themselves, or even think about it. It's not, as I understand it, that they are genetically gifted. While many veterans develop PTSD, many do not. Many veterans, about 11 a day by the last thing I've read, commit suicide, but many more do not. They work through it. Like Sharlene, they're "resilient."

After her visit with a therapist Sharlene said she really started to reflect on what it was that made her so resilient.

"That's when I started self exploration, trying to figure out the different path that I took from my brother. And even though we experienced a lot of the same circumstances, but in different ways given our genders, they were equally challenging circumstances nonetheless."

Some of us are more resilient than others. Most of us have to work at it. Sharlene has studied it extensively and now, as a certified coach, she teaches others what she's learned about it from both her time in and out of law enforcement.

Since I walked away from my dark day, I've started exploring options as well. One thing that both Sharlene and I found we had in common during our talks was writing, journaling. Another was how we thought about, or saw things.

Expectations

"I think a lot of my resilience came from not accepting the low expectations others had for me," Sharlene said. "When I went back and looked at everything that had happened to me, when the psychologist told me he didn't know why I hadn't killed myself, I think I finally arrived at the answer—because nobody ever expected much of me in the first place. As a Black woman, I was already at the bottom of the barrel in the eyes of the world. Add being poor with no privilege, or access to it, and a police officer too ‑ none of that gave me cool points. There's a famous quote by Malcolm X that states 'the most disrespected, neglected and unprotected person in America is the Black woman.' My experience leaves me no room to argue with that. So I learned to rely on myself and refused to let myself down.

"Even when I became the victim of a crime, the police just blew me off when they came to the house. Ours was the headache house on the beat, a location cops try to clear with as little effort as possible. I guess I ultimately realized at some level that if nobody expected anything of me or believed I had value then why would I want to prove them right and fade away quietly. As circumstances became progressively worse, I would think about a prior challenge I'd gotten through and know that if I got over the last one, I could manage the next hurdle too. Each time that happened, one success built on the last, and my resilience became a habit, a built-in thing I didn't have to consciously think about each time. It became a part of me.

For me, not having support systems or external resources made me develop personal resources and confidence in my ability to turn any circumstance around. I just came to regard every experience, good or bad, failure or success, as a learning opportunity. All of it was a blessing.

"For me, there was nobody to disappoint except myself. And I wasn't going to disappoint myself. So I think that's why I never thought about suicide. It's like somebody said, 'I didn't come this far just to come this far.' I didn't go through all these things growing up just to go through all those things growing up. They were learning experiences that helped me grow and develop insights to better support others down the road," Sharlene said.

Who are you living to impress? Sharlene got it right—when you're not trying to impress your partner, the department, your family, or your peers, when your only competition is yourself, you're not going to go into that deep funk when things go wrong.

You know you're doing okay, or will be okay, because your only competition is yourself. You pick yourself up and try again. That doesn't give you the license to be lazy or below average. Set some standards for yourself based on the job, and your goals. Make them challenging but achievable.

For instance, Brian was just a beast. He was just the best police chief, the best guy. He'd say "you have the ability to change an entire department for the better or for the worse."

And he changed it for the better. If you did your job and you worked hard—he had your back. But if you were a rod, (Retired On Duty) and all you wanted to do was complain, he'd hold your feet to the fire. He'd say, "Go do your job first and then come complain."

He completely changed the whole morale of our department. All of us have theories on why he committed suicide, but he never left a note and we never really got any closure.

Where I'm going with this is I was going through that hard

place. And I realized that it wasn't suicide. Was it a sacrifice? And so I started looking at it more as a sacrifice, like he was sacrificing himself for his children and for his family and I started to get it.

There I was, getting pulled out of undercover work. The new chief didn't believe in narcotic work. And I was just so passionate about what I was doing that getting pulled hurt deeply. He took me out of undercover work, put me on an internal investigation and on midnight patrol. I did not want to do that. I was in a world of hurt. All my life I was able to adapt to everybody else's preferences and wishes. I was able to be a successful undercover cop because I was so flexible and adaptable, but this was too much to ask of me.

An undercover cop was who I was, what I did. Now my marriage, my identity, this was all getting stripped away from me. I was about to lose my job. I didn't want my kids to see me fail. I couldn't justify a suicide, so I started looking at it more like a sacrifice, like if Brian can do it. If he can sacrifice himself as strong as he was, then I can do it too. That's my reasoning for why I wasn't really committing suicide. I saw my actions as a sacrifice for my kids so that they didn't have to live and see their father be a failure.

And that's what depression and PTSD did to trick my brain into saying "you're doing this for them."

The voice in my head was telling me, "You're going to be strong for your boys." And, I had to shake through that. I had to realize that suicide was not a sacrifice and that voice was wrong.

The true sacrifice would be addressing the problems and living with them, no matter how painful. By facing those problems and trying to resolve them as best I could, I'd need to revisit the things I learned at Clearview. That was the sacrifice—feeling my feelings, and doing what I needed to do to fix them.

Taking the easy way out and putting the gun in my mouth, seemed honorable. After Brian died, like I got it. Nobody ever said, "He's so weak." No one said that. I said to myself, "he's not weak."

"He was doing the honorable thing," was less painful than, "He couldn't deal with it," and that's how my brain slowly started to trick me into thinking that that suicide was okay—choosing the less emotionally painful option. Like I said, the painful reality was, I just didn't want my kids to see me fail anymore. I didn't want to see me fail anymore. Failing was not about who I believed I was and I couldn't handle it.

Part of the higher rate within law enforcement is we're in this role where we're solving everybody else's problems every single day. That's our expertise, but then when it comes to our own life, we don't do very well at it and that is how we define failure.

The thing I came to realize was that none of that stuff we experience is really a failure. It's just a different phase of your life that you're going through. You're beginning over, starting over and changing your focus, your career path, and your identity. Everything I've learned in life I've learned by failing at it first. I just had to remember that.

Retirement and Suicide

"I don't want to be a cop anymore." Choosing to leave police work was the scariest and yet the best decision of my life. I was a good old boy, and I mean that in the best of ways. I was the pride of the police department and the pride of the undercover world. Yet, in the flash of an eye, after Brian died, a new chief took over. He didn't like drug work and more importantly, he didn't like me. Knowing he had no respect for me, and that he was happy to put me to grinding on midnight patrol shifts after an internal investigation on a timesheet issue, was a huge blow to my ego.

On top of that, I was dealing with Brian's suicide, my divorce and my lack of passion for the job overall. I simply didn't want to do this anymore. It was the same feeling I had upon graduating from high school and knowing I didn't want to go to college and keep playing games. Deep inside, I just knew something had to give, something had to change. I just didn't know exactly what that something was.

Chief Russo didn't take the actions he did in an ethical, fair, or good way. He knew I was struggling and he really added to the pressure. As you can imagine in the undercover world it's not a 9-5 job and you really don't have timesheets.

Your timesheet would say nine to five every Monday through Friday but we don't actually work those hours. And so it was kind of an unspoken rule in the drug task force that you just sent your timesheet in at the end of the week with 40 hours on it. If you worked over 40 hours, you kept a mental note on it. If there was a day where nothing was happening you went home early.

So I submitted a time sheet and during that week in question there was a SWAT training, and I showed up late to the SWAT training because my flight was delayed on the way back from a public speaking event.

Chief Russo was also on the SWAT team. He knew that I didn't show up until about 10 am. However, on my timesheet, I put 9 to 5 as instructed, even though after that SWAT training I had worked until about 9 pm on several undercover buys. My reward for working extra time? An internal investigation for falsifying a physical document initiated by someone I considered a friend.

I remember that feeling of not being the golden boy anymore. For two months, I was on desk duty wondering if I had a job or if today was going to be the day I was going to be fired.

I was interviewed under the Garrity Rights with my union representative present. I had my undercover cell phone dumped and I was treated like I had the plague. After the internal was completed, Chief Russo ruled against me. He stripped me from the SWAT team, pulled me from the drug task force and gave me several unpaid days off from work.

What really hurt though was the drug task force turning their back on me. During the course of the internal, the commander and assistant commander of the Drug Task Force repeatedly reached out and showed their support for me. The same bosses I bled for, risked my life day in and day out for, lost my family for, told me, "We have your back Griff." Then they didn't.

When the internal was over and I was considering legal action, I reviewed the interviews with those bosses. I know this may surprise you but they DID NOT have my back. The commander said "we never authorized any one to "flex their schedule as Detective Griffin indicated." Wow!! Once again my proof (emails, texts, timesheets) did not matter. What was fair, what was right did not matter. I was right back in Principal Garrity's office being suspended.

One more blow. *"And he carries the reminder of every glove that laid him down and cut him till he cried out....but the fighter still remained!"* I was banished to midnight patrol in Keene, New Hampshire, the small 40,000 person town from nine at night to seven in the morning. Just months prior I was laundering money for the cartels and buying and selling dope and busting dealers more than anyone else on the force.

With the lessons I'd learned in life, I got out of bed and stopped feeling sorry for myself. I went to work and did my job. I found a new passion. I poured every ounce of energy and passion into public speaking and training other law enforcement officers the ins and outs of what made me successful. Byron believed in me. He believed that I was special and I will always be forever grateful to him and his wife Sabrina for their belief in me.

Fast forward a couple months and I had a two day *Fighting Fentanyl* class in Hampton, NH. This was a private class and I'd been working on it for months. Each registration was $250 and I had 50 people registered for my class. This was some much needed money to get me back on my feet and I'd worked really hard to get it. Are you sensing a theme here? I bust my butt, do everything right, and then..."it's not fair."

I marketed, I called agencies, forwarded my resume and the outline of my class to everyone and every agency in the Northeast. The date of the class was November 5th and 6th, which was a Monday/Tuesday. My leave request had been submitted and approved months prior to the event. I set up hotel blocks and a dinner for the attendees. In the week prior to the class, the media reached out to the Keene Police Department about this Fentanyl training which was being conducted by one of Keene Police's Officers and asked to interview me. That request was denied. That Friday, Chief Russo found me and said "Can we talk for a minute?"

"Sure Chief, what's up?"

"I'm cancelling your leave for next week?"

"What do you mean? I've had my leave request in for months and I have 50 officers from all over the country coming to town to hear me speak." I could feel the heat beginning to rise and the chorus to the old, "It's not fair" song began to play in my head.

"You have court on Monday, you were sent a subpoena several months prior which you didn't respond to," Chief said.

"I never received that subpoena and no one has reached out to me or followed up." With a court date on Monday, normal protocol is the prosecutor will meet with the testifying officer to go over questions and answers. I found out later it was a misdemeanor drug case from two years prior which had already been continued three times.

"Sorry, your leave is cancelled." The tone and his lack of empathy was obvious. This wasn't about work. It was personal to him.

"Chief, I'm not going to be there."

"You will be there," he said. I could hear the arrogance and presumption spewing from him.

"No, Chief I won't."

Later that day I learned from the host agency that someone from the Keene Police Department had reached out to him and began questioning him as to the timeline, process and logistics of the class.

He called me and said "Watch your back Griff...someone is gunning for you." I found out later it was the same Lt. JM who initiated the original internal investigation.

I began to pray about the situation. I began to use all the tools and resources I'd learned from the age of 14 up until that time. I recognized on some level this was another crucible, a testing by fire to melt away the dross and debris and see what pure gold remained in me.

This was bigger than the department. It was bigger than Chief Russo. I could hear Joe C telling me to step forward and be the leader he knew I was. I was calm. I was prepared. I had done what I thought was right. I had gone to my class and taught both days, missing my court date. I'd committed to Byron, gotten permission and done everything by the book. An adverse action would not be fair, but I was ready for "not fair." I was prepared to take action and take control of my life, and my future.

On Wednesday, I knew what was going to happen. I mentally asked Brian for strength to do what needed to be done. I prayed and asked the Holy Spirit to speak through me and give me courage to do what needed to be done.

Wednesday morning arrived and at 9 am my desk phone rang.

"Matt, we need to see you in the Chief's conference room," said the voice on the phone.

The moment of the scariest decision I would ever make was finally here.

I walked into the conference room praying for strength and guidance, still somewhat unsure of what I was going to do, holding out hope that it was going to be something other than the formal process of putting me through another internal investigation. Even as I write this, my stomach goes into knots.

I knocked on the door and a voice said "come in." It's exactly what I thought it was. A Lt, two Deputy Chiefs and Chief Russo. Here we go, I thought.

"Have a seat, officer Griffin." I did as asked, my face stone cold, no emotion, no fear, no intimidation showing.

An awkward silence and a pause followed as I was seated. Then Chief Russo spoke.

"Officer Griffin, we need to inform you of the initiation of an internal investigation..."

I wasn't doing this again. I was prepared this time. Fool me once, your mistake. Fool me twice...My mistake.

As the Chief began to speak again I interrupted him. I stood up from the chair and I began to talk.

"Steve, (Chief Russo's first name) we've worked together for a long time. I've been here for a long time. Anything that you've ever asked me to do, I've done it and done it better than anybody else. When you asked me to ride the bike and make arrests, I made 110 arrests in six months and received an award for my efforts.

"When you asked me to go to the high school and take the SRO position, I did it. I then wrote the cyber bullying policy for the state of New Hampshire, and I changed the entire climate and morale of the high school. When you asked me to return to patrol and work DUIs on midnights, I did it. And for the next nine months, I wrote over 100 DUIs and received an award by the state police for my efforts.

"When the department asked me to go undercover, I went undercover and I did it to the best of my ability sacrificing my pay, my marriage and my family to stop the flow of fentanyl into our state. I was awarded top undercover officer for 2015, 2016 and 2017.

"But I can't live like this anymore. I can't walk on eggshells. I've worked my ass off for this department and there's not one person sitting here that can tell me I didn't do my job to the best of my ability.

"Since we are talking about numbers, by my count we have seven openings here at Keene Police....now we have eight, here's my two week notice." I reached into my pocket and laid my resignation on the table, turned and walked out and never looked back.

You may wonder if I'm still upset at the way I was treated? Am I mad about the internals or Lt. JM lying to advance his personal agenda? Am I upset about the anonymous email sent to Byron or the phone call to the host agency?

Absolutely NOT. God is great. He knew what He was doing and it has turned into the best thing that has ever happened to me. I created a successful consulting company, became a national training instructor and most recently was hired by one of the best Law Enforcement companies in the world, Axon.

I know that a lot of cops end up killing themselves after they retire because they're not doing "the job" anymore. They're lost. They don't have anywhere to go or anything to do, at least nothing that makes them feel as strong and as much as part of a team, and a culture as police work did.

They turn into old cops talking about the glory days. Active duty officers don't have much to do with them other than on veteran's day or something. They're out of the game. The same thing happens when an officer is permanently injured. What are they going to do, where are they going to go? Thankfully, not all officers flounder.

Mark Sigfrinius was a Seattle Motorcycle Patrol Officer in 1989. He made a routine traffic stop and was shot by the driver, a fugitive from justice. The driver was a felon who had killed a man in New Mexico and he was not going down without a fight. As Sigfrinius confronted the driver, the man shot him in the chest. The bullet passed through him and severed his spinal cord. In spite of his injury, he fired back, forcing the felon to flee on foot where he was later captured. From what my editor, who worked with him, told me, it was a hot day and he'd chosen, on that one day, not to wear his bulletproof vest.

Sigfrinius could have gone into a very dark space, and lived there with no one blaming him for doing so, but he didn't. A Christian, he recovered from the wound, but didn't regain use of his legs. He would be a paraplegic and in a wheelchair for life. He didn't let it get him down. He left the police force and he and his wife moved to Goldendale, Washington where he found another life—as a three time mayor of the town. He still had his hand in police work since he was the mayor, but he focused on a new passion—community and connection.

If you're at retirement age, or considering taking early retirement because of all the things happening across the country with the defunding of police, I have to warn you. Get something to do in your retirement, before you retire. Don't take just any job. Take one you can embrace and be as passionate about as you were police work. If you can't find such a job, create one. Become an entrepreneur. I've heard of a women officer retiring and starting a drone business to help with search and rescue and crowd management.

Others take up training police dogs, or turn to computer technology that keeps them in the law enforcement arena and engaged with the people they identify most with.

I am a Solution Specialist on Axon's Virtual Reality team. I demonstrate and speak about how to use VR to train officers on the indicators of a mental health crisis as well as speak to agencies through PLET. What has all this got to do with suicide? Having a life outside of the force, having something or someone you can turn to if you become unable or unwilling to deal with the stress of the job can be a lifesaver.

What happens when you're taken offline against your will, or whether you choose to retire because of an incident? The end result is kind of the same. All of a sudden you go from being everybody's hero, the alpha and detective or undercover guy, to being retired. And it's like, now what is your purpose? What happens when you don't have a purpose anymore?

What happens when you find out your whole identity is wrapped up in the job and now you're not there, you're not needed, even not wanted. There are younger, stronger, more highly trained officers coming up, anxious to prove themselves, just as you once were.

Sure, you're remembered, but that fades in ten years, or maybe even five, no one will remember what you look like, or what you did —not really. Other than being a wife, or husband, or a mother, father, or a friend, you'll find yourself asking, "What am I really passionate about?" And if the only thing you're really passionate about is police work and now you're not doing that—the hit to your self-esteem, your sense of purpose, your life—it's all going to take a nosedive. You can only play so many rounds of golf, or clean your weapon, or take the grandkids out for ice cream just so many times before you're bored. Now what?

What do you do after you retire, how do you find that next thing that you're passionate about doing with your life? I'm passionate about God, about sharing my testimony, my story and helping officers, veterans, first responders of all kinds get help so they don't pull that trigger.

Sharlene Jones transitioned to corporate security. She also teaches and coaches about resilience, journaling, and how to facilitate critical conversations. She took her experience and skills and created a full, fulfilling life outside of police work. So did Byron. So did I.

If you can't be a cop, or you've been a cop and you're retiring, or thinking of leaving the force in the face of all this "defund the police," and force reduction stuff going on, you have to, as Ramon said, "have someone or something to love outside of police work." You combine that identity that defined you for 20 or 25 years—that of protecting the public, and you find a way to a new passion, whether it's inside or outside police work.

There is a vocal minority of people that are taking away the honor and the integrity behind the profession. That vocal minority that wants to defund the police has no concept of what that means, but their demands and protests start to strip away the thing we've been so committed to for most of our lives.

So we're seeing a lot of law enforcement suicides after people retire. But we're also seeing a lot of younger officers taking their lives because they came into a job they thought was honorable and had integrity. Then they go through something, let's say it's an officer-involved shooting, and now they're going through a media frenzy and being villainized for something that they were trained to do, and did by the numbers, by the book, and were perfectly legal and justified in doing.

But because of social media and people who don't understand the rule of law, or how things work, or what officers are trained to do and see that the general public, with no training or experience gets to have a larger say in police work than the police, they're disillusioned and get bitter.

Their department may not stand up for them. The leadership is nonexistent or weak, or politicized and they're left to fend for themselves. They back off and instead of thinking how can I stop this bad guy, they think, "How will social media act if I stop this bad guy?" They stop responding. They get depressed because they're losing the passion and integrity they had for a job they believed was ethical, righteous, and fair.

I know that there are a lot of issues out there about how law enforcement responds and what social media says. But you know as cops, we tend to really over-invest in our profession. And when we don't train our younger officers, our millennial generation or the generation after, on how to deal with this new face of policing, we have a problem. So we try to resolve it. That's the type A, driven, leader personality in us. We do a great job in the academy of training our guys in the black and white of the streets, but not in explaining that not everything is black and white.

In the undercover world, nothing was black and white. There was never a drug deal that went just as it was supposed to go.

If I was supposed to go to the Walmart parking lot at 10 o'clock for an ounce of weed, it was always 10:30 and half an ounce of weed. I think we've got to do a better job of training in that gray area. Don't just teach the procedure the officer has to follow. Teach recruits to think about how this is going to affect them and what they are going to do about it to ensure they're doing their job and not getting thrown under the bus for doing the job as they were instructed to do it.

I had a baby, and I had a two and a half year old die in my arms. I remember all the shootings and dead bodies and everything else. But that single incident with Benny was the most traumatic for me. And I couldn't ask anybody for help. I wasn't prepared for the nightmares that I would have afterward. Yet, I wouldn't do anything differently.

I would replay that day over and over again, asking what could I have done differently? I needed to know, to hear, to be trained to realize that wasn't a good path to start down looking for answers.

We refuse to try and ask for answers in those gray areas. We don't talk about how these things are going to affect us, because once they do affect us, then we enter that red zone where we're not the only ones affected by this trauma.

Ramon told me his divorce deeply affected him too. "I wasn't sleeping. I was having nightmares and not sleeping. I'm waking up exhausted and I'm going into work and I'm irritable. I'm not on point. I'm not switched on. I take that same level of anxiety and irritability on every call that I go on and that's the problem. Depending on what the call is, or how it goes, I probably add to the burden and irritation I'm already carrying. If that weren't enough, then remember, we're held to a higher standard out here. We have body cams that are videotaping every moment of a 10 hour shift. At some point we wake up and realize we're living a life that we didn't subscribe to. We signed up to serve and protect, not to be micromanaged by non LEO critics and desk jockeys."

Younger officers don't understand how to go ask for help. They don't say, "What I saw and what I did and what's happened to me outside of work is really affecting my home life, and how I deal with things at work. I need help."

Unfortunately what happens is they don't talk about it. They don't get help. They stuff everything down inside and assume it will eventually go away, that it's part of the job, or that there's something wrong with them that this stuff is bothering them. And so their work product suffers and in turn, they compound those problems.

Because the work product suffers now they're being demoted, or they're being put on an internal, or even worse, they get distracted and they make a bad decision, or a really bad decision that costs someone their life.

Now, not only is the profession that they're so passionate about, the thing they wanted to do—to help people—feels like it's turned on them. That identity of being the hero, or the helper, or the guardian is being stripped away from them, even by their peers. And no one tells them it's not them, it's everyone who goes through this. They just don't speak up because they don't want to end up in the same boat as some of their colleagues—at risk of being thought weak and losing their career and their identity.

When I think about it, it's like the sharks in SARs. They tell you, "don't be last," knowing full well someone is going to be last, even if they've done the best they can, they know they're going to be hosed no matter what.

I think that's a major problem. If you seek out help and that gets back to the department, and then you have to go through an assessment to come back to work, there's that fear whether it's a rational fear on the department's side or not.

I like how Sharlene put it.

"With the identity piece (around being a cop) I think I was almost insulated from that, because my experience was at the intersection of my race and then my profession. When I'm in blue, I'm not black enough for Black people and not blue enough for LEOs.I exist at an intersection where neither identity is a tailor fit, which is probably a good space to be in, because then you really have to dig deep and know who you are *at the core* of your being independent of your race and independent of your profession.Maybe that's what allows me to see both sides with some objective clarity.

I started journaling heavily again after the George Floyd event. I've journaled my entire life. I had the idea that journaling could be a good option for officers because it gives them a tool where they can start the process of self-analysis and discovering their own answers without initially reaching out to someone. Maybe that would be a good first step for them.

"After George Floyd's death, I started teaching a method of journaling I refer to as soul writing. One of the groups I facilitated the workshop with was the National Organization of Black Law Enforcement (NOBLE). It was an insightful session for even me as the trainer because many of the people there were expressing the same thing that I described earlier — the challenges that come with the intersection of race and profession. The impacts of being Black and a police officer really came to a head after George Floyd. Intimately feeling the pain of the Black community but then having to put on the uniform and enforce the law from the blue side, while also understanding at some level that you need to be in that uncomfortable space to effect change and hopefully prevent future incidents, is a unique and extreme amount of stress. I don't think many departments recognize, understand or acknowledge the unique experience and stress placed upon officers of color. .

"People have said after my workshops that they were surprised to learn you could do so much with journaling. I teach 12 different techniques to cover a variety of opportunities. It helps people get their thoughts out of their head and onto paper, for a better vantage point to reflect on ideas and to see their thought process in a tangible way beyond the noise of the incessant chatter that often goes on in our minds. Journaling can be a transformative and empowering process because you control how you start to figure things out without anyone looking over your shoulder, or judging you."

I agree with Sharlene. I think that's a major piece of the puzzle. That's a huge piece of the mental health roadmap. Byron, the founder/CEO of PLET, at a national conference said ,"We've got to take away that first step, that barrier to officers getting help."

"We've got to figure out how we take this first step of saying, "Hey guys, I need help." Nobody wants to say that. Nobody wants to raise their hand because there's so much indecision about that. There's so many unknowns that happen with that first step. If you're brave enough to say, "Hey guys, this really affected me. And I'm struggling right now. Like mental health or suicide of depression."

When you say those words, nobody knows what's going to happen next. You have a pretty good idea based on the culture but you struggle with the thoughts.

Are they gonna take my gun? Am I going on light duty? Are they going to commit me? My passion is trying to take away that first step, but I think you've just hit on it. If we can introduce something that gives them the tools to analyze themselves and where they're at, and how to take an objective look at what's happening, that's a great first step. I've included a bonus chapter at the end of this book to get you started with journaling if you're interested. I've found it's really powerful.

My newest thing is called spoken word poetry or slam poetry. And It's my thing, my writing. I just love it. I'm doing a slam for mental health awareness and it just kind of chronicles through like the times of my suicidal period. But for me, I was taking the bad out of my head, putting my feelings and thoughts on paper and then reading it and letting other people see those emotions.

I'm not saying "I need help," in this. I'm just voicing my

emotions. There's no value statement to it. That's why it's so power-ful. It's just what it is. Just words on paper, that's it. I don't have to clarify. I don't have to explain or justify anything. It's the things that come out of my head. I'm allowed to do that whenever I want, and nobody can take my gun away because I'm putting words on a paper. I don't have to qualify any of these emotions.

They don't even have to be mine per se. It's just what I'm hearing or feeling at that time. It's just something cathartic about writing. Everybody has this mental block about writing. One of the first things Sharlene teaches people when they come to the journal work-shop is a writing sprint. She calls it "writing dirty". It's writing without any regard to spelling, grammar, punctuation, syntax, or anything you'd worry about in a formal document.

The only requirement is that you have to continue writing for five minutes without letting the pen come off the paper. There's no topic. Anything goes, just get it out. It's like a mind dump and people are amazed at what comes out on paper when they don't have to abide by the rules. When there's no punctuation when it's just words it ends up being the springboard for future, more structured writing. It functions as an ice breaker for a lot of people. She also tells cops to consider when they have that emotional or traumatic call, before going 10-8 to take the next detail, do a writing sprint for five minutes. We all spend at least that much time shooting the shit with each other after a hot call. If there's not an immediate urgency to get to another call just take a couple minutes to get the thoughts out of your head and onto paper. It just takes the edge off the pres-sure a bit so it doesn't get dragged to the next call.

When I started public speaking and getting on the stage, I loved the training aspect of it, but what I really loved was telling my story. My whole life, I never got a chance to tell my story, like the things that happened to me growing up and, and, you know, and Brian's suicide and my ex-wife and, and everything else. It was therapy for me to express myself that way. Connection, expression, it happens when you get alone with yourself and a journal.

Sharlene is a strong supporter of journaling. She said, "I think a major piece of the roadmap is giving first responders the ability to write dirty (without all the grammar and punctuation rules), to get the rough spots out of their head and onto paper, to see it from a distance and then move on. I think writing is an effective gap measure or first step to getting help in a culture where people are hesitant to publicly raise their hand for support. The idea of journaling may conjure images of a teenage girl with a diary with a unicorn and a pink lock on it but once people learn the variety of techniques they start to feel empowered to take their wellness into their own hands. I stumbled upon journaling myself as a vulnerable kid navigating some tough circumstances. I started writing really young, using it as a way to rewrite the bad stuff that happened. I had power on paper to change any circumstance I wanted.

"It would be nice if everyone had the support that wellness commercials are made of, but even without it, I know it's possible to make it through because I did it. If I can overcome circumstances, alone, circumstances that would bring a psychologist to tears, others can do it too. Lack of support is not an absolute barrier to wellness. Find a way. Write. Talk. Change careers, get help. But take care of you."

She made me think. She made me realize what I've been doing my whole life is to tackle the "it's not fair," thing and let it go. I look back and see I needed to prove everybody wrong to make me right. How screwed up is that? What I needed was not to prove to everyone else I was right and things weren't fair. I needed to focus on Matt Griffin and my happiness, my character, my life, my decisions and how I was going to quit being a victim and take control of my life and future. That might or might not include police work or some extension of it. Things can change — God's got a plan and all I can do is trust Him.

Along the way I got a mentor that was down in Philly. He was about 75 years old, just a great man. He and his wife Carol were never able to have kids. And I was down there for dinner one night and Carol looked at me and she said "When are you going to start dating again?"

I said, "I'm good. I don't need anybody else in my life. Like, I'm straight, everything is working out."

I was uncomfortable with her question, so I was crab walking back into a space where I was isolating again, protecting myself, not connecting. I'd just come through all these dark times, and I was learning that connection and support and purpose was key to healing. Yet, here I was throwing up walls and keeping people at arm's length when I felt uncomfortable. And she said something to me that stuck with me.

She said, "Matt, just think about how successful you are now and how passionate you are right now with everything that you're doing now. Now imagine that you are able to share that with somebody else who made you better."

And she said, "because if you find that person that makes you better, all the success that you're having, you're going to double it and it's going to make you feel that much better."

She was right. I took her at her word. Now I've been dating an amazing woman who makes me a better man every day.

It doesn't matter who you are, where you are, what you're fighting. You can get through it. I wonder what would have become of my kids if I'd succeeded and left them without a father to teach them it's okay to hurt, and cry and talk about your emotions. What paths would they have walked down, believing their own father didn't think it was important to be there for them? I shudder at the thought.

I wonder who my girlfriend would be with now if she'd never met me. I wonder how many people my talks for PLET have reached, how many men or women put their guns away and started believing that suicide wasn't a solution.

Suicide is like putting down a great book, or walking out of an action movie without seeing the end. You never know what happens, how the plot twists, or what could be because you've checked out. Don't check out. Ride life to the end. Trust God. Ask Him to show you what He has in store for you. Believe.

CHAPTER 9

The Fighter Still Remains

"In the clearing stands a boxer,
and a fighter by his trade
And he carries the reminders of every
glove that laid him down
And cut him till he cried out
In his anger and his shame
'I am leaving, I am leaving,'
But the fighter still remains."
~ Simon and Garfunkel

Let's see, extreme poverty in childhood, getting my butt kicked more times than I can remember by gangs, bullies, rich kids, and anyone who felt the need to take me down so they could feel better—been there. Fought there. Won and lost there.

Drug rehabilitation in High School, joining the Navy, SAR training, undercover life, the aftermath of numerous traumatic accidents I witnessed, including a suicide right in front of me as I lunged for the man's gun, bodies I dealt with, the loss of friends to drugs and suicide, four kids including one with special needs, divorce and an almost successful suicide. Trust me. We all have challenges—even the 'golden haired boys' and beautiful women who seem to be blessed with talent, looks, opportunities and 'privilege.' You know who you are. The outside of the book doesn't tell you what the story inside is.

People who looked at me my entire life saw the star lacrosse player and athlete, the "successful cop, undercover guy, SAR, person," someone who was able to blend, succeed, and bust bad guys better than anyone else. But, I was closer to the edge of the abyss more times than I like to remember. I rose from the ashes with faith and perseverance and God's grace, but that didn't mean the abyss closed over. I just managed not to fall in. My four boys have come closer to not having a father more times than just the near suicide. An accidental overdose of fentanyl after a big drug bust almost killed me, but also showed me yet again that God was watching over me.

Josh

Career criminals develop bad attitudes towards the police early. By the time they're in high school they have a special hatred for police. That hatred makes the hair on the back of the necks of both the cop and the criminal stand on end when they see each other. It's mostly a mutual thing—and it makes for interesting and rewarding arrests, but also for a wide range of stressful emotions.

During my time on the police force in Norfolk I spent time as a School Resource Officer (SRO) at KHS. I encountered Josh, who was just such a teen criminal. My interactions with him would almost kill me.

I'd been chasing local drug dealers like Josh for years. While I was the SRO at the local highschool, Josh was a student. I remember him walking through the halls of KHS and when he saw me in uniform he'd give me the middle finger as forcibly and flagrantly as only a teenager can.

"Your time is coming Josh!" I thought. I was not only older, wiser, and more seasoned in the way of drug dealers than Josh, I was hungering to bust him as well, for a reason I'll share shortly.

I'd watched Josh for some time. I'd watched him graduate from local marijuana sales to selling heroin and ultimately fentanyl. About two weeks before the incident with him that would push me from zero to 200 in an instant, I saw him coming out of the Marriott Hotel.

I admit, from my former undercover days, I could tell Josh was good at what he did—selling drugs and evading arrest. I wondered if I would have ended up where he was had I not played sports, and wanted out of the ghetto. Like I said, Josh was smart. He knew the game and how to not get caught and how to minimize the damage if he did. He knew not to carry more than he was selling. He knew how to run, evade, hide, and lie. He had a promising and lucrative career ahead of himself as long as he kept his edge and didn't slip up. I planned to be the cop that broke his winning streak and his edge.

As Josh left the Marriott, I Immediately called for Andy, one of my younger proactive police officers, to try and make the traffic stop, which he did. I started helping him with the stop and running the interdiction part of it. Even though Josh was cornered, he wasn't about to admit he was caught. His arrogance knew no bounds.

"Stop fucking with me Griff, you're not gonna get me!" he sneered at me.

I ignored him and ran a dog around his gold Lexus. I got a good dog hit on the vehicle. For non-police readers a 'good hit' essentially means that our police dog was able to smell the presence of narcotics in the vehicle. A dog's nose is so sensitive it can pick up on the smell of narcotics that was in a vehicle, even if it's been removed. It's like if you or I walked into a room where a smoker had been smoking. The tobacco is long gone, but the smell is not.

With the dog's alert on narcotics that in turn gave me probable cause to search the vehicle. While Josh and the officer making the stop cooled their heels, I typed out the search warrant and had it signed by the Judge. I came back to the car with Josh's comments in my head. I was saying "C'mon God, just give me a little bit here, enough to put this POS away."

I ripped the car apart and didn't find anything in it. However, when I opened the trunk of the vehicle I found a notebook. I was hoping it would be a ledger (drug sales, prices, money owed etc). However what I found was even worse. It was an undercover officer (and a father's) worst nightmare.

On page one, I found my name, dob, address, undercover vehicle, personal vehicle along with my license plates and cell phone numbers both personal and undercover. On the rest of that page were all of my undercover partners' names, descriptions and notes about each. along with descriptions of how they looked.

"Well done Josh," I thought. You've done your research. I was fine with that. No law against knowing your opponents. But the game changed as I kept turning the pages. After the names and descriptions of my undercover team, were the names and descriptions of my four sons. Names, DOBs, mother's address and where they went to school.

I went from zero to 200 in a hot second. This was not okay. Why does a major drug dealer have my kids' names in a notebook in the back of his vehicle?

Up until that point it was a cop against a drug dealer. The law against the criminal. Good versus evil. Now my kids were involved. Was he going to do something to my kids if I pinched him?

This stop suddenly became personal. I wanted to take my badge and gun off and go knock on his forehead and demand we settle this like men. "Are you gonna do something to my kids if I catch you?" I wondered only briefly before I looked up from the book and saw him sneering, a smirk on his face at seeing my anger at the information in the book. My dog had gotten a whiff of narcotics, but we didn't find any drugs. Josh won this round, but I vowed to myself he wouldn't win the next. We kicked him loose and I watched him drive away, my stomach churning with anger, fear, and worry for my kids' safety.

"I'm patient Josh," I thought as his car faded out of sight. "I can wait."

And that's what I did. I waited. Just like in some cheesy western shootout I knew we'd meet again at the OK Corral. I might lose the battle, but I wouldn't lose the war. Thankfully I didn't have to wait long.

A couple weeks later my phone rang. It was my number one at the Drug Task Force. "Griff, we got you a new undercover car." (UC)

"Sweet!" I thought at first. Then I thought about the "Black Max." The 1999 Black Maxima UC car was a part of me. All black and murdered out with tint and a sound system that rocked the vehicle and anything next to it, it fit my flow, my image, and my ego. It had served me well for the better part of a couple years.

Number one insisted. He said "The Maxima is done, too many miles, too many repairs." I said okay and drove my last drive with Max. On the hour and change ride up to Concord, NH I talked to the car and told him I wouldn't let them chop him up. I assured him that he'd been good to me, it was just time to go our separate ways, and it wasn't personal.

I got to HQ and tossed the boss the keys to the Max. In turn he handed me the keys to my brand new rig and pointed over in the direction of the adjacent parking lot. "There she is," he said....

I looked over towards where he was pointing and didn't see anything resembling a UC vehicle so I said "where boss??"

"Right there in the middle..."

He pointed out the new vehicle I'd be spending countless hours in over the next couple of years.

"Are you fucking kidding me?? No way, give me my keys back...."

"I'm not driving a RAV 4!!!!" I yelled.

"C'mon boss, look at me. I have cornrows and a lip ring. How am I supposed to do drug work in a RAV 4. (no offense to anyone with a RAV4. It just didn't strike me as a UC car.)

"Sorry Griff, you'll make it work."

"Yea I guess I'll change up to skinny jeans and Chuckie Taylors, I'm sure there's some deranged soccer mom selling dope somewhere," I said. I couldn't have been more sarcastic, but he ignored me.

I got the Rav 4 on a Wednesday, so on Thursday I went into work and sat down across from Brian and and began bitching. Why wait, right?

"B, what the heck bro, I've been killing it. How they gonna give me a Rav 4 bro."

"You'll make it work Griff, you always do. You're one of the best cops I've ever met."

He continued. "I tell you what, you've had a long successful week, we have an interdiction day coming up tomorrow. (That's what happens when President Trump calls your state a drug infested den. You get a bunch of grant money to target drug dealers and users which we termed "interdiction days.")

"Come help us on interdiction day tomorrow and at 3 pm, I'll cut you loose. I know you don't have your kids this weekend and you're heading to Massachusetts."

This was huge for me. As a regular schedule I was working until 5 p.m. and then sat in 95-S traffic trying to get into Boston to see my girlfriend at the time.

"For real, B?"

"Yea go ahead Griff, help us for a couple of hours and get the boys some arrests then I'll comp you out at 3 pm."

"Hell yeah. You got it B." Rav 4 or not, I was pumped. The next day, I showed up for the briefing at noon in the roll call room at Keene PD. Everyone went around the table with the list of targets for the day and what they were going to do. At the end of the briefing, the Lt looked at me and said, "Anything to add, Griff?"

"Yea if you guys see JF (Josh) out here, he's driving a 2007 Gold Lexus license plate 3479923, don't stop him. He knows the deal and will bug out. Just hit me up on the radio and I'll take care of it."

Everyone nodded and we left roll call to go out and fight crime. A couple of arrests and several hours later 2:45 pm rolled around. I begin heading towards the border. I was excited, I had a fun weekend planned. I was meeting my girlfriend and her friends at an awesome bar with live music. I came to the roundabout in Keene and sure enough here comes Josh's 2007 Gold Lexus entering the other side.

I fully expected him to see me and roll down his window and flip me another bird to let me know I was still #1 in his book, but this time was different. He didn't notice me. He didn't even blink an eye in my direction. I was as good as invisible.

"Lets fucking gooo Rav 4!!!" Best undercover car in the world. So instead of live music, my girlfriend, and cold beer, I wheeled around and followed Josh into town. On the way I watched him pick up a local drug user. This same drug user had just been arrested by yours truly several days prior. He had just been released on bail. Yep, this was going to be it.

I watched Josh pull his Lexus into downtown Keene. The entire time he was driving, I watched him searching his side and rear view mirrors. He was looking for the black Max, he knew if this drug user was working then the black Max would be out here somewhere. He pulled into downtown Keene, and sat there for the next 15 minutes.

I called everyone off to make sure no one spooked him. He pulled out and did what we call a "hot run." Essentially, he makes several right turns to see if anyone is following him. This guy was good. I remember thinking if he put half this energy and effort into a regular job he'd be a millionaire by the age of 25. But Josh's passion was poisoning our children's bodies with hard, hard drugs. He didn't care who he sold too, or what happened to them afterwards.

I stayed chill and hung back to see what he did. He may have been feeling invincible, but I was feeling invisible—knowing what was about to go down if I could be patient. He pulled back into downtown Keene, parked for about 15 minutes and to my surprise did another hot run, this time going the opposite way, staring intently in his side and rear view mirrors. Unfortunately for him the black Max wasn't out there. I grinned. Instead of the Max, he should've been looking for cornrows in a soccer mom's car. I couldn't stop grinning. It was just getting better and better. I could almost taste the coming bust.

Once he was done with his second hot run, I called out on the radio and asked for a cruiser to make the traffic stop if he moved again.

A trooper drove into downtown just as Josh was leaving. He turned on the lights and sirens and Josh pulled into the St. Bernards church parking lot.

The trooper approached the vehicle and spoke to Josh for a minute then spoke to the passenger. He decided to run his dog around the car. I watched as he got Josh and his passenger out of the car and allowed them to walk away from the stop.

I began calling out on the radio for him to stop them, knowing that they were holding on their person. Josh would never be so careless as to leave drugs in the car some place let alone bring out into public more than what he was going to sell.

Unfortunately, the trooper didn't hear me. Josh and his passenger just scrolled off into the night. The trooper's dog returned another positive hit for the presence of narcotics and the vehicle was towed back to the police department. Still, I was sick to my stomach about the missed communication and a chance to search Josh and his passenger.

After about two hours of typing up the search warrant, it was finally signed by the judge and I headed back to the sally port where the vehicle was being kept. I wasn't all that optimistic about my chances of getting anything, but you never know.

Paul Gifford, my partner, was waiting there for me and I went to the driver's side while he went for the passenger's. The dog hit indicated the center console was of the most importance so I immediately dove into the center console. I ripped it open after saying a quick prayer only to find it completely empty. "Just give me a little bit..." I kept asking God to just give me enough to put this guy away.

Then Giff opened up the passenger door and tried the glove compartment and found it locked. I walked around with the car keys in hand. I unlocked the glove compartment and BAMMMM!!!! There it was!! The answer to a prayer. A half kilo of heroin and fentanyl and $8,000 cash in a plastic bag.

I had caught him on a re-up. I began screaming "HELL YEAH!!" at the top of my lungs and tackled Giff into the partition between both sally ports. Then, all of a sudden, I didn't feel so great. I figured it was just the adrenaline rush wearing off or my tackling Giff into the partition. Whatever. It would pass.

We scooped up the narcotics, cash and everything else with evidentiary value, and went to the detective conference room. As we were packaging everything up, I continued to feel light headed. Giff looked at me and said "Griff...you ok?"

I remember looking at the clock on the wall and when he said it for a second time, I looked in his direction and my eyes stayed on the clock for another half second.

"I'm gonna head to the bathroom, bro, I'm not feeling so hot."

Giff said okay and told me he'd continue packaging and paperwork.

While I was sitting in the stall of the Keene Police Men's locker room, the room began to spin. It spun in a way that reminded me of the many drunken Navy nights laying in my rack in a foreign country after one too many rum punches.

It was all I could do to pull my pants up and go splash some water on my face. I got to the second of two sinks in the locker room and the room was spinning about 180 degrees. It finally dawned on me. "I'm exposed!!" I said in my head.

"Shit....what am I gonna do?" I tried to splash water on my face but I knew that wouldn't help. I sat down on the floor of the Keene Locker room and began to pray. "Please Lord, let someone come in here and find me."

180 degrees turned into 200, then 270....I didn't have much time left to get help. Then I looked up and noticed my patrol locker was unlocked and was only about two feet away. I knew I had narcan in my cruiser bag inside my locker. I crawled over to my locker, I couldn't stand up. I grabbed the narcan from the front pouch of my cruiser bag and hit myself with it. I sat back and watched as the 270 degrees...became 200...then 100...then the spinning and light head-edness was gone. I felt almost instantly better. I stood up, splashed

some water on my face and went to find Giff. Answered prayers again.

Before that day, I had not been in my patrol locker in over a year, yet it was open, unlocked. By the grace of God. By the grace of God there go I. God's timing, and another puzzle piece fell into place.

Remember the RAV 4? Well, at the end of the interdiction briefing, the LT told everyone we would be on State Police channel 2 for comms. I remembered the RAV 4 did not have an undercover radio installed in it yet so I ran to the locker room to grab my patrol portable radio. With the portable I could communicate and hear what was going on. It took me about 10 minutes that day to just remember my combination—something I never would have been able to do under the influence of fentanyl.

Coincidence? Maybe...Or maybe God was watching over me. Maybe God had a plan for my life. Well, not maybe. He *definitely* had a plan for my life. What I was beginning to learn was that God doesn't just answer the big prayers, or the little prayers we think we need to have answered—like giving me a drug bust I so desperately wanted. He answers the prayers that will put us on the path He has planned for us. He "brings all things together for good to those who love, honor, and follow Him."

God had a reason for giving me the home run I prayed for as a child. He had a reason for not bringing Benny back to life in my arms. He had a reason for the Rav 4 exchange. He had a reason for Ben picking up the phone on the night I was waiting for the clock to strike 00:00 so I could kill myself.

To the average eye, there's no rhyme or reason for why God answers the prayers He does because answered prayers aren't about what *we* want. They're about what God has planned for us.

Sometimes answered prayer isn't about getting or finding the right answer, or having someone walk into a situation to save us. God used Ben when I was sitting in my Yukon waiting for midnight. That night God answered my prayers for peace in my life, but in a different way than I could have ever imagined. I thought death was the way out and through. God showed me it wasn't.

When I definitely didn't want to die, I asked God to send someone into the locker room to find me and save me. Someone did find me. It was me. I found myself. I found the courage to realize how short life is and how quickly my four boys could have grown up without a father. I found the need and desire to search out and understand more about faith. Unfortunately, it took a couple more life or death situations, my plan to kill myself, and lot of love and support I didn't know was out there, for me to look up and say "Thank you God."

I do believe God watches over us. He has a plan for each of us. And, if we screw up that plan, He says He "works ALL things together for those who love/follow Him." He can bring the best out of the worst we do to ourselves.

Kendra moved on, but I have another woman in my life now. Kendra and I still talk every week about the boys and we'll always have that connection. While writing this book I started a new job with Axon, the amazing folks who brought us tasers, body worn cameras and virtual reality training to help our officers go home safe every day. I'm still doing public speaking for Byron and the PLET, raising four sons, including one with special needs.

I'm still learning — from my boys, my new girlfriend, the officers I keep in touch with, and the new officers I meet through work. I face new challenges every day. Some are extremely stressful, others—not so much. But as long as any of us are here on this earth, that's going to be a given—that life is hard. It's harder for some, and some have more resources than others, but we all have our challenges.

If you're still reading this book, I want you to know that you're not alone.God has a plan for you too. There's hope for tomorrow no matter how crappy life looks or feels like today. Today's problems are today's problems, and tomorrow's problems are tomorrow's problems. Don't let them compound, and don't ignore them thinking they're going to go away. Even if you bury your head in the sand, the ocean still rolls in.

Focus on one thing, one issue, one task at a time. Open a line of communication with somebody, preferably someone who truly cares about you. Remember, everyone is struggling. Everyone. If they say they're not, they're lying. They may not be struggling at that moment, but at some point they have struggled, and they will again.

If you're on any kind of social media, then you know someone is hating on you for absolutely no reason other than they can. Ignore them. They don't know you. They're trying to get a rise out of you. Even if you're not on social media, some troll out there who needs to see you fail so they feel like a winner, is going to be throwing shade and hating on you in some way, somehow. It's a fact of life. The more public you are, the more likely you are to collect haters. It's part of the package.

Officers, like those at the 7/7 ambush in Dallas in 2016, were killed by a gunman who never met them, and didn't know them or anything about them, including the fact they had families and people who loved them. To the shooter, they were simply police officers. He was pumped up with hate against all police officers. He hated the uniform, hated the profession, hated everything the police stood for.

It wasn't about honest hate for a person he knew. He didn't even know the names or backgrounds of the officers he killed. For him, it was about the uniform. It was surprising then to learn that Micah Xavier Johnson, the 7/7 shooter, was an Army Reserve Afghan War veteran. A veteran! He was simply angry over police shootings of Black men. My point is, "haters gonna hate." It's not fair. It just is. Don't get sucked into that hate and take it personally. It's not personal. When you learn that you'll relieve a ton of stress. Next? I know guys who were at the 7/7 shooting, and at most of the other incidents I talk about here.

My point is, don't let the memory control you. Take control of it. Check in on each other. The anniversary of a death—even one by natural means, a divorce, the loss of a child, any trauma is painful. It's painful every year. The fourth of July never passes when I don't remember or hear Brittany screaming, "Save my firecracker!" Benny would have been 18 this year. The pain and the memories never, ever go away. The pain is always there, just maybe a little less raw. Check in on people. Find out their date—whatever it is, and check on them before and after and on that date. Don't just jump on social media to say, "Happy birthday."

There are all kinds of anniversaries and not all of them are happy ones. It's not painful to have people ask. It helps. We want to remember, to talk about the good times, and to get that pain out and let other people's concern and love wash over us. It's healing and comforting to know people care years after the fact. It can get pretty lonely when you are the only one, or the only one of a handful of people, who remember.

There's not a day I don't think about Brian. When I was applying for the job I have now at Axon, I left my last interview and prayed, and told "Brian," or my awareness of him, "Make it happen Brian." Whether or not he had a hand in my getting the job I can say God absolutely did. I got the notice shortly after that prayer that I had the job. If all I can do is speak to Brian through God, I'll take it.

People don't "get over it," whatever "it" is, after a year. They hurt every year. They hurt before and after the date. They begin to feel apprehension as the season, the month, the day grows closer. They hurt when they remember special anniversary dates of things they did with a loved one—their first date, when they met, when they graduated, or whatever. They hurt when it passes, remembering the event and the days after.

If you're going to care about somebody, even if you don't keep in touch the rest of the year, check on them on those dates. Reach out. Tell them you know they're struggling, dealing with "the date" (of the divorce, of the death, of the suicide, of the loss) and say, "I know it's the date of ____, and I'm thinking about you, wanted to see how you're doing, and see if you want to get a beer or a burger, or come over and just hang."

Be there for them. Have that difficult conversation. I don't mean you have to "be a therapist" for them. But do be a friend. I see a lot of guys who truly care about their friends, but who don't take care of each other because they're having a hard time asking that question, "How are you doing today?"

They don't want to hear the answer because then they think

they'll have to "deal" with the answer and most aren't ready to do that. Go by their house/apartment or wherever. Order a pizza or take out and watch a movie. Go for a run. Work out.

Take a walk. Be there. You can do that. Just being with Ben that night, just talking, laughing, sharing stories and catching up with him saved my life.

I know. I know. We don't want to hear from our buddies that they're suicidal, or depressed because we're scared of how we're supposed to respond to that confession. Do we joke? Do we get all serious? We want plausible deniability if they do kill themselves. You don't have to be a shrink, or a therapist, or know all the right things to say or ask. You just have to care. I talked about my navy career and the best friends I found during that time in my life. Cole Hyland was one of them.

There were six of us in that two bedroom apartment. Cole was the even-tempered, funny, intelligent, kind-hearted in every way, roommate. Every year we still all catch up with each other. Most of the time it's in person and it's something I look forward to. We grew up together. We all came into the Navy at 18 years old without a clue. For the next six years we matured, got married, had kids and were there for each other through the best of times and the worst of times.

I can say without a shadow of a doubt that they are my best friends in the world. None of them care about anything other than whether my kids and I are doing ok. Several years ago, I was doing some LEO training outside of Chicago (where Cole is from). I sent him a text to see if he was available to meet for dinner. Once I found out it was two hrs away, I told him not to worry but he insisted. He said "I never get a chance to see you."

So Cole drove two hours to have dinner and beer. He asked how I'd been and I began to tell him how I left the police department, the undercover life, and finally about suicide. Cole sat there and listened to me. For almost an hour, I rambled on about my life, my situation. I stopped to catch my breath and Cole looked at me and said "you know my brother was a cop right?"

I actually didn't know his brother was a cop. I thought it was his twin and he said "No my older brother Graham." He began to tell me about Graham and his struggles with substance abuse and financial problems. Then he dropped the bomb.

"He killed himself, Griff."

Stunned, I just sat there and looked at him.

"What? Cole, I didn't know brother. I'm so sorry." Cole went on to talk about how Graham was larger than life but struggled to get out of his own way. We talked about his life and things he went through as a police officer, husband and father.

"I knew it was gonna happen, Griff. My mom passed away shortly after he killed himself." Stunned again. Here was one of my best friends in the world and I didn't know any of this. I felt terrible. I felt like I let him down.

"I'm sorry bro." Is all I could manage.

"I tried everything I could to help him. Every phone call I got from him was like- here we go again, what did Graham do."

Cole and I talked for hours. I could see and hear the pain in his voice. I could hear the questions he had no answers for. I wish I could've given him the answers but I didn't have them either. I didn't know what to say other than to just listen.

I asked Cole if I could interview him for the book. He said yes, and we spent another two hours on the phone talking. As we talked we healed. We healed together. He knew I cared and I knew he needed to speak. He needed to have a voice and speak for Graham. I needed to hear his story and connect with him over what he'd gone through.

Sometimes there isn't an answer. Sometimes we don't have to resolve every problem we face. It's a tough lesson to learn as a first responder. All day and every day we are given problems and our job is to resolve those problems. Some problems can't be resolved. Sometimes we need to learn the answer to the hardest of questions is to sit, listen and love. Love the person, love being with them because sometimes that's all that's needed.

I learned that from Cole and I am forever grateful for our friendship and the lessons I've learned from him. Just listen. Just love.

You don't need to fix people. You don't need solutions. You just need to say, "Hey brother. I care about you." I know it sounds simple, too simple to work. But it does work.

I was talking to my editor and to another friend about some things they were struggling with. The advice I gave them went back to my SARS days. Whatever it is hanging you up, or overwhelming you, just get through the next minute, the next hour, the next task. Don't think about the end of the project, the overall goal, the depression that pushes you to end your life or do something stupid. Don't think about graduating SARS. Think about the one thing you have to do next. Do it. Grind on. Then do the next thing. One thing at a time. Pick out what it is and grind on it until you finish it. Then pick the next thing and do the same.

If that's the only advice you have to give them, then give them that.

Say, "Hey man, I know everything sucks right now. You're feeling like there's no way out but killing yourself. That's a permanent solution to a temporary problem. Don't do it. I care about you. You're loved. There's light at the end of this darkness. Let me help you get through the next hour, hell, the next 24 hours. Just give it 24 hours and see what happens. If it gets worse, we'll give it another 24, then another, but it's going to turn around. It always does." Then stay with them. Talk. Listen. Care. Help them troubleshoot what's driving them to end it.

For me, the feeling that drove me to suicide was feeling like I was such a loser that my boys would never speak to me, love me, or respect me again. The people I loved the most, cared for the most, wanted to connect with the most were the very people I believed (falsely) that I couldn't connect with.

I couldn't see past the shame and humiliation I was feeling. It all kept adding up and piling on. I wasn't used to losing so much I couldn't get back up and "come away leading the pack." I knew, somewhere, what I needed to do. In my head I learned all the lessons through school, SARs, and Clearview.

But I needed space, and like hundreds of others, I sought that space in solitude. And isolation and solitude, as good as it feels to wallow in our pain alone, leads to suicide. There are other ways to get space without leaving your support or your community of people who care about you.

Take a leave of absence. Go on vacation. Take sick leave. Quit your job (my ultimate solution) and find something else that will allow you to use your training, experience, and passion for helping. Take the space you need, but don't shut out the people you need. Connection is vital.

For most of us "quitting" the job isn't an option. But "leaving" is. I LEFT my job in policing. I CHOSE to do something else with my life. I took control of my life, my future, and who I was in that moment and I moved forward. That's resilience. That's bouncing back. Hell no it wasn't easy. I was scared, I wondered how things would work out, if they'd work out. All I knew for sure was that suicide would keep anything good from happening to me ever.

I kept returning to memories of getting my ass kicked by Rob C, to SARS training, to Clearview, and to my brother telling me, "When they throw you to the wolves, you return leading the pack." That ultimately felt far more motivational and stimulating for my type A personality than "ringing the bell" on life.

There are a lot of "explanations" for the meaning behind the song I quote at the beginning of this chapter. The lyrics talk about the narrator as someone who was deeply scarred by the experiences he has had as a young man. He "left his home" and "family" when he *was no more than a boy.*"

I "left home" essentially when I made the choice to join the US NAVY. What everyone wanted me to do was go to college, get that nice expensive piece of paper that says "bachelor degree," play sports and play the game of a lifestyle that had already failed me. What I wanted to do was get away from what everyone else wanted for my life, and decide what I wanted for my life. I didn't know much about real life—beyond blending, fitting in, and pleasing adults who seemed to think they knew what was best for me. I didn't know what God had in store for me, or where I'd end up, but I quickly learned the Merry-Go-Round of life doesn't stop for newbies. The different cultures, boot camp, "A" school, it would all become another eye opening experience.

The song goes on *"...cut him till he cried out In his anger and his shame, I am leaving, I am leaving," But the fighter still remains."*

This isn't just a song. It's semi-autobiographical, and a part of Paul Simon's life. It's burned into my heart too. Those lyrics are my lyrics. The song says the narrator of the song left home under some vague pretense that life on his own would be better than wherever he came from, but ultimately it wasn't ("a pocketful of mumbles, such are promises"). The narrator is seeking out prostitutes and seems desperate for some sort of connection, no matter how low. I turned to the arms of another seeking answers, connections, solace too. I get it. It was a bad choice for me. Very bad.

In spite of all the things that happen to this guy, he keeps standing. The *"fighter* still remains."* When the whole world dumps its misery, hate, criticism and worse on us, the fighter still remains.Whats inside you and who you are don't leave you. Like everyone else, Paul Simon tells music magazines he was doing his best, but says in interviews that he was being unfairly criticized.

"I think I was reading the Bible around that time," he told one music magazine that's now offline.

"That's where I think phrases such as "workman's wages" came from, and "seeking out the poorer quarters." That was biblical. I think the song was about me: everybody's beating me up, and I'm telling you now I'm going to go away if you don't stop."

One of the verses that doesn't get as much air time as the one I quoted above is the fourth verse:

"Now the years are rolling by me, they are rocking evenly. I'm older than I once was, and younger than I'll be; that's not unusual, nor is it strange. After changes upon changes we are more or less the same. After changes, we are more or less the same."[1]

That's why the song resonates with me. "After changes upon changes, we are more or less the same." And as the years have rolled by, they're rocking more evenly. Things have changed a lot. I've changed a lot. I now wear a suit and tie, not cornrows and a nose ring. I have a different relationship with a new woman. I still have a friendship with Kendra—she's the mother of my boys, whom we're still raising together, just not as husband and wife. "Changes upon changes, we are more or less the same."

All my life I learned to "fit in," to survive, but all that time, except for Clearview, I didn't learn to truly and deeply connect with people, to feel my feelings, and to respect and listen to them.

There's a difference between surviving and connecting. Surviving is about not getting "taken out." Connecting is about finding peace, relaxing and letting people love you and allowing you to love them.

Connection with people necessitates being vulnerable, open, feeling your feelings and sharing them with those you care about, and who hopefully care about you. I wasn't doing that with Kendra. I wasn't doing that as a cop, or with Brian, or even with many of all the many people I called friends. I worked hard to fit in. I "belonged," but no one knew me because I didn't know myself. I couldn't even share my feelings, my grief with Benny's parents, my friends. I hid it all until God helped me find myself.

Now I connect with my sons, and we have real talks, share real emotions. I cry, I'm there for them when they cry. I love them, I kiss them and hug them.

They are my sons. I'm not going to hide behind that overtly masculine culture that tells me I shouldn't hug and kiss my sons, or be real with them. I don't like the culture that tells me I should pretend to know everything and not be weak and admit I don't. The fact is, I tell my sons, I don't know the answers, but we can figure out the answers together. I can't explain how powerful and moving that is. To think I almost left these guys behind to figure life and death, love, and God out alone makes me quake with how close I came to not having the relationship I have with them now.

I've learned they don't care about my failing, or falling, or losing, or not knowing. They love me for me as much as I love them for who they are. It's so powerful I can't put it into words. We've talked about what happened, and what didn't happen that night. They've read my suicide note. I look forward to talking about it more as they get old enough to grasp it as adults.

I'm "age appropriate" with them about the suicide now, but I don't hide it. They need to know people, even their dad, fails, feels down, lost, and sad. They need to know that it's okay for men (and boys) to cry, to hurt, to need to be comforted, and to talk to someone who loves them. They can come to me with anything. I'm their father. I finally get it about "God our father." He loves me and my sons so much more than we can love Him.

You can't hide anything from God. He knew us before we were born. There are more than 100 verses in the Bible where God tells us He knew us, He planned us, He shaped us before we were even a glimmer in our parent's eyes.

"Before I formed you in the womb I knew you, and before you were born I consecrated you; I appointed you a prophet to the nations." ~ Jeremiah 1:5.

"Your eyes saw my unformed substance; in your book were written, every one of them, the days that were formed for me, when as yet there was none of them." ~ Psalm 139:16.

But there's more. God is all about connection—including connection with yourself. Connection with others, with God, is vital to our health and well being. It's essential to our becoming resilient, to our getting through the tough times, the times that drive us to contemplate suicide.

I learned recently that over the last 10-15 years research shows that people who are "more resilient," are also less likely to commit suicide.[2] It's not an absolute answer, but learning resilience, which includes learning to connect, is a way to help keep that darkness at bay.

Learning resilience, connecting with friends and family—and I don't mean just the camaraderie of "the brotherhood," of veterans and LEOs. I mean a connection with another human being that guarantees when you say, "I'm having nightmares," they don't freak out, or pull you offline. They don't report you, or force you to quit your job. They listen. They hear you. They support you, encourage you, and help you through the rough times. That's connection. The greatest connection I had turned out to be someone I'd known my whole life, someone who loved me so much, but who I didn't notice unless I wanted something.

True love, God's love, is the connection that saved me. He'd been there beside me all along, waiting, listening, watching, knowing. I'm surprised by how many officers and first responders I know who think about, worry about dying, or getting killed while on the job, but most of them haven't ever thought about what would happen next, after they died.

Heaven is a real place. It's a kingdom, God's kingdom. He sets the rules and the laws about who gets in there. You don't get in by "being good," or "doing good." Your entrance depends on whether you believe in Jesus Christ, accept Him as lord of your life, and follow Him. That's what it takes to get into heaven. It's free, and no one is so "bad" that they can't find forgiveness.

Heaven isn't all angels sitting on clouds strumming harps. That's not biblical. The Bible tells us heaven will be a place where we work and interact, only without hate, evil, sin, corruption, or all the things that have screwed up this life. You won't have wings, you will have purpose. The alternative is, well, horrific. In hell there is no light, God is not there, and you're in eternal pain for eternity. If you don't look at God for any reason other than to avoid hell, that's a start.

CHAPTER 10

Changing the Culture

If you always do what you always did,
you will always get what you always got."
— Albert Einstein

Awareness is step one. No one is going to change police, military, or emergency services cultures overnight. Culture change begins with baby steps. It begins with the people inside the culture. If the people don't change, the culture doesn't change. You can't force people to change their culture. It has to be their decision.

You can lead, and let the changes flow down. But you can't change people by ordering them to change. You inspire, motivate, or show them a greater vision. Officers want to be the best. If you're in a leadership position, you're the best one to effect that change. Someone's got to step up and be the first one to change, not just talk about change.

As I wrote this book, I was looking at how culture change happens. I grew up around leaders, coaches, military officers, police supervisors and disciplined structure. I know how deeply rooted military, sports, and police culture are in the male psyche. I know the culture is not going to move leagues in my lifetime, but maybe it'll change in the lifetimes of my four sons. You know what I mean. I want my sons to grow up in a world where they don't have to stuff their emotions, or hide their feelings—and they don't have to emasculate themselves, or look, act, or dress like women to have the right or society's approval to express themselves.

From the moment that we are selected as candidates, and we step through those academy doors, raise our right hand, and invest months of our lives into our profession, we begin to learn, change, and adapt to this culture. They hand us our badge for the first time after all our hard work and training, sweat and tears. We're totally invested in being police officers, or firemen, or medics, or soldiers or sailors, or Marines or Coast Guard. How can we not embrace the culture?

The cultures of some of these organizations goes back for more than 200 years. They are proud of who they are, and what their culture is. They are not giving up those deep seated, dearly beloved history around their warrior and tough guy culture easily—nor do they necessarily have to. Simply adding to the culture with understanding about trauma and the impact on mental health will do so much to enhance and enrich that culture.

Lisa Jenkins, a pastor writing an opinion piece for The Daily News in New York wrote, "One of the things that we fail to realize is that we can pass as many laws as we want designed to bring about change, but unless the actual culture changes, then we're back to square one. Culture is not something you can see or smell. You can't touch it. But you know it when you experience it. Simply put, culture is socially transmitted and learned behavior. And people are socialized into culture in any number of ways."

She was writing about NYC police corruption, violence, and a toxic culture in general in the city. But her words about culture and how we're socialized into it ring true across the board. She asked, "Do I want to defund the police, the group that is protecting my community?" Or do I want to change the culture?"1 She chooses to change the culture, not defund the police. It's going to be hard to do.

In small ways cultural change is definitely being considered in many smaller to mid-size departments—especially around mental health issues.

Studies are being done, and the subject is being raised as more and more officers continue to die at their own hands. The suicide of the four officers who were at the DC January 6, 2020 protest on Capitol Hill has brought new attention about this issue around the country. I found a lot of papers, reports, studies, and commentaries on police mental health when I started writing this book. I was trying to understand my own path towards suicide, why I slipped, as hundreds do each year, into such a dark place, and why some of us emerge from the darkness, and so many don't.

I believed from the first moment I was able to see clearly what I had almost pulled off—my own death—was rooted in cop culture and in not admitting weakness. A culture that denies men and women in police work and as first responders—the right to experience or express their emotions in a healthy, open way, is a deadly culture.

The stress of bottling up all we see, hear and do on the job, coupled with the stress of our personal lives, is too much for any healthy human being to process without professional help from time-to-time.

As I've looked around at the men and women I know, I can see those who are lucky enough to have a partner who understands, who's there for them, who isn't afraid to hear about the things they see. I assumed they had sort of a live-in therapist, at least someone who could listen and be supportive, but that's not necessarily so.

When April Scherzer woke to the sound of a gunshot and her 36-year-old police officer husband, Max, dead in their home, she wasn't surprised at the response of the police department. As they had done on the few occasions Max was brave enough to ask for help, they ignored him.

"The first thing you get when you marry a police officer is the blue family. You become part of that group. And I felt like after Max killed himself that me and the kids kind of got kicked out of that police family," April told NBC news in October, 2019.2

Prior to Max's suicide, the Westampton Township Police Department in New Jersey, where Max worked for 12 years, gave a presentation on mental health. Max asked for the psychologist's phone number afterwards. The department promptly confiscated his gun, sent him home for 30 days, and told him that a department-affiliated therapist would have to clear him to return for duty. He wasn't given any assistance, or referrals for assistance, April told NBC News.3

Max's PTSD may have started after seeing a car crash and catch fire. Max tried to pull the driver out of the vehicle but was unable to do so. He could only stand there and watch the man burn alive, unable to help him, April said.4

The nightmares, and the self-medication started shortly after that, she said. Max didn't get the help he deserved when he was alive, and he didn't get the typical funeral and respect an officer killed in the line of duty gets. There was no flag, no memorial, no recognition of his devotion to the department for over a decade. The sad thing is, this is typical and most officers don't realize it, or if they do, they're in denial about it.

Jeffery Smith, one of the Washington, DC officers who committed suicide after January 6, said he was in physical and emotional pain and he asked for help. He wasn't happy with the care he received at the Police and Fire Clinic for his physical or emotional pain. He was waiting for his follow-up appointment. But at that appointment, rather than being cared for, he was ordered back to duty the very next day, January 5.

His wife Erin Smith told USA Today, "...the District of Columbia government, so far, has taken the position that for some reason, because my husband's injuries were emotional, invisible, he didn't die in the line of duty. It's time for the mayor, the Metropolitan Police Department, the D.C. government, and other departments and governments around the country to recognize that silent injuries, these deaths, even when at a police officer's own hand, are a direct result of the job they have been doing. Their deaths are in the line of duty."

These women are fighting back. Their husbands may be gone, but "the fighter still remains."

Police Officer Jenn Kennedy is another officer who fought and won. Jenn lost her police officer husband, Dave, to suicide on February 17, 2014—three days after Valentine's Day. As I had done with Benny, she too recognized the address that came across the police scanner. Only it was her house, not a friend's. Her daughter had called 911. The call went out, and that's how Jenn learned of her spouse's suicide. She responded to the call, and found him on the floor. I can't imagine a more devastating call.

Dave and Jenn met, married, and worked at the Springettsbury Township Police Department and served there 13 years together. They were both officers, but she said Dave could never share the darkest of the things he saw prior to meeting her. This is not unusual. Many first responders, influenced by the cultures where they work, choose to protect those we love from the horrors that we battle—whether they are likely to understand or not. She stayed on the force after his death. She wasn't/isn't fighting the culture as much as she is fighting for awareness about mental health.

Before coming to the Springettsbury PD, Dave had worked undercover as a narcotics detective in Baltimore. Jenn believes that's where Dave's issues began.

She never got an answer to what he saw exactly. She told Anothony Machcinski of Our York Media that all she knew was that the incidents were "horrendous." Jenn was one of the lucky ones. Her police department didn't ignore her, and didn't treat her loss as many departments do—by ignoring his death or her grief. Instead, Dave's death inspired Daniel Stump, the Police of Chief at Springettsbury, PD, to look for solutions. After attending several conferences, Stump told Our York Media, he developedSpringettsburyFit, a seven-part holistic program aimed at helping an officer's mental health.5

There are many departments across the U.S. who value their officers and treat them fairly and compassionately. But there are more who don't. If you're lucky enough to be working with one of the compassionate ones, stay with them. However, still look for something or someone to love, or be loved by, outside of your job. Keep your passion, but understand that there are no guarantees, which is truly sad given the passion most LEOs and first responders have for their jobs.

We're so invested in who we, as newly minted officers, firemen, EMTs, first responders and military personnel have become as a result of our training, and the academy, that we sometimes don't realize that the profession we've held in such high esteem, doesn't feel the same about us. These departments frequently and deliberately put distance between officers who experience depression, PTSD, nightmares, sleeplessness, or trouble functioning because of trauma or stress.

Fresh out of the academy, we also often fail to realize that we're now held to a higher standard in our personal life, as well as in our professional life. We are groomed to buy into and support the existing culture, and not to talk about change. We're so freaking excited to be "a cop" that we don't want anyone pointing these things out. We think that PTSD, depression, a horrific incident, will never happen to us.

Sadly, if you stay in the job long enough, it probably will. Why? In part because of what we experience and because we work in a centuries-old culture that demands it be that way. From the warrior culture to the "thin blue line culture," to the unspoken or unacknowledged culture of our police roots — that policing began as a way to control minorities and the poor; that police culture is as old as slavery and originally organized to control slaves. If you thought changing the culture in a Fortune 500 company or corporation was difficult, you don't even want to stare into the abyss of centuries-old military and police cultures.

I'm not against military or police cultures. On many levels, I'm proud, honored, and humbled to have been a part of them and to have served. They have protected our community and country and our freedom. They are cultures that promote ethics and character even if they don't always support them. They're not snow white. There is corruption, and there are bad cops. That's true in any and all professions—but police officers carry guns and get more attention when things go wrong.

However, they do, as a whole, make our country strong, and for the most part, they get or keep bad guys off the street—although that's changing as courts and the system kick criminals back onto the streets faster than police can process them.

What bothers me is that so many agencies do what they do at the expense of the men and women who make up the ranks of the more than 18,000 police agencies across the U.S. The majority of these agencies (more than 15,000) are organized at the city or county level and could affect tremendous changes if they chose to.6

That's why I tell officers, "respect the job, embrace the job, honor the job, and do the job to the best of your ability, but don't marry it." When you put all your focus in your work, or "all your eggs into one basket," with no outlet for your life outside of work, then you are setting yourself up for failure.

When you experience work related challenges and you have no alternatives, no support, and that basket suddenly breaks free, and those 'eggs' break all around you, you can feel your life is over. I felt my life was over. I'd worked my tail off, succeeded, and yet still failed, not because of anything I did, but because of the same power, pull, and political games being played. It was high school all over again. It's not fair, but it is reality.

I know other officers who felt or feel the same way. Is it fair? Sometimes being pulled offline is fair, sometimes it's not. It's not so black and white as it seems.

Let's look at the other side, your supervisor's side. Let's look at the culture that exists, and how it needs to change. It's true that Officers with mental health issues, PTSD, and stress can pose a risk to themselves, their colleagues, and their communities. That's a fact. No one wants to hear it, but it's a fact.

According to an article written by Bengt Arnez, in The Journal of

Police and Criminal Psychology, "A person who is subjected to continuous stress has a reduced ability to regulate emotions and behaviors.7 One study found 34 percent of law enforcement officers demonstrated partial PTSD, that is, a person who has sufficient symptoms of PTSD to cause impairment.8 Officers who have impaired decision-making abilities can pose significant risks of injury or death to themselves, other officers, and civilians, as well as increased litigation risks for their agencies.

We've all experienced subjects during our work, on patrol, who were emotionally impaired, mentally ill, depressed, angry.

That reality that our emotional state impacts our decision making cannot be ignored. Someone who isn't mentally prepared to deal with their emotions, the job, and what they need to do every day is a risk to themselves and their partners. What else is your supervisor supposed to do if they learn you're not functioning at 100%? What would you do in their shoes?

Do you want to be on a tough call with a partner you're not sure will be able to handle a critical event, or handle it correctly, or worse yet, who freezes or faints, or runs? What's the solution? I think it's going to take more than just pulling officers offline, or sending them to therapy, or encouraging them to leave the force if they're having a bad day, or a string of bad days. It's going to require deep and wide-spread culture change.

Judith Anderson, a health psychologist whose research focuses on the biopsychosocial mechanisms by which stress impacts health and occupational performance, argues that "By creating an organizational culture that embraces mental preparedness and provides the tools for stress reduction, an organization can help to develop and maintain resilience within its ranks."9 That means officers can have a bad day and take appropriate actions to deal with what's going on—just like normal people outside law enforcement do, take a healthy break, yet keep working without the stigma and career-killing sanctions.

Imagine a culture where community mental health and police mental health both matter. If you've been a cop for any amount of time, you're going to be at a different place mentally, psychologically, and experientially than the officers around you—especially younger officers, or those from a military background.

Ramon Batista explained how he came to the job very naive (as most of us do), but within a few years, he experienced a huge change in his ability to empathize with others, and realize how important a supportive community within the department became to him personally.

Ramon Batista; the Roadmap for Success

"For the life of me as a young cop, I didn't have the skillset or the capacity to have any empathy for what my coworkers were going through when they were getting divorced. I didn't understand it. And so when, when those things would unfold in front of me with friends or guys that I knew, I would just sit back and scratch my head and kind of go, what's the big deal? I mean, so what, I don't understand why you're a wreck over your wife or marriage or whatever.

"That indifference and lack of empathy lasted until I got married. I'd been dating this girl for two or three years, but my marriage only lasted a year. And so then the marriage ended. Bam.

"Wow. I suddenly, finally got it. My marriage was falling apart, and I was suddenly going through a divorce. You think about it all throughout the day, you go to bed thinking about it, and then if you sleep, when you wake up, you wake up thinking about it. It really is hell and I would never wish a divorce on my worst enemy.

"So it wasn't until I experienced that kind of emotional and psychological roller-coaster, that I realized why those guys were all torn up. And at the time, it seemed so important to me that even if it really wasn't like that big a deal, what they did for me was.

"My close friends around the department kind of closed in on me and made sure that I was okay. They were calling, they were checking in on me. They were sending me messages, or talking to me and basically showing me that they were the support system for me, that otherwise, I didn't have.

"That's when I finally started understanding the trauma that can happen when you're going through all the stress of work stuff on top of your personal life stuff. You gotta be spot on. I'm getting a divorce, and all of a sudden, you know, one of the legs of the stool is missing. My personal life was in shambles. I started to pay attention to that and how being connected and having a community that cares about you matters, how it can get you through those tough times.

"There was another situation with a guy that I knew, and was close with, worked with, who didn't have that same kind of community I did. He discovered that his wife had been unfaithful to him and she was seeing another guy. And so he lost it. He went to where she was and he killed the guy and then he turned the gun on himself and killed himself. This was before we had any kind of real help from the police department with respect to coping with personal issues. So whatever my friend had been dealing with, he had maybe told his friends, maybe not," Ramon said. "But it ended badly."

"So that's kind of my history of how I came to really care about mental health. I had firsthand experience with it. That's why it's so important that our frontline folks are healthy and able to go out and be the best they can be, but only if they're mentally and physically fit in order to deal with the stressors that come with a 20, 25-year career.

"From the early stages of this thing, I can tell you that there was a stigma around mental health. I can remember as a younger cop that you couldn't ever have anybody within your circle, your Sergeant, your command staff, or whatever unit you were in, even suspect that you were mentally unfit to go out there and do the work. Remember we're the ones that go out there and fix these issues for everybody else. We are expected to be 100% at all times no matter what's happening with us personally.

"If you were having problems, you didn't even bring it (mental health issues) up ever, anywhere. If you did ask for help, then it's 'hold on, wait, why is he asking for help for something the rest of us do on a daily basis?' The first question people are going to ask is, 'what's wrong with him?'

"You never wanted to be the guy that they were asking that about because that's chipping away at the foundation of the thing you love —the job. The fact that you might not be 100% because of your divorce, or because of something that happened to you on the job, or if you were affected by anything that could somehow jeopardize your position and take it away from you, that kind of talk wasn't allowed —even in your own head! So, you never want to talk about that. You didn't talk about that.

When I was going through my divorce I never said anything to anybody about struggling. Guys just knew and took it upon themselves to be there for me. It wasn't until I got to the Mesa police department that I realized there's so much more we can do and can continue to do around mental health.

"I think that peer support programs are very, very important. I think that they are a critical component of this whole wellness foundation in law enforcement," Ramon said.

"But one of the things that I think that is of ultimate concern with a peer wellness program is that there has to be confidentiality. So that if I'm going to you and I'm telling you about what's going on, like, you don't repeat that story because if you do and you say it to the wrong person and then it, then it starts to kind of take off on its own, that's no good. The victim, and this whole thing is going to be me, the person that needs help. But now you're the subject of rumor and innuendo. And I think that can be very damaging, more damaging than what you're actually going through.

"I never looked at a day in law enforcement, and I don't know many people that do, and thought that our work wasn't something that we were so proud of—even when it was dangerous and stressful. From the time we're in law enforcement, until we're not, we're a police officer, or a state police officer, or a sheriff's deputy. We're law enforcement. This is your badge, this is your oath. This is what we do.

"We protect each other, we protect and serve our community. It's just hammered into us over and over our whole career. It's the honor and the integrity and the loyalty that's built into the profession that creates a lot of pride. So, I'm asking you this, 'Do you think that's part of the way that we're brought on? Should it be?

"Remember the onboarding procedure of going through the academy, and the field training officer program? Then there's the choir practices after you make it out of field training and things like that and the pride that you have in that. It all works together to form a very strong culture of not asking for help. I wonder if all those little things tie in a little bit to the stigma of not being able to ask for help. Without a doubt, I know it does," he said.

I wholeheartedly agree with Ramon. Culture, the unspoken, unwritten rules or whatever of police and first responder, veteran training are subtle and all pervasive. From the movies we watch as kids, to the video games we play as teens, and everything the media reports on, police are tough guys who can handle the stress, and they do not cry. That's only reinforced in our training.

"When I went through the police academy, there was a fantastic police psychologist, Dr. Kevin Gilmartin. He wrote a great book that talked a lot about our tendency as officers to over-invest in our profession," Ramon said. [Emotional survival for law enforcement: A guide for officers and their families,]

"What's so unfortunate about that over-investment is that we put all this energy and effort into this job that we love, that we honor, respect, and always try to do our very best in, but we don't realize the job is not in our control. It's always in somebody else's control.

"I remembered that when I finally got to be an assistant chief of police. There were those times when you had to take somebody offline because they'd been in some type of critical event and needed some distance.

"They have a really bad accident, say a shooting. You take them offline for their own mental health, although they're not looking at it that way. You asked me whether in some of these situations if the members themselves have an option, and I'll tell you that what I've found is that by and large, they did not. Even if they'd done the right thing. They did not have an option about how it was handled.

Someone else did. So there you go with that whole loss of control of something that you really care about.

"I was always very mindful of how taking someone offline would come across. I would take the time to talk to people on a one-on-one basis. I would explain, "Hey, you know, you're going to be okay. We just have to go through this process. I'm going to try to get you to a good place during this period where you're not on patrol.'

"I was sincere. I meant it. I would make sure that I wasn't trying to put somebody in the place where, where they were like a square peg in a round hole, and the assignment didn't line up for them. I remember one guy specifically that had been in a shooting and man, you know, we really try to make sure that we put them in a place that was kind of fun, kind of cool for them to recover.

"And it was a cool place, but it still wasn't back on patrol where he wanted to be. Even that assignment, which was a plum assignment, and a nice break, where we gave him some additional training, and put him into a great group of people with a lot of camaraderie, wasn't enough.

"After a few weeks of him not being where he needed to be, where he wanted to be, he was sad. It was getting to him. He wasn't with his guys and that impacted him more than the shooting.

"I think that the work that needs to be done really goes back to what I was telling you that Dr. Kevin Gill, was telling us early on, that you have to understand that there's somebody else that's going to be in control of this thing you love—this law enforcement career, which is essentially your entire identity. And you have to be able to acknowledge that when something happens to take you offline, and it's not a matter of if it happens. It's a matter of when that happens. Some bureaucrat sitting up in the command staff office will make a decision that impacts you adversely, fair or not, justified or not. This is true across the board. There is someone who is always going to be above you, someone with more accountability and insight or not, who is calling the shots. It's going to impact you more if you're not prepared for that reality," Ramon said.

I thought back to my three-day suspension in high school. and how lucky I was at 14 years of age to experience that very lesson of someone else controlling the shots. Some people are 24, or 34, or 54 years of age when they wake up to that reality. Knowing, and having experienced that several times in my life, gave me time to prepare my exit strategies when the career ending time came. And that's what it is.

Something happens, right or wrong, justified or not, righteous or not, and you're pulled offline. You lose your position, post, gun, badge, and career, and you have to think about what's next. Someone doesn't like you, your politics are wrong, your faith is wrong. Or you can be liked and respected, but someone else wants your spot and they have a powerful ally who can move you aside to make room for them. I was the best person for the job in high school, but not the most politically connected. We know what happened there. Live and learn.

Here's what bites. You can't just lose it all and expect to survive. You need that exit strategy. You need a backup plan. You need community and support from people who care about you. You need to believe in yourself and have a core belief that no matter what these people say, you're going to survive.

So when the time came and I was pulled offline because of a personal action by people who didn't like me, I wasn't surprised. I saw it coming. I was prepared. I knew what to say, and I said it. I chose to leave. I wasn't "forced out."

If you're thinking you're the only one, or you and I are the only ones who got thrown under the bus, or jerked around, or pulled offline for no just cause, think again. It happens to thousands of officers every day.

"Yes, this is an amazing career," Ramon told me. "It's honorable. But, you have to remember, you're always going to have a boss and the situation could arise where they're going to pull the rug out from under you. Even if you're doing all the right things, saying all the right things, and have all the boxes checked, you have to be ready for the unexpected. Because inevitably, because this is such a litigious, public, political, and dangerous job that, inevitably you're going to be in a position where you're going to be faced with something like that. It's just completely unnerving, especially when you're young and you don't know what the hell is in the store for you down the road.

"So I think building resiliency, having someone or something you love—and who loves you—outside the job—is critical," he said. "Have somewhere to go when you aren't going back into the agency —someplace you love, someplace where you can be proud of yourself."

Again, I agree with Ramon. I didn't realize it at the time, but I'd been focusing on, and was so over-invested in who I was as a cop, as an undercover officer, as all things related to police work—I hadn't taken time to focus on who I was outside of all that.

One of the things that was so helpful in my life later on, whether it was taking on a side job speaking to officers, or any other side businesses or playing lacrosse, raising my sons, was my passion for my interests outside of law enforcement. I was passionate about law enforcement, but there was always something else. For me, it was still about helping and protecting my community, and my brothers and sisters on the force.

If I could impress anything on people, especially younger cops or those heading into retirement for whatever reason, is to have more passions than just police work. I get it. You're 22 years old, this is all you ever wanted to do. You're so gung-ho on the job you can jump buildings in a single bound, and stop bullets and speeding trains. I get it. I felt the same.

Police work is awesome and hopefully you'll have a long, successful career. But be prepared for trauma, for crisis, for things not going as planned, and don't let it funnel you towards suicide or depression. You're better than that. If you're counting down the months, or days, or even years towards retirement, the same is true. Have something you're walking towards, not just something you're walking away from after 20 years. You don't know when, where, how, or why your mental health will fail.

I remember there were 33 of us in the academy and an instructor walked in and he talked to us about mental health. And he said, "you know, by the numbers, there's 33 of you here and statistically speaking, one of you will shoot and kill somebody in the next two years."

He was right. In the next two years, two of our guys shot and killed somebody. And both guys are no longer cops. They weren't prepared for the fallout, they weren't prepared for the interviews. They weren't prepared for the societal response from the shooting. So many things combined that they didn't talk about in the academy.

My academy was six months long in Virginia Beach. It was a day academy, meaning we went home every night. So a lot of times we would hang out, we would drink beers after work and things like that.

We talked about what that instructor said that day. I remember one kid that actually wanted to be "that guy" who shot someone in the line of duty. He wanted to be involved in a shooting. He got his wish, he shot and killed somebody. I remember him over a beer during that day we "got the talk." He was saying, "you know what, I can't wait for that. I can't wait for that opportunity (to shoot a bad guy). And if my number is called and I'm picked, and I gotta be put in that position, then I'm ready for it."

The odd, twisted, truth about a righteous or justified shooting as I said before is it is almost looked upon as a badge of honor by other officers. Your buddies slap you on the back and congratulate you for "taking out the trash," especially if it's a righteous shooting with a very bad guy who gets taken out.

I was speaking with an Officer who had been involved in an OIS and after he was cleared and returned to full duty an older police officer saw him before roll call and said "what's up killer" with a high five motion. He said, "man, I wasn't ready for that."

Meanwhile, you're mentally and emotionally torn. You're feeling all kinds of guilt, even if it is a righteous shooting or you're defending yourself or someone else. You're not sleeping, you're feeling the effects of PTSD, you want help, but you can't get help because everyone is telling you how great you are. You're hearing that you did the right thing because you were involved in "saving a life." You wonder what's wrong with you that you don't feel like a hero.

A deeper part of you knows taking another's life, no matter how bad they were, is a big deal, not some video game score. And it eats at you. Some part of us thinks that's a good thing—that we did what we're called on to do, even when it means killing someone. But if you're an emotionally normal person, not a sociopath or a psychopath, you're going to be conflicted.

It's going to affect you emotionally and mentally and you probably won't want to ask for help—believing it will resolve itself somehow. I think that has to change. We do a great job in law enforcement of checking in on someone for the first week or two after an incident, whether it's a shooting, an accident, or a partner's suicide. We imagine the grief will magically heal in a matter of months.

So, after a few weeks, or months we let it go. We expect that person, once they are cleared from the incident and the approved period of "grieving" to be back to "Full Duty," and functioning at 100%. It fades in intensity for us, so we assume it does for them. After all, "Time heals all wounds," right? We truly believe they are fine.

Trust me, they are not. When that six-month or one-year anniversary rolls around, it hurts. Check on them, put the date in your phone and say "hey buddy, I know today sucks for you but I want you to know I care and I'm here if you want to talk, chill, have a beer, or whatever."

March 9, 2017, is that day for me. It was both Brian's death and my wedding anniversary. I began speaking about checking in on our people after an incident and shared "my date," and my losses and people took it to heart. On March 9th, 2021. I woke up around 8 am and looked over at my phone to find over 100 text messages from people all over the world. The tears flowed down my face. If you are one of those people reading this who messaged me, please know your messages and love helped shape the passion and theme of this book. It takes a village, a community to overcome the forces of satan.

Attitudes have to change about other things too. Departments need to look out for their people and do the reasonable, common-sense thing.

There was an officer named Scott, who was a great cop, an amazing person, and a dedicated community protector. Scott had put an unauthorized night sight on his weapon. And during the course of a shooting he was in, that unauthorized night site was what saved his life. But because the agency hadn't formally approved it he was pulled offline and sat on an internal post for almost 18 months—over a night sight. He was pulled offline, not for the shooting, not for the way he handled himself, or the situation, which were all by the book, but—over a night sight that ultimately saved his life. He got to the point where he said, "I don't want to do this anymore." And we lost another good cop.

I have seen the situation where amazing officers have reached a really quick breaking point after just one shooting. They have one encounter and they are practically body slammed into the realization of how close they came to dying, or being wounded, or being crippled for life. Either that or they see someone else who was killed or crippled and they decide police work is not for them.

Maybe they've been shot, maybe they were just shot at, but not wounded. But they realize they could have been killed. Being a police officer suddenly gets real. Their loved ones realize it, their kids realize it. And what would have been a perfect career from someone moving in the right direction and suddenly they're checking out of police work way too early because there's no one there to walk them through it, to give them the help they need, to answer their questions or help them examine their fears.

"One of the things that I noticed as a young cop," Ramon said, "I was always asking for more, like, I always wanted more. Give me more training, give me better equipment, give me a better under-standing of what I can or can't do and what situation, you know, and deliver it to me, not like I'm an idiot, but deliver it to me, on a level playing field.

"So the end goal with that was always the fact that, hey, if I can give officers the best tools to navigate a sticky situation without putting themselves in a situation where they have to do something that is lawful, but awful, then I was going to do everything I could to try to make sure that they had the training and they had the best equipment," Ramon said.

"In three decades, I saw that when you get into a shooting, that when you make a decision and end that life, or the course of somebody else's life forever, and I don't care how tough we come across and how tough we say, we are, you are now going to carry that for the rest of your life. You're now going to carry somebody else's soul with you for the rest of your life. I wish every situation was like, you've got an armed gunman, you know, holding somebody with a gun to their head and, you did the right thing and you saved their lives and countless other lives.

"I mean, I wish it was that clear cut because then that would make acting on that situation much more palatable.

For the majority of us to say, 'Hey. I had to make that decision, I had to do that because there were no other options for me, is painful, no matter how justified our actions were. If it was literally, you know, him or the victim, because the bad guy was about to kill again or shoot or stab me or whatever," would be the best outcome.

"It's so much easier to just say policing should be black and white, you know, like 'Hey, the guy had a gun to a woman's head. I had to do what I had to do.' The reality is those things just don't unfold like that most of the time. So I wanted to make sure I protected the officers from those scenarios and helped them try to make the best decisions they could.

"The trouble is, we're looking at incidents where fault and decisions about how to act are not that clear cut. Until all the body camera footage and the departmental investigation comes back, we can't be sure. We have the public and the courts getting months to weigh the possible causes of action the officer had less than five seconds to consider. And that officer is offline for months waiting to hear whether they did the right thing or not.

"I knew that even if the officer knew they'd done the right thing, and physically survived the incident, which they likely would, could they survive a criminal investigation for homicide because they killed somebody? Would they be able to survive mentally and emotionally? Would they be able to live with the decisions that they went through and had to make because of what unfolded? There were many times that I dealt with people who decided to commit suicide by cop. How do you explain that to the public?

"The guy comes out with a gun, they're pointing it in the direction of the officers. And this person has already made their intentions well known about what they want. They want the officer to pull the trigger because they can't. They're going to take out a cop if the cop doesn't take them out first. They're literally putting the officers into a kill or be killed decision.

"There's no good outcome there. The one guy that's got to pull the trigger in order to put that scenario to an end, I felt so bad for them. I would have the conversation with them upfront. I would say, 'Hey, look, you know, that person couldn't do this thing (suicide) on their own. So they decided to go put it out on somebody else—and today that somebody was you. I understand that that was not what you wanted to do today, but, but that was something that somebody else predicated and initiated and forced your hand to do.'"

"I said that to them because I needed them to understand that I understood them, and I understood what had happened. I knew that my five minute talk was not going to be enough, but I wanted them to know I cared about what they were going through, and that I understood what they were going through."

"Of course they needed more than my talk. But I hope it helped him. I hope it was a spark of hope in the darkness. They needed to have professionals that came around and also talked them through that issue, but I hope that five minutes was something positive and supportive. I hope it gave them some hope," Ramon explained.

"Matt, I was always worried about losing officers in situations where they would reminisce over an action that they took—usually a legitimate action, but then ruminating and questioning whether that action would develop into PTSD, or harm their career, harm their personal life, or lead them to substance abuse.

"If that happened, then we would lose a good person and I just didn't want that. I wanted to give our guys the tools to succeed no matter what, no matter what the color was, no matter what the situation was. I wanted them to have every opportunity to feel calm, prepared, and supported.

"So the issue with discipline is this, and I think it's important that during the course of any type of administrative investigation, or allegation of misconduct that the organization has to work with— like triple time overtime—in coming to a conclusion with what the hell happened. Whether or not there's any discipline to be meted out needs to happen as quickly as possible, once fault or no fault is obvious. Because the mental wellness of our officers having something like that hanging over their head and expecting them to be just fine and dandy is impossible. It's unbearable.

"When investigations drag on you know, into days, weeks, and months like you describe how yours did, that is completely irresponsible on the part of the organization. It's irresponsible because the agency is causing a ton of strife and additional concerns and weight on the officers and their minds and everything.

"The officer has an internal investigation looming over them about whether or not they did something wrong. We're talking about things like time sheets, or being professionally inappropriate in a way where an officer should be disciplined—not a critical incident like corruption, or excessive use of force or whatever. And you know, what, all of us are wired to think, or ask, 'Hey, tell me, are you going to find that I, that I did something wrong? If so, what? What's going to happen?'

"I think that what needs to occur is transparency around the issue of discipline. People need to know, 'hey, if I break some citizens cell phone, or scratch their car, and it's my fault, what's going to happen? Like tell me now what's going to happen.' That should be spelled out. Like there should be clarity with respect to discipline. It shouldn't be a cruel ongoing guessing game.

"They shouldn't be walking around wondering when the hammer is going to fall for something minor. It goes back to building resiliency with the officers from the onset and then the internal organizational changes that have to happen. So that when, when something like this comes up, those matters are resolved promptly without the department dragging their feet about what's going to happen. If the officer does something wrong or not, at the end of the day, guess what, no matter who you are, this is what your response is going to be.

"In the end, I talked to so many different officers because I've been on a lot of internals. The longer your response takes, the longer it continues, the more that officer is going to separate himself from the administration and from his brothers and sisters that he works with. The longer the investigation goes on, the higher and higher the wall is going to get between him and his fellow officers. And the harder it's going to be to break that wall back down and integrate them back into patrol and back into the brotherhood.

"This is what we're trying to accomplish. And you know, that's huge. They get put through the meat grinder in a situation like that, over some fairly minor incident, and you expect them to bounce back and be like, 'Hey, you know, I'm a top notch police officer here. I'm going to take it on the chin and I'm still going to care about the things you tell me to care about. I'm going to be active. I'm going to do all that.'

"No way you're going to see that. You're going to get back an angry, disgruntled human being who feels they got jilted, cheated, and thrown under the bus for doing their job. Everything they just went through is unexpected, they couldn't have seen it coming. They were kept in the dark. Police departments have an opportunity to make that right. Police departments have an opportunity to avoid that pitfall. I want to see that happening."

Ramon and I had such great talks like this, I wish I could just write a book about all we talked about. By the way, he has coauthored a book called, Do No Harm, with Mark Ziska, on "hiring and supervising for character" if you want to read more of his thoughts on changing police culture.

Some of this stuff is just so easy and obvious. Some of it is beyond complex. I get it. Obviously I've put a lot of time and a lot of thought and a lot of effort into changing the culture around and I'll continue to do so. It all comes back to mental health and mental health training or mental health evaluations. I'm back and forth on whether evaluations should be mandated after an incident like a shooting, or where life and loss of life, or truly brutal incidents happen.

I ask friends inside law enforcement and outside, "Do you think that mental health evaluation should be a regular part of a police officer's everyday life?" I think in situations where you know that you have officers working specific details that are really tough they should be mandated. I mean situations where people don't even want to talk about them because they're so horrific.

Ramon said, "Yes, exactly. Like you have a squad of detectives that have to work on these really traumatic things—like child abuse comes right to mind. Rape, murder, suicide. I figured out over the course of decades in policing that compassion fatigue is real. You have a detective that works in a unit like child crimes. And after a while, it's like, believe it or not if you're not getting regular check-ups, you get to a point where you are just going through the numbers. You're numb. You've walled off your humanity, your compassion just so you can get through the day.

"You're just going through the motions and you may not conduct that additional interview, right? You may not go to whatever business to try and see if there's video there because you're burned out. You're tired. You know, this is like the upteenth child abuse situation you've seen in your mind, you're thinking society is so screwed up, and this is just what they do to children.

"I mean, I don't know what happens, but those kinds of things are real. And I think that if you have detectives and officers in these high risk units, you need to make sure that there's a program in place where you are putting them through some type of decompression. You can't wait for them to come forward when they're starting to feel overwhelmed. It might be too late. You have to insist on regular checkups. Maybe that involves an evaluation, a chat with the department psychologist, you know, whatever it is. But there has to be some kind of formal program for folks like that.

"Now when you're talking about everyday patrol officers, I think there are different ways that you can tackle that. I'm not so sure that it's a situation where, where I would say, okay, every six months, I think it's mandated, or maybe once a year, it's mandated that uniformed officers are gonna have to go through some counseling session regardless, or maybe not.

"But I think that there are, you know, modern day mobile applications that when an officer's got downtime and can look at where they are, that's a start. Remember, if we've done our homework in that organization and elevated the issue of mental wellness and support for people that are needing it when they need it, it's going to make a difference.

"Even more, there's no stigma attached to it. If there's a mobile application that they can seek out on their own and confidentially get assistance for personal issues, I think that's totally doable. There are other areas and situations that come to light because of reports and incidents their supervisors are aware of. I think that it should be mandated."

I think that so long as you bring up mental health in a respectful way in terms of the people you're dealing with you can help them see the value in getting people help without stigmatizing the process. You can let them know they're a part of the decision-making process of how that program is going to work. I think then you're going to have a greater chance of success with changing the culture. If you don't, and some of those officers decide not to conduct that extra interview, decide not to go check for that additional footage, and leave evidence in their desk, instead of checking it into evidence then, when those things start to rear their ugly head, that person's going to lose their career.

Aside from the malice that's occurred to the victim of the crime, everybody loses. The victim's friends and family lose. The officer and the department lose. My opinion is that the law enforcement and military culture has to unveil the mask of mental health to protect not just the officer, but the community. We've got to have evaluations and mental health training in a non-stigmatized, healthy, supportive manner. I think if we begin to look at it a little bit differently and change the perception on what mental health training is we can make a huge difference.

It's possible to do this in the academy or in any type of training where there's that opportunity. I remember when I went to undercover survival, and basic narcotics we did a ton of scenario-based training. During that scenario based training, they taught you to close your eyes and picture the situation before you go in.

For instance, I'm making a controlled purchase of fentanyl. I close my eyes. I put myself in that role. I would go through a mental checklist of things that could happen or what could be said to me and how I would respond to it. It worked.

I think if we're able to unveil a little bit of that psychology, and take away the cloak of mystery behind mental health training, officers could see it's just another aspect of training that will help them do their job better.

Whether it's as simple as the Sergeant or Lieutenant for that shift doing their annual eval saying, "Hey, you've been involved in several critical incidents that I'm aware of. I just want to check in with you. I want to have a conversation on how you're doing, how you're doing personally, as opposed to professionally. I want to open the door and let you know we have avenues to help you. We want to let you know that this is part of what we do now as part of our training."

This shouldn't be a witch hunt, or a chance to sneak up on someone and find out if they should be taken offline. It should be legit, authentic, and honestly trying to help create successful critically thinking officers.

When you see the evils of this world on a daily basis, things can go south in a hurry. We have to have a roadmap for success. Compassion fatigue impacts officers at all stages of their careers.

Compassion fatigue is real. Supervisors and officers alike see it every day. Compassion becomes commonplace to you. Whereas the first time that you go to an ICAC situation and you see a five-year-old being sexually assaulted your emotions are through the roof. You want to climb into that video camera and strangle somebody. But after two years you're like, okay, it's just another pedophile doing what pedophiles do.

I think if, as a culture, we're able to change the perception of mental health training we can change the culture. One of the last things Brian ever said to me was, "Matt, if you're not mentally prepared, you're not physically ready."

I've used that in a lot of different aspects of my life whether I'm mentally prepared for a phone interview or a phone conversation, or going to my sales job, or whether I'm mentally prepared to step up on the stage and pour my life out to 250 people that I've never met before. Being mentally prepared is just as important as being physically prepared. Could it be as simple as changing the term from mental health training to mental preparation?

We put a lot of time and effort into physical preparedness. We mandate PT tests, but I think it's also important to say, we're also requiring you to be mentally fit as well. You're going to see more trauma in one day than most people are going to see in a lifetime. Regardless of whether you think you're going to be okay or not, someone needs to say, "we want you to know that this job will have an effect on you. And when it does, we're here to listen. We're not here to take your gun away. We're not here to mandate you to go see a psychologist or to look at ink blots, but we want you to know that there is a process for it. And the process starts with your immediate supervisor or, or if you're not comfortable with your supervisor, then there is a list of options for you. I want to mentally prepare you to be a successful police officer.

Right now, officers aren't asking for help they legitimately need and deserve, because of the stigma. And with the way the media and society are thinking about officers right now, the stigma is even stronger. Society is ready to demonize any officer they think wasn't acting at 100% capacity.

They don't care if the officer is traumatized because of riots, or ambushes, or deaths. Their goal is to bring that officer down, to discredit them, shame them, humiliate and destroy them because some organization is hell bent on defunding or destroying the police because of their own agenda.

No officer is going to see that and say, "Yeah, I think I need to see a shrink," because some departments are telling their officers to "stand down," and not do their job and not complain about it. Morale in many agencies is in the toilet because officers are not being allowed to do their jobs—they're ordered not to do their jobs. I don't know an officer on the planet that would admit to stress, or PTSD, or feeling overwhelmed under those circumstances. They'd rather retire early, or as many have done and will do—they'll kill themselves for lack of an alternative.

Yet, we're telling them as leadership and as administration, we want you to get help. We want you to be mentally prepared, so you're physically ready. We want you to be a critically thinking successful officer every day, day in and day out. But they're not stepping up to the plate with the resources, the support, or the trust that needs to happen.

If we can flip the script on how we present mental health training to our younger generation and look at it as mental preparation, then I think we can begin to move that needle. The officer's attitude hopefully will be, "they're not saying, 'I'm weak.' They're asking me to do a mental health checkup to ensure I'm prepared to do my job the best I can."

My public speaking involves talking about "what is it about mental health? And, and a lot of times it comes back to that same stigma I've been pounding on throughout this book. LEOs tell me, "I can't ask for help." So, if that is the overwhelming reason we're not providing mental health training is the officer doesn't feel comfortable saying "I need help, because if I ask for help, it says

'I'm weak and I'll be taken offline," there's got to be a better solution.

Why don't we take that burden away from them? "Okay, we understand that you don't want to ask for help, but we're going to provide you help because we love you and we care about you. And whether you want it, or not, or think you need it or not, we're going to give that to you. And in the majority of the time, it's your choice on whether you want to engage in that opportunity."

Organizationally that kind of change has to occur from top down so that the members know that they're going to be handled a particular way and that it's okay to talk about it.

The supervisory core has to understand that this is a part of their duties and something that they have to do. Organizationally, this has to be supported from top for it to be successful. There's a real variance in the capacity and the understanding, and the skill set of frontline supervisors.

There's such a wide gap in leadership regarding how to best provide support for the stress that first responders face in their work. It will take time to reframe and retrain how to recruit and promote people within a culture that understands the model of providing mental health support for their staff.

Officers need to know that there are opportunities for them to go to somebody without penalty, without the stigma, without reducing their agency's confidence in them.

I'm fortunate. I think I only had a handful of really bad supervisors in my life. Some were so bad I would've never been caught going to them and saying, "Hey, you know, I'm not feeling so good. I need to talk to somebody."

There's no way I'd have done that because they would have sold me down the river. Some have managed to do that even when I excelled in my job. I shudder to think what they would have done had I admitted my feelings and plans at the time, or not been capable and high performing.

There are people, supervisors or whomever, who will do anything to throw an officer under the bus. That's the risk with hanging everything on supervisors. Some are fantastic, so it's not impossible, but I'm just telling you it could be a challenge to weed out the bad apples —most of whom are surrounded by other bad apples. It's not going to happen overnight.

Society's response to LEOs and the effect on mental health is generally awful, unless they've been impacted personally by the challenges of someone they love.

Sadly enough, it's the mentally ill in society who end up being killed or abused by responding officers. That doesn't help reinforce the idea that being mentally ill isn't a bad thing. The Treatment Advocacy Center says, "People with untreated mental illness are 16 times more likely to be killed during a police encounter than other civilians approached or stopped by law enforcement." 10 They're more likely to be harmed or killed because police and first responders aren't trained to recognize and respond to the mentally ill as much as they could be. Axon is helping with a program that helps officers understand mental illness and what it's like for the person suffering, but that's just a start. Changing the culture, changing the way departments respond, and what their policies are, will take people like myself speaking up, and raising awareness. Hundreds of departments around the country are starting to change. Laws are being enacted. But the conversations among those on patrol, first responders, and chiefs have got to continue to happen. I hope this book sparks that movement. This is not a book about how to do that. I'm only able to write about my awakening, and my experience with mental illness and health. I'm willing to speak, to talk to chiefs and LEO groups, and to carry the message. But you have to help too —even if it's talking to family and friends, or passing this book along, or journaling, or speaking up and talking to a friend who may be suicidal. Little actions can make big changes.

I can't repeat myself enough, the stigma around mental illness has got to stop, or at least change significantly, and it starts with awareness, training, and change on a personal level.

Obviously law enforcement and the military aren't being seen in the best of light these days, and there's a lot of societal challenges between communities and police. The divide has never been stronger between society and police. The stigmas and fear around the mentally ill are growing. So, how do you think that affects a patrol officer or a police officer or a military person who wants or needs to get mental health help?

So you're involved in the shooting, or you're involved in some type of traumatic situation and society gets wind of it. If it goes viral, as a police officer you have officers thinking, "if I pull the trigger, I'm going to be under a lot of scrutiny. I'm going to be an overnight internet sensation, and not in a good way." They may lose their right to own or be in possession of a gun or other weapon. In some states, they may become the focus of red-flag laws.

[Red flag laws are state laws that authorize courts to issue a special type of protection order, allowing the police to temporarily or permanently confiscate firearms from people who are deemed by a judge to be a danger to themselves or to others. Relatives or friends concerned about a loved one who owns one or more guns and has expressed suicidal thoughts or discussed shooting people is one source, but anyone can report another. They're well intentioned laws, but as with many laws, easily manipulated to punish the innocent.]

Worrying about YouTube or Twitter instead of whether the guy is pulling a gun, or about to kill your partner has caused officers to either fail to take the action they should have taken—or take less action than is needed to control the situation—all because they're worried about how it will look to the public watching a citizen's cell phone video, even though the officer's actions are justified and legal.

I often wonder how that possibility has affected the mental health of the military and the police. I think that social media can definitely have an adverse impact on folks because they feel as though nobody has their back.

Think about the work that police officers do day in and day out. They didn't create these laws. They didn't create this justice system —a system where sometimes you wonder aloud whether or not there's equity. You know, they didn't create it. They didn't create it, but they're tasked with working within a system that was created by other people.

It's incumbent upon leaders, judges, police unions, and police leaders in the criminal justice system to stand up for what is right, not what is politically expedient for them. They need to start the work of addressing some of these shortfalls. At the same time agencies need to be authentic and transparent with the public about the changes that need to happen so that the public can begin to see the truth. When a police leader speaks, they represent their organizations, and they need to do so ethically, morally, and accurately.

If the public believes them, they're going to support them. The message would be even stronger if you could get labor organizations to stand shoulder to shoulder with police leaders and mayors and city managers, and to echo this message of "okay, we understand we're working on it, we're trying to fix it."

At the same time, we need to build resiliency and understanding into our frontline officers, along with the awareness that their mental health is a legitimate issue, not a stigma to avoid. We have to fix it. We have to work together to improve how we're doing things. You know, thousands of people across this country are marching in solidarity against police abuse. You can't just turn a blind eye to that. You can't just say, "Hey, all those people that are out there, they're crazy. You know, they're all Antifa."

You do that and you start to sound like a crazy person. So you have to acknowledge that there are issues and that we have to address them, and we're going to do it together. And at the same time, try to insulate your folks from the fringes.

Tell your people, "I'm going to do everything I can to make sure that you are trained well, that you are equipped with the best training, technology, and tools we can provide," and mean it.

You have to let your people know that you have confidence in their ability to do their job, because you know that at the end of the day, they're wired a particular way that makes them who they are, willing to run into burning buildings and help strangers and protect their community.

219

Police officers and first responders are passionate about what they do and what they represent. But at the end of the day are they going to drive by some suspicious activity because, oh, you know, "I don't want to be the next social media sensation and lose my job."?

The job of supervisors, the job of department leaders is to go out there and continually push the ideal of, "Hey, you gotta go out there, you gotta do your best. And I'm going to do everything I can to make sure that you're equipped to make the best decisions, and I'm going to support you when you make them."

Your option of not supporting your officers is getting a robot to do the job. Do you really want a robot? No, you don't. Because the robot does policing like a robot.

If you have robots and someone runs a red light the robot isn't going to listen to any excuse the person gives them. They're going to get a ticket. If a robot sees you jaywalk. He's going to stop you, detain you and write you a ticket no matter what you say. And if you have to pee, you're going to pee in your pants because that robot's not going to let you run to a bathroom.

Cops are human beings, not robots. They're going to make decisions that sometimes miss the mark. They're doing the best they can with the information they have at the moment they make it. They don't have the luxury of five different camera angles, and a person's criminal or life changing turnaround in their hands, or hours to weigh and calculate the outcomes of their decisions like the Monday morning quarterbacks who haunt social media feeds.

If you're a surgeon, or doctor, or attorney, can you imagine every minute of your work life and your decisions being recorded?..

We understand what could have happened during that situation that led him or her to make those decisions. But then, society doesn't understand that because they've never been in that situation. So they see something and on face value to say, "holy crap, I can't believe that that officer just made that decision at that time, right there with what I see."

No one in their right mind, without any training or understanding of what is happening in front of them, would lean over a surgeon's shoulder and say, "holy crap, I can't believe that surgeon just did that!" because they read online or Reddit that that's not typical. With no understanding of what's happening in front of them, people are so quick to make life and death criticisms about the police it stuns me.

I think it's incumbent upon leadership to be more progressive and assertive in saying, "This is what happened. We're reviewing all the videos, and we're looking into it. Please withhold your reactions until we have all the facts."

People are going to have an immediate, usually visceral reaction. That's the society we live in today—instant offense, even at things that are legal, justified, and prudent. This is where the Chief of Police, or public affairs says, "I understand your initial reactions—of anger, fear, disgust, disbelief, but understand that there may be some other things that happened during the course of this event that we don't know yet. We're looking into it." Then they have to follow through. No hiding, no spinning the facts, just be honest, authentic and bite the bullet and stick to the truth no matter what the outcry, or how many social media views. We have to stand up for what's right and honorable.

When officers say, "I did what I knew was right. And nobody has my back on this." Then that creates this culture where it's essentially police versus society, and worse, police versus suits and supervisors.

And that's what I really want to change. I think society's response to LEO's and, and LEO's response back to society has really changed for the worse because of the lack of transparency and the lack of leadership.

"We bring it on ourselves a lot of times," Ramon said. "For better or for worse, sometimes police chiefs and deputy chiefs are like, you know what, I'm not getting involved. I'm not putting my face in front of the camera until I have every lick and shred of evidence. And I understand what is going to happen to my officer. I understand why they acted like they did, but at the same time you've got a human being who made a decision in a traumatic situation, in a split second. You know, and there's gotta be some measure of innocent until proven guilty.

"That's the standard for the community, 'innocent until proven guilty.' It has to be the standard for police officers as well. A lot of times fileadership has to step up to protect their officers demanding that they be allowed to complete their investigation into the situation.

Yes. Change the culture. If the leader doesn't get out there and begin explaining what they can, and being the voice of reason, then for a part of the population who is always going to be angry, they're going to take advantage of the situation. They simply use that negative energy in their next encounter with a police officer.

Look no further than Rodney King or George Floyd to see how the actions of those officers made the lives of officers across the country miserable, or resulted in their death. We're trying to do the right thing for officers that are just out there trying to do the right thing every day, day in and day out.

Whether you're a supervisor, or Police Chief, or a probie or a rookie, make a difference. Shift the culture by being compassionate. Send out the good energy. The life you save may be your own, or that of a fellow LEO or first responder.

1. Jenkins, Lisa. 2020. "OPINION Don't defund the NYPD; renew its culture." NY The Daily News (New York City), July 25, 2020. https://www.nydailynews.com/opinion/ny-oped-dont-defund-nypd-renew-its-culture-20200725-gumydapn4rhwffpvpuvswsvjuy-story.html.

2. NBC News. 2019. "When a police officer dies by suicide, what help does the spouse get?" October 21, 2019. https://www.nbcnews.com/news/us-news/when-police-officer-dies-suicide-what-help-does-spouse-get-n1069316.

3 . Ibid

4 . Ibid

5 . Our York Media and Anothy Machcinski. 2019. "5 years after responding to husband's suicide, cop opens up to fight stigma." Our

York Media. https://ouryorkmedia.com/stories/5-years-after-responding-to-husbands-suicide-cop-opens-up-to-fight-stigma/.

6 . U.S. Department of Justice. 2016. "National Sources of Law Enforcement Employment Data." bjs.ojp.gov. https://bjs.ojp.gov/content/pub/pdf/nsleed.pdf.

7 . Bengt B. Arnetz et al., "Trauma Resilience Training for Police: Psychophysiological and Performance Effects," Journal of Police and Criminal Psychology 24 (2009): 1–9.

8 . Ibid

9 . Police Chief Magazine. n.d. "Share Resilience as a Department Cultural Initiative." PoliceChiefMagazine.com. Accessed September 4, 2021. https://www.policechiefmagazine.org/resilience-as-a-department-cultural-initiative/.

10 . Treatment Advocacy Center. n.d. "People with Untreated Mental Illness 16 Times More Likely to Be Killed By Law Enforcement." https://www.treatmentadvocacycenter.org/. Accessed August 29, 2021. https://www.treatmentadvocacycenter.org/key-issues/criminalization-of-mental-illness/2976-people-with-untreated-mental-illness-16-times-more-likely-to-be-killed-by-law-enforcement-.

CHAPTER 11

What Saved Me Might Save You

*"Though the Bible was written over sixteen centuries
by at least forty authors, it has one central
theme—salvation through faith in Christ."*
- Max Lucado

I 'll just cut to the chase here. What saved me was the thing that almost destroyed me — an innocent death, and wondering why horrible, horrible things happen to people. Feeling Benny's last breath in my mouth wasn't just air. It was a life. And it was the life of my friend's child. All lives matter, but having a personal connection to that life is harder to bear. Connection is the core to everything that happened to me. It's how I got through life, why I wanted to take my life, and how I found my purpose.

Connecting with Ben the night I wanted to die, gave me a sense of community, even just that one friend was a sip of water in a desert, and boy was I dehydrated.

I'd left Dave and Brittany's home, and the body of that little boy, angry at God, and wondering if there even was a God. All the things I heard and practiced about a "higher power" during my teen rehab, all the church I'd attended, all the prayers I'd prayed as a child were forgotten.

My anger, despair, and an overwhelming feeling of hopelessness left me conflicted, but driven to know the answer. Why, if there was a God, and if He was real, then why did He let bad, horrible things happen to good people, to innocents, to children, to Benny? My questions drove a wedge between me and God and our connection.

After Benny's death, I sat in my bedroom for weeks crying and wishing I had responded to the call sooner—wishing I had done something a little different. After beating myself up for weeks on end, I turned my anger back to God. If God is so powerful, so loving, so caring, then how does God allow a little boy to die like that? Why doesn't He intervene?

The nightmares of the scratch marks on the wall where Benny struggled to free himself haunted me then and still do. I couldn't reconcile what I learned or knew of God with what I was experiencing, and had experienced.

Things didn't make sense. Life, God, love, hope, nothing was making sense. Drug dealers lived and thrived and the innocent died.

My whole life I had gone to church. Every Sunday I sat in Catholic church and went to CCD either during or after the service. The church drove home the fact that Jesus and God were constants in life and weren't to be questioned. So, I remember feeling the power of Jesus early in my life. He was not only there for me in church, but on the baseball field too.

I played in the little league world series when I was 13 years old. That experience, that summer, was one of my fondest memories growing up. My team traveled the entire summer of 1992—first to Jersey City, then staying with host families in Royersford, PA for regionals and ultimately going to the Little League World Series in Houma, La.

As fondly as I feel about that summer, I still remember the not-so-great aspects of it—like our coach. Coach was a difficult person. He used to scream and yell and if you made a mistake he put you down and made you feel like you were worthless. Sound familiar?

Unfortunately, I can see his face and remember his name almost 30 years later.

His son was on our team and I remember feeling so bad for him that he had to deal with this man every day of his life. Well, you know the inevitable happened. In a very important game—I dropped a fly ball. Second baseman Franky came running out and I came running in. I failed to call him off and the ball fell to the ground. One run was allowed and I received the error. After the inning was over, I came running into the dugout and Coach began hammering on me. "You're a disgrace to this team!!!" he shouted. It didn't matter that I was doing the best I could, and hustling my ass to get the ball.

Everyone was looking at me. I sat in the dugout and cried. Yep. Thirteen year old me couldn't handle it and I sat in the dugout with tears streaming down my face.

I went home that night and I prayed. I prayed that I would hit a home run in the next game and when Coach came out to shake my hand I would have a message for him!!

God would have to answer my prayer if it was going to happen. I'd never hit a home run before in my life. I was a good hitter but not a power hitter—mainly singles and doubles. If I was going to hit a home run it would take a miracle.

I prayed for hours and hours...all throughout that night and the next day, right up to my turn at bat.

"Please Lord, let me hit a home run....Please Lord!"

It was the bottom of the second inning in the next game. Runners on 1st and 3rd and I walked to the plate. The home run was out of my mind as I got to the plate. All I wanted to do was make contact and get the RBI sacrifice fly.

First pitch came from the pitcher. I swung and crushed a three-run home run over center field.

As I came around third base, my team lined up to congratulate me at home plate and there was Coach with a big smile on his face and an outstretched hand. I took his hand and whispered "Who's the disgrace now?"

I thanked God that night for an answered prayer. I knew He hit the home run, not me. Most importantly I knew He was listening and had heard me. He answered the prayer of a child to hit a home run. That made Him real and personal to me.

Fast forward 15 years and I was MAD at that same God. I was angry and most importantly I was lost. I felt like God can't be ok with this. How, why, where is the silver lining? How could He grant me a home run, but not save the life of an innocent child?

How can a loving, powerful God allow a two-and-a-half-year-old boy to die by a window blind cord? So, I yelled at God. I cried. And then I cried and yelled some more.

I made a decision that January in 2006. I decided I was going to investigate. I was going to investigate whether or not God was real and if He really did love us. I wanted to know whether Jesus was legit or maybe just a made up fairy tale. I mean I was a cop right? That's what I did. I investigated crimes, I collected facts, I determined truth versus lies and cause and effect. I was a trained investigator so why not do the same thing in real life?

I started researching, looking for books, articles, anything I could get my hands on. I was an unbiased investigator trying to find the facts and the truth. So after a couple weeks of research I was invited to a baptism for my friend's son. I was the first person there and as I walked in, the usher handed me a welcome bag. I was like "cool, thanks." I took my seat and looked back and saw that he wasn't handing them out to everyone, which I thought was weird. I was the only one he gave it to.

That night I looked in the bag and found a book called *More than a Carpenter* by Josh McDowell. If I remember correctly, it was a short read, only about 115 pages. What McDowell had done was document his own journey on whether or not a literal Jesus walked the earth and did all the things the Bible said He did.

The book was evidence based and it made sense. A switch went off somewhere inside me. I decided that Jesus was REAL. The mere evidence that Jesus Christ walked the earth is overwhelming. He existed. He was a real man in a real body with a real life who walked, and taught, and healed, and loved. Then He died on a cross in the most brutal manner possible—a full Roman crucifixion—while His mother and best friend watched at the foot of the cross.

Whether you believe he is the son of God or not is up to you. Many of you reading this already know He's real. Others are on the fence, some will not or do not believe. There's still something in this book for you.

But I believed and I wanted to know more. So, I attended Lancaster Bible college and received my bachelors degree in Bible studies. It was one of the most amazing things I have ever done in my life. During my time at LBC, I went on two mission trips and saw the hand of God working in Belize and the US.

But, the fire that burned in me throughout that time left me after my divorce. I felt like God had once again abandoned me in my time of need. Brian's death, my divorce, the failures that hit me one after another, beat me down farther and lower than I'd ever been beaten before. Even in SARS training I never felt as hammered and in such total and unrelenting pain as I did then.

But, I look back now and I can honestly say with a full heart that God was holding me in the palm of His hand during that darkness. He was there with me the whole time, even if I couldn't feel Him there.

I was finally able to make peace with Benny's death. I was able to make peace with Brian's death. I was able to look at the pain and suffering I saw as a police officer, and that I heard from others, and I could finally see God's hand at work. I can't understand why God would allow those things to happen but maybe He was saving Benny from a life of pain. Maybe He was using his death to get my attention. I don't know. I don't have an answer or even a "maybe" as far as Brian, but I know I think about them both everyday.

I told Brian's story again yesterday and realized how much he's impacted my life. But I also realized it's not my place to know or to try and connect the dots that God has sprinkled throughout my life. It's my place to have faith that it was God's plan and that one day I will know the reason.

Just like maybe all the turmoil and trauma I saw and went through in my life was His plan for me and my editor, and the people and interviews we did, and the people I've met since writing to be connected through this book. So, I sit here writing. I'm sharing my life and can feel His hand/His voice guiding me and guiding you as you read this. There is nothing you have done that He can't or won't forgive you for.

My walk in faith hasn't been easy and it hasn't been sunshine and roses. What I can say is that my faith has given me peace. Peace that He knows what He's doing and I don't have to know the reasons for things, even horrible things, to trust Him or His plan for my life. I believe in the power of prayer.

As a public speaker, I've finished every presentation with my story about Brian and the struggles of my family. I ask for prayers for my son and I've watched the Lord answer those prayers and help his mother and I find the right doctors and medicines. If you've given up on God because of people in the church, or because someone harmed you, or you've seen "too much" or experienced too much trauma, or not been the person you want to be, I ask you to reconsider God. I ask that you read "more than a carpenter" and look at the evidence. Because, "...*with Him all things are possible.*" Matthew 19:26.

If you're wondering if God is real, not just for me, but for you, ask Him. Ask Him if He is real to show you He's real. Ask it with all sincerity, and He will answer. God gave us free will. He's not going to come barging into your life demanding to be served and acknowledged. Yet, He's there for you no matter what you've done—waiting for you to ask Him to help. There's nothing you've done, said, thought, wished, or imagined that is too bad for Him to forgive, if you just ask.

When I was sitting there in my Yukon, with my gun, with my suicide note, about to leave four sons of mine fatherless and confused, God was with me.

When I reached out to a young man threatening to kill himself I was inches and seconds shy of stopping him. He actually killed himself in front of me as I reached out to take his gun away. God was there watching, and hurting, too. I sat by this young man's body, next to the blood and the brains, alone, for several hours while waiting for backup and other services and investigators to arrive. I had time to think about a lot of things.

When my wife told me she wanted a divorce, when I heard Brian had committed suicide, throughout all the times of my life that I've failed, tried, succeeded, and ignored God, He was there.

Matt Griffin isn't special. He's just a child of God. The Bible says God knows when a sparrow falls to the ground, and He knows the number of hairs on our head. He's God. Of course He knows. And He cares. And He listens. And He loves. Jesus Christ came to earth, a promised Messiah, and died to save us from the death we were born for because of sin.

I'm not a preacher, but I am a believer. I know for a fact that God had a hand in Ben making that phone call when he did. I know for a fact that God had other plans for me, plans I'm still not entirely aware of right now.

I believe I was called to write this book. I believe I was called to tell you I've been where you, or someone you know or love has been, or is. I've been in the middle of that dark, dark night waiting for 00:00 so I could permanently check out. I wrote the note, I cried over the thought of never seeing my kids again. I grieved for all I had, all I had been, all I was losing and I truly believed that by taking my own life I'd be leaving behind a better life for everyone I cared about.

And as much as I believed at the time I was right—I was wrong. And if you're thinking that now—that the world, or your world, or family, or ex would be better off without you, you're wrong too. What you're leaving behind are people who love you and care about you—whether you know it or not. You're leaving them to deal with the pain, wondering why they didn't see it coming, and why you didn't say anything. You're not doing anything brave, or manly, or responsible by checking out. You're leaving nothing but unending, lifelong pain, not peace, behind. Don't do it.

Get through one more minute, one more hour, one more day, one more week. One of the things I told myself somewhere between getting to Ben's house and that cold beer, and our talk was, "If dying is a good idea today, then it will be a good idea tomorrow as well. I can wait." I told myself that every day, every night until I decided maybe dying wasn't the answer after all. And I started looking at that light at the end of the tunnel. I started not *just* listening to people like Ben say, "I love you man," I started hearing it. I started believing it. Most of all, I started living like I believed it.

You may not have a Ben, or a Byron, or a Ramon, or a Sharlene or anyone in your life that understands police work, or emergency medical services, or the military, or what happened to you. You may not have a wife or husband, or even an ex-wife, or ex-husband who cares or that you can connect with. You may or may not have kids, or even a dog, who is going to grieve with you. But you will always have God, the being who created you, who knows you better than you know yourself, and who loves you, and has a plan for your life, and who wants a relationship with you.

He's real. Trust Him on that. Give Him a chance. It's the hardest and yet the easiest thing you'll ever do, but that 30 seconds of surrendering your life to Him lasts for an eternity—literally. Here's all you have to do:

Admit to God That You're a Sinner

Sin just means "missing the mark, doing things that God says are wrong. Sin is disobedience. God is our father, a loving, omnipotent parent. If I tell my kids not to do things, I don't do it to kill their buzz or make life less fun for them. I do it to protect them. If I say, "Don't do drugs," it's for a reason. I know what they don't. I know what drugs can do to them and can lead them to do while under the influence.

They have to trust me on that. When their teenage bodies are on fire with hormones and puberty, and peer pressure, and all the things they see on social media, or at school, my saying "No," isn't going to make me the cool dad. But I care more about their lives than I do about being the cool dad. Fortunately, most of the time they trust me, even when it doesn't feel good to obey me. God's the same way. Trust Him when He says what you've done, what you're doing, what you're contemplating doing, isn't the best thing for you.

He says, "For all have sinned and fallen short of the glory (holiness) of God." You aren't alone. We're all sinners. We've all disappointed God. Admit that and you're halfway to heaven.

Accept Jesus Christ's gift. He literally bought us. It's not like He paid our bond and gave us a get out of jail free card, but then we have to go back to court for trial and sentencing. We were sentenced to death before we were born, and on our way to hell before we accepted Him and His gift of eternal life. He paid the price God demanded. His death forgives and covers all sin for all mankind—including me, you, and anyone else you know or don't know.

He paid the fine and did the time in hell so we wouldn't have to. That's what the cross was about. It was a blood sacrifice for us so we don't have to pay for our own sins — which no amount of money or good deeds on earth could do anyway.

Home stretch brother, or sister. Home stretch. Finally, repent. I know that sounds like an archaic word, but all that repent means is "Stop digging the hole you're in any deeper." It means stop doing the things you know are wrong and start living your life like He intended, listening to Him, learning what He expects of you, and loving Him with all your heart, mind, and soul as you start to realize what Jesus did for us.

You won't get it all at once, or you might. Start going to a church that preaches the word of God, from the Bible. Run from anyone who focuses on a prosperity gospel that teaches God is an ATM or a Santa Clause to give us all we want. Run from anyone who focuses on solely man-centered inspiration, or a "have happy-thoughts" philosophy. Find a church that teaches the Bible from the Bible. Keep looking at churches until you find one. I was told once — if you find a perfect church, don't join it cause it won't be perfect anymore. Go online and watch YouTube preachers like Chuck Missler, Thomas

Horn, Jack Hibbs, Greg Laurie. Perry Stone. Read websites like GotQuestions.org, or Buy a Bible and read it daily. Pray—which is just talking to God. You don't have to say anything fancy or flowery. Talk to Him like you'd talk to a loving father who cares deeply for you.

And that's it. Done. Moment by moment, hour by hour, one day at a time. If you're thinking today is a good day to die, then remind yourself, if it's a good idea today it will be tomorrow and don't do it. Give yourself another day. Give God a chance. Give life a chance. Let go and give your pain and sorrow to Him. My story isn't finished and neither is yours; in spirit or in person, know that I stand with you. Choose life. Choose happiness. Choose faith. Your testimony begins today. Go within and you'll never go without! Minute by minute, hour by hour always remember.....

There is a light at the end of that dark tunnel and...You are loved.

EPILOGUE

I want to ask you a favor. We all know someone who is struggling. We all know someone going through a tough time. Whether it's divorce, job loss, internal investigation, a shooting, a death in the family, finances out of control, whatever. Reach out. Help me smash the stigma around mental health and asking for help. Just pick up the phone, send a text and say the things that saved my life:

"I love you, I care about you, I am here for you."

BONUS CHAPTER: SOUL WRITING

Journaling for LEOs and First Responders

*"Life is like an onion; you peel it off one
layer at a time, and sometimes you weep."*
- Carl Sandburg

What if there was a way to channel your fear, anxiety, questions, and concern into a place where you weren't judged? What if you could freely express yourself where your supervisors couldn't decide you'd be better off without your weapon and riding a desk? What if this was legal, relieved stress, and centered you on those days the world wouldn't stop spinning? What if you could find solutions, be heard, and still maintain your job, culture, and career without worrying about whether or not someone was going to gossip, or say the wrong thing to the wrong person at the wrong time?

What if you could do this without a therapist or any other human being needed in the process? There is such a thing. It's called *Soul Writing*—which, I know, sounds like a 12-year old girl and a pink diary covered in unicorns and glitter, but bear with me. It's actually the art of journaling. It's the simple act of doing what people, especially military and business leaders, have done for years—keeping a personal log or notes about their life, their day, their challenges, or their thoughts.

Journaling, or writing from the soul, whatever you want to call it, is an especially powerful way for LEO's and first responders to function and work through job issues, or tough times when you don't feel or think you can or will ever feel again. What you write about doesn't even have to be traumatic. It can be any issue at work, or in your personal life. It can be "slam poetry" like I write (see end of book), or it can be bullet points, or just thoughts. Grammar, spelling, all that doesn't matter. Just get the words down on paper.

The world, heck, the workplace, is full of chatter, gossip, and shade from everyone. There are social, political, religious, and opinionated people that will tell you how you should live, feel, think, and react to life with or without your asking. If you limit yourself to the expectations of others, and neglect your own desires, you're riding a speeding car towards a brick wall, or facing eating your gun in the future.

Any unsettled feelings you might feel deep inside you, from anger to fear, to rage, or sadness, will go unaddressed or unexplored for fear of judgment by others until you can't take it anymore. At that point you'll either check out, or quit the job.

The simple inability to relate a feeling in a way others can 'get it,' the way you intended it is more common than you know. Getting the kind of support we need during our initial unsteady steps after a bad incident is critical if we're going to survive it. That's where soul writing/journaling comes in.

I met Sharlene Jones just as I started writing this book. The things she described about how to journal, and how to get to the core of things really struck home with me.

She's already given this officer journaling class to the National Organization of Black Law Enforcement Officers (NOBLE). And she gives it to private clients, her coaching clients, and any agency who is interested. It's a one-day seminar and it's powerful. Yes, I'm strongly plugging it.

Sharlene has "been there" when it comes to trauma, both

personal and as a LEO. Her brother was an active shooter in California. After a not very good start in life, he was on the straight and narrow. He was working a job, had started turning his life around and was doing well when he snapped. He left work, returned with a gun and took a course of action where that didn't end well for anyone.

The media doesn't share the backstory of a former felon trying to make things work, but finding no solution, chooses a permanent one at the end of a gun barrel. Three strikes and you're out. Sharlene took a different path and it made all the difference.

She spent fourteen years in law enforcement as a Deputy Sheriff and then a Police Officer with two Northern California law enforcement agencies before transitioning to international corporate security. During her time as a LEO, she served as a Special Victims Detective, Hostage Negotiator and Team Leader of the Crisis Negotiation Team. Writing made a difference for her, it's made a difference for me, and it can make a difference for you.

It's not just Sharlene and I who advocate journaling. Numerous studies have shown that writing about trauma, or "expressive writing" is powerful. According to *Psychology Today,* writing can "help people confront emotions they were avoiding and cognitively process what's happened to them. There is also some evidence that revisiting difficult emotions in a controlled way can help people move past and heal from those emotions."[1]

Soul writing, or journaling, makes your thinking and feelings visible to you, but not to others, unless you choose to share your writing.

Soul writing allows you to tune into your inner wisdom. Sharlene says, "It gives you a private seat at the table with your soul where you can listen and share thoughts and feelings that are hard to verbalize., You get to have a conversation with your soul, your truth, your ultimate guide—you." It's healthier and longer lasting than pounding down a six-pack and crashing to escape the pain.

Soul writing is not therapy or a replacement for therapy. It's a tool for officers and people in critical incident situations, who have experienced trauma, or who are in jobs where they aren't quite ready or able to put their experience into coherent words or concepts.

It's for people who want to explore the gray area between who they are and who they want to be, what they have and what they want, what they feel and what they know. It's a way to explore your feelings without sharing them with others until you're ready. It's like practicing a speech, a request for a raise, or any difficult conversation in a mirror before doing it in the real world. You control what you say, when you say it, and how you say it and who you share it with. If you choose to do that.

You don't have to be an expert writer to benefit from writing about what's happening with you, or what you're thinking or feeling. In fact it's better if you forget everything you learned in English class. You get to throw away the rules in soul writing. Nobody will be judging your grammar, punctuation, or paragraph structure. There's no audience for your writing unless you choose to share. The only requirement is that you write your journal by hand. No computers.

Research in neurobiology, psychology and brainwave function have shown the advantages of putting pen to paper in contrast to typing or dictation. You can even break or change a habit by simply changing your handwriting. So, pen to paper. No typing.

If you have time for a cup of coffee a day, you have time for soul writing. Write while you're having your coffee. You don't have to choose between them. Benefits can be realized in as little as five minutes a day.

Sharlene said she spent a career in law enforcement where she was taught to accomplish control over her feelings, frustrations, and challenges through a simple "ask, tell, take, formula."

Like she told me, "That strategy didn't always go over well on the job but was even less effective when it came time to confront my own soul. My 'core self' couldn't care less about the authority my uniform symbolized or my "command presence." Instead, I found the formula that worked for me was: open, ask, listen, and follow-up. That's what led to the clarity, alignment, and growth that helped me thrive. I believe it can help any officer or person willing to take the time to do a debriefing with themselves via journaling." The steps are simple: Open, Ask, Listen, and Followup.

Open: Open up. We've all asked suspects and witnesses to do this while we scribbled notes. You know what you want—truth, facts, feelings, what they saw, what they thought happened, what they "know" happened. Open up. Let it all out. Tell your journal everything. Don't question or edit, or second guess yourself. Don't worry about grammar or punctuation. You're the only one who is going to read it. Just write it. Get it down on paper. Do it in code if you're worried about someone finding it and reading it. But do it.

Ask: When you come to the end of a sentence, or paragraph, or page, then stop. Ask yourself, "What else?" And keep writing about what comes up. Ask, "What do I believe happened?" Ask, "What am I feeling?" Ask, "What just happened?" When you get it all out on paper, look down at what you wrote and ask, "Is it true? Do I know beyond a shadow of a doubt that it's true?" And then write what comes up. When Benny died, if I'd been writing then, I'd probably write, "Could I have done something different? Was it my fault for not getting there sooner?" I would have written about how angry I was with God, and about whether or not there was a God. When you write it down your subconscious can't bury it somewhere it will fester and rot and come back to haunt you. It's like a cold case. Five years from now all the evidence is there in your journal. You can say, with the insight that comes with time, "I did everything I could."

You can play detective with yourself. Ask the hard questions. Give yourself the hard answers. If you doubt yourself, or feel good about something, write it down.

Listen: You're a cop, or first responder, or .... You listen to people every day. You hear the BS, the lies, the panic, the grief, the anger, the accusations, the questions. Do as much for yourself. Listen to what you're feeling and can't seem to put it into words. It's okay to write, "I was such a jerk. They were such a jerk." Be honest with yourself. Listen to what you're thinking, good or bad. This is a judgment free zone.

Follow Up

Write until you can't write anymore—whether it's five minutes or five hours. Let what you've written sit, unedited. Come back to it in 30-minutes, then the next day, then the next, or on your day off. Let it sit and percolate. Sleep on it. We all know how we see and feel things change when we get some distance between the event, and our reaction. Go back and follow up with how you're feeling and what you're thinking days after the event. Then go back and look at that. Make decisions and set goals. Review them. Take actions that you need to take. Maybe you need or want to write a note, or call someone, or have a conversation with your partner or spouse.

Debriefing is defined as a conversation between two or more people. We've all been to one. The supervisor talks about what happened, what actions were taken or should have been taken, where you screwed up and where you did good things that won you a lot of "attaboys."

Unfortunately, even though a debriefing is designed to help us come down or process stressful events, there's not often a lot of real talk happening in those either. You say what you need to say, or are expected to say about the event, but it doesn't get all touchy feely. Other than the usual pep-talk and admonition to "speak up if it's bothering you," — like that's going to happen (not) —there's not a lot of opportunity to get to the things that might be bugging you. You don't share the dark stuff and neither does anyone else.

There may or may not be an agency psychologist there, depending on the incident. Either way, the thought processes involved in a particular incident or situation, whatever the outcome, good or bad are broken down, picked apart — or not.

Debriefing is supposed to encourage an individual's reactions, reflections, and performance on the actions and thought processes they went through. The goal of the debriefing is to incorporate improvement, insight, and growth into future performances.

With journaling you're debriefing yourself. You're asking yourself about your feelings and actions and you're looking at them without fear of losing your job, or being considered weak. You become the person asking the questions, and answering them. Writing it all down in a journal puts you in control of the outcome of examining any thoughts or feelings you may have. It puts your feelings into a form where they can be read, observed, and contemplated without fear of judgment, reprisal, or adverse action taken against you.

You can start journaling with the simple act of buying or grabbing a blank notebook and a pen and starting to write. Write as though you were in a one-on-one debriefing session.

I do a form of writing that Sharlene and I call "writing dirty," instead of "riding dirty," let's write dirty. Take 5 or 10 minutes and put your thoughts on a piece of paper and then look at how they came out. Step away and grab something to eat, or drink. Then come back in a few minutes, hours, or days and take a second look. What you'll find you've written down is normally very different from what you thought was going on in your head. It's expression in its simplest form. Writing it down instead of replaying it over and over in your head gives you the ability to release it, let go of it and move on from it instead of suppressing it.

Here's what I do. Unplug from the world. Cell phone, tv, computer, tablet etc. Turn it all off and breathe for a couple of minutes. Grab a pen and paper and set a five minute timer. Write whatever comes to mind. Whatever thought, feeling emotion just write it down. It doesn't have to be sentences, it can be thoughts. It can be whatever it is you want it to be.

So, "real talk time." That's what I call it with my boys. No BS, nothing chatty, just real talk, real topics, real feelings. If you don't get to the root of whatever is eating at you, you'll never get rid of it. It's safe to put it in the journal. Lock it up, use code words, whatever, just write.

This is me. Laying it on the table and putting myself, my thoughts bare for you to think about and reflect on — my hope is that it resonates with you. My writing has blossomed into what is called spoken word or slam poetry. I perform my life for you through words and actions. See my website for more information. I've placed the words of my "Slam Poetry, Journey to Midnight poem" here for you to read.

They say when you die you see it. A light at the end of a tunnel
Like a train coming at you in the darkness
A bullet flashing suddenly, in a parking lot.

It's 10:02 p.m.
March 17th, 2017.
The gun in my hand feels almost weightless. It's been two weeks since my
partner committed suicide. Combine that with my ex putting all the bank
accounts on ice and this is a bitter mixture.
The kind where you just have to tilt your head back fast,
Close your eyes and hope you don't notice
the burn of the shot.
This tunnel only moves in one direction.
One way down.
One choice and not even one thing left to live for.
Tired of the strain of sons seeing their father as failure
Again and again.
I have to be strong for them.

0000 is midnight in military time. And my time is up.
I wrote my suicide note; the final words
All that will be left of me.
It reads like a poem.
"You won't understand, I know this. But please understand
that I love you more than anything. You are my light in bad
times, my sunshine every morning."
I won't see the sun again cause In two hours, it'll all be done.

Its 10:24 p.m.
They say when you die
Your life flashes in front of you like a movie.
This is my movie;

I remember walking through the halls of Morristown-Beard like I was being led through the gates of academic heaven. Thinly sliced lawns and carefully spread veneer of prestige. An opportunity. A chance to advance.
The "scholarship" kid used for athletic achievement. Just lucky to be there. Trading t-shirts and sweatpants for blazers and khakis. I thought sports would make me an equal but fitting in meant playing a different game. Going undercover. Walk like you have the money. Designer jeans, designer drugs...
Fight to be seen through the lens and culture of privilege. Blend in and Disappear. Honor roll and athlete but most importantly an outcast.

My parents found weed under my bed and my family sent me into the mountains to find a Clear View, but I couldn't see the forest through the trees.

At night in the woods, all you can find is yourself and all you can see is the darkness. Still and frightening. Sounds like you've never heard before, Like voices of leaders you never knew you needed.

Joe C told me If you go through it, you'll get through it. We are all addicts. You just need to learn how to deal with it. Feel the problem from your head to your toes and proceed.
What you are to be you are now becoming...
Choose!

It's 10:51 pm.
The chosen identity, the cornrows, the tattoos, the beard, they can be removed but the job never scrubs off.
You learn how to survive. how to fit in. Adapt and overcome. But what they are really saying is suppress. Here I am again lost in a sea of ignorance. Undercover, but like my brothers we don't ring the bell. New costumes. New clothes, new rules, I excelled in all of them.
Do you remember your first dead body? I do.....
I saw more trauma in one day than most people will see in their entire lives. Suck it up. Shut your mouth. Can someone tell me if it's going to be ok? Can someone say the nightmares will go away.
If you're not strong enough to see it then it's not the job for you!

Mechanical disposition- worn like a uniform that never quite fit. Get the job done and leave it. But it never leaves me.

Save my firecracker...Save my firecracker...she screamed. The last breaths exhaled from the 2 year old during CPR.

Like the hollow eyes of men with guns to their temples. Those Last moments embedded like bullets in skulls and drywall. The flash and noise of violence. blood spatters and shattered bones. My voice echoes between screams. The last voice they will ever hear.

"Take a breath. Just talk to me. You don't want to do this".

Smiling family photos on walls of the person that was alive only seconds ago.

*We are taught to normalize nightmares as an occupational hazard
Speak crisis like a learned language.*

*Those Midnight patrols. Starting with roll. You never know when someone is going to wrap their car around a pole. Bloodshot eyes, and all the lies
What difference am I making if life is so random? Am I really helping anyone? What is this all for?*

*Its 11:13pm
I read the note again:*

"Life is funny, you're on top then you're under the rock. Financially, emotionally they never coincide. My demons have finally won. The skeletons have become more of me than the person I'm proud of."

*We are all one step away
One choice
One accident
One mis-step
From having ourselves lost to our own darkness.
Addictions take our hands and tell us we are worthy of feeling good again.
That we deserve even the slightest moments of relief from the secrets we have been forced to carry. The silence we have been told to shoulder.
Always someone's friend, a co-worker, a spouse, a daughter. Anything to smother the pain. Whatever pain you have. Everyone is an addict.
So close to the edge.*

Always dancing on the blade so close to our throats. The needles are so close to veins. Just to feel anything
Else.
I am not immune, withdrawal through pills prescribed for the pain.
I feel the pull to forget.
I know the pleasure of wanting to escape this pain. These memories. These broken pieces I have gathered up that could resemble someone worth saving, but sometimes mirrors break under the weight of their own reflections.
I want peace. So tired of trying to catch shadows and calling it living. Don't be weak. Hold it in. suppress the pain. Be strong. Make the right decision.
The gun in my hand feels heavier now.
It's almost time.

It's 11:45pm
What you are to be you are now becoming. That's what Aristotle said
Who am I?
I read my note again
"Even when the curtain closes for us all, the show will live on.
I've lived the best life I could, but it wasn't good enough."
I wasn't strong enough
I can be strong now.
I want to see the light
Maybe the light is never coming
Maybe the only light is the one here
The one I hold in my hand
A flash in the dark
A lightning bolt
Choose
Choose
What you are to be
You are now becoming
I am becoming free of the memories I was trained to swallow
Like the knot in my throat
The canary in the coal mine
Why can't we talk about this?

245

Countdown begins. I'm tired.
I am ready to leave this all behind.

11:58...
11:59...
And it happens
A flash in the dark
Not from my hand
My phone...Someone is calling
The last voice I will hear appears: a friend, Ben.
I answer
"Matt let's get together"
I've got something to do
"Just for an hour"
Maybe tomorrow
I think of my body
Slumped over the steering wheel. The police officer at the scene
A scene I have seen
So many times before...
I decide
OK, I'll come by
Because Tomorrow is still a good day to die
Tomorrow turned into a week.. A week turned into a month and month to a year!
All it took
Was one person to be there
One person to tell me
It was going to be ok.
I won't say it gets better
It just gets easier
But if you go through it, you'll get through it.
This is for you. To all the men and women, mothers and fathers, sons and daughters, law enforcement and military alike, who didn't get a chance to see the light!
Who didn't have the sign posts to lead them to get the help they needed

#1 leading cause of death in the police and military is not homicide.
It's suicide
The casualty of the job is the violence we inflict on ourselves.
The expectation that we are immune to trauma sentences us to silence
We are the ones others call to get help, but who do we call when we need it?
Call me...Call me
Weakness is made in your ability to admit you are human? No, that's strength!
We are tough enough to talk about it. We are strong enough to ask for help.
There in the dark
When the pressure pushes you down
Realize that you can make it
One step at a time
Moving through the woods at midnight...You will find the path
With every person you share with
With every story you put down
With every boulder you drop
One by one
You will discover dawn.
The tunnel isn't the end
Because the only way out is through.
There is a horizon ahead for you. And there you will find the light.
Please connect with me through my website *www.journeytomid-night.com*

RESOURCES

For Leos, First Responders, Veterans

There are hundreds, if not thousands, of suicide hotlines, websites, and resources around the country. Some are national, some are local. But they're there and they want to help. This is not an exhaustive list of websites, but just some I know about or have heard about from others. If one doesn't have the help you want, try another. Sometimes the people answering the phone are having a bad day, or may have just lost a caller, or be in the middle of their own issues (it happens). Many of the people who staff these call lines are volunteers. They hear a lot of things and are at risk for their own issues at times, just like us. Give them the benefit of the doubt if you experience a bad encounter. For additional resources, check my website: https://journeytomidnight.com.

The National Suicide Prevention Lifeline is open 24 hours a day, seven days a week. They have help in both English and Spanish. Their number is 800-273-8255. There is no cost to call any suicide hotline. Options include:

1) Lifeline: Call 800.273.TALK (8255)
2) Crisis Text Line: Law enforcement text BLUE to 741741,
Others text TALK to 741741

3) Call 911 for emergencies

4) Blue Line Support 855-964-2583

5) Copline 800-267-5463

6) Cop2Cop 866-267-2267

7) Check with your department for services including peer support

CLASSES AND COURSES

Soul Writing

The art of journaling and self-debriefing about incidents, concerns, feelings, or thoughts after a shooting or any other death event, or trauma. If you'd like more details or information about soul writing contact me at: *Soul Writing*, the course or the book, teaches you how to.

Sharlene Jones

Sharlene spent fourteen years in law enforcement as a Deputy Sheriff with the Contra Costa County Office of the Sheriff, and a Police Officer with the San Ramon Police Department before entering corporate security. During her time as an LEO, she served as a Special Victims Detective, Hostage Negotiator and Team Leader of the Crisis Negotiation Team.

She received her formal education from Georgetown University, the University of San Francisco and the University of Cambridge. She received her real-world education growing up in diverse communities where she learned to understand, value, and assess a variety of perspectives to engage in crucial communication to mitigate crises and facilitate understanding.

Her combined formal and real-world education form the solid foundation on which she is uniquely qualified to facilitate critical conversations, affect change, and deliver results in any environment. Her passion is amplifying diverse voices and transforming adversity into opportunity.

Contact Sharlene at: SharleneJones@protonmail.com for more

information about bringing the LEO Writing course to your department, or about buying her book on journaling.

BOOKS

Ten Things to Do
Before You Commit Suicide

There are many books about suicide and suicide prevention, or the families and siblings of those examining a family member's suicide.

A good, free download by Becky Blanton is on my website: *Ten Things To Do Before You Commit Suicide*. I strongly suggest you download it and read it, or give it to someone you think it might help.

In Whom I Am Well Pleased, a memoir by Edward Byrne, attorney, survivor of NYFD son's suicide https://edwardtbyrne.com/in-whom-i-am-well-pleased/

Ed did what no parent should have to do—survive his son's suicide. Several years after his son, firefighter Matt Byrne, hung himself from a tree in the family's backyard, Ed wrote a memoir about his experience as a parent, and about his son's journey through addiction and firefighting after 9/11. The book, entitled, *My Son, In Whom I Am Well Pleased*, is finished, and currently in search of an agent. His first book, *Love's Not Over Til It's Over,* is available on Amazon.

WEBSITES

The following websites offer either counseling, assistance, emergency help, or other services. Please read each description thoroughly to see if they offer what you need before contacting them. Some require email contact and others offer 24/7 telephone or chat. Some are for the family/friend survivors of suicide, others are for those feeling suicidal.

Badge of Life

BadgeofLife.com

Phone:1-800-267-5463 Copline

Our mission is to educate and train law enforcement about mental health and suicide prevention. No more broken cops or cops' families.

Bluehelp.org

Phone: None

It is the mission of Blue H.E.L.P. to reduce mental health stigma through education, advocate for benefits for those suffering from post-traumatic stress, acknowledge the service and sacrifice of law enforcement officers we lost to suicide, assist officers in their search for healing, and to bring awareness to suicide and mental health issues.

Bluehelp.org offers comfort and honor to the families, friends, and LEO's who have lost an officer to suicide. All officers, regardless of method of death, deserve thanks; and all their families deserve your support. It is the mission of Blue H.E.L.P. to reduce mental health stigma through education, advocate for benefits for those suffering from post-traumatic stress, acknowledge the service and sacrifice of law enforcement officers we lost to suicide, support families after a suicide, and to bring awareness to suicide and mental health issues.

Make the Connection

https://www.maketheconnection.net/

MakeTheConnection.net is an online resource designed to connect Veterans, their family members and friends, and other supporters with information, resources, and solutions to issues affecting their lives.

MENTAL HEALTH TOOLKIT
For Family of Veterans

Resources

https://www.mentalhealth.va.gov/suicide_prevention/prevention/index.asp

https://www.mentalhealth.va.gov/suicide_prevention/docs/OMH-074-Suicide-Prevention-Social-Media-Toolkit-1-8_508.pdf

This is a great resource for veterans and families of veterans who want to know how to respond to posts on social media. Includes sample tweets and posts from suicidal veterans along with appropriate responses.

Mission 22

• Website: https://mission22.com/home
• Phone: (503) 908-8505

• Mission 22 is NOT a crisis organization. They offer treatment for Post-Traumatic Stress and Traumatic Brain Injury and all of the issues veterans are facing today.

Mission 22 supports the veteran community with three main programs; veteran treatment programs, memorials, and community social impact. Mission 22 provides treatment programs to veterans for Post-Traumatic Stress, Traumatic Brain Injury, and other issues they might be facing. It organizes events and builds memorials to create social impact and awareness for these issues. Mission 22 serves combat veterans, those injured in training who therefore could not deploy, and victims of MST. Mission 22 also has an Ambassador volunteer program for people to get involved as well. Ambassadors educate the public on veteran issues, help get veterans into Mission 22 treatment programs and create resources in their communities. Through these three programs, it enables a push for the betterment of our community and support when veterans need it the most, right now.

National Suicide Prevention Lifeline

The National Suicide Prevention Lifeline is a national network of local crisis centers that provides free and confidential emotional support to people in suicidal crisis or emotional distress 24 hours a day, 7 days a week. They recognize everyone's struggle is different and so they provide specialized assistance for youth, Military, Law Enforcement, Veterans, Native Americans, Suicide survivors, LGBTQ+, Loss Survivors and more.

Their Website:

https://suicidepreventionlifeline.org/

The Lifeline provides 24/7, free and confidential support for people in distress, prevention and crisis resources for you or your loved ones, and best practices for professionals. They also provide a chat feature for the deaf and hard of hearing.

Suicide Prevention Resource Center

https://www.sprc.org/

https://www.sprc.org/organizations/action-alliance

The Suicide Prevention Resource Center (SPRC) is the only federally supported resource center devoted to advancing the implementation of the National Strategy for Suicide Prevention. SPRC is funded by the U.S. Department of Health and Human Services' Substance Abuse and Mental Health Services Administration (SAMHSA).

• SPRC Steering Committee
• SPRC contact information
• SPRC advances suicide prevention infrastructure and capacity building through:
• Consultation, training, and resources to enhance suicide prevention efforts in states, Native settings, colleges and universities, health systems and other settings, and organizations that serve populations at risk for suicide.
• Staffing, administrative, and logistical support to the Secretariat of the National Action Alliance for Suicide Prevention (Action

Alliance), the public-private partnership dedicated to advancing the National Strategy for Suicide Prevention.

• Support for Zero Suicide, an initiative based on the foundational belief that suicide deaths for individuals under care within health and behavioral health systems are preventable. The initiative provides information, resources, and tools for safer suicide care.

UCF Resources
https://ucfrestores.com/about/

The University of Central Florida Restores, or UCF Restores, began as a government-funded research initiative in 2011, but has grown to serve as a resource to the Orlando community, the state of Florida and beyond. UCF RESTORES' unique approach to treatment – includes the first-of-its-kind three-week intensive outpatient program – combines exposure therapy, emerging technology, one-on-one and group therapy sessions to realize unprecedented success for those suffering from PTSD.

The Rosengren Trauma Clinic at UCF RESTORES provides clinical treatment services to first responders, veterans, active-duty military, survivors of military and civilian sexual assault, and community members experiencing PTSD and trauma-related concerns. Services are available at their clinic in Orlando. Their team of behavioral health experts use evidence-based treatments that utilize technology to effectively treat trauma and PTSD.

OTHER RESOURCES

The Marshall Project
https://www.themarshallproject.org/

Although NOT a site for those in crisis, or having suicidal thoughts it's an important website. The Marshall Project, (named after the late Chief Supreme Court Justice Thurgood Marshall) is a nonpartisan, nonprofit news organization that seeks to create and sustain a sense of national urgency about the U.S. criminal justice system. They have an impact on the system through journalism, rendering it more fair, effective, transparent, and humane for both officers and inmates and those who work with them both.

NOTES

PROLOGUE

1. . The History Channel. 2021. *Columbine Shooting*. New York, NY: The History Channel. https://www.history.com/topics/1990s/columbine-high-school-shootings.

2. . https://www.abc10.com/article/news/school-shootings-effects-on-police-still-largely-unknown/507-a4e8d5b7-7121-42c5-a558-088d3be3ad24

3. . https://cops.usdoj.gov/lemhwaresources

4. . ABoyrava, Abe National Public Radio (NPR). 2017. https://www.npr.org/sections/health-shots/2017/06/12/531751457/a-pulse-nightclub-responder-confronts-a-new-crisis-ptsd

5. . Aboyraya, Abe. National Public Radio (NPR). A Pulse Nightclub Responder Confronts A New Crisis: PTSD.

    https://www.npr.org/sections/health-shots/2017/06/12/531751457/a-pulse-nightclub-responder-confronts-a-new-crisis-ptsd

6. . https://ucfrestores.com/

7. . FireRescue1. 2021. "5 Years Later - Pulse Nightclub MCI Highlighted Need for First Responder Mental Health Support." FireRescue1. https://www.firerescue1.com/mci-mass-casualty-incidents/articles/5-years-later-pulse-nightclub-mci-highlighted-need-for-first-responder-mental-health-support-F3yVAPRgc6cKs5sd/.

8. . FireRescue1. 2021. "5 Years Later - Pulse Nightclub MCI Highlighted Need for First Responder Mental Health Support." FireRescue1.

    https://www.firerescue1.com/mci-mass-casualty-incidents/articles/5-years-later-pulse-nightclub-mci-highlighted-need-for-first-responder-mental-health-support-F3yVAPRgc6cKs5sd/.

9. . https://www.flyertalk.com/articles/why-is-suicide-such-a-problem-in-the-tsa.html

10. . Hilliard, Jena. September 14, 2019. *New Study Examines the Tragic Relationship Between Police Officers and Suicide.* https://www.addictioncenter.com/news/2019/09/police-at-highest-risk-for-suicide-than-any-profession/

11. . The Chicago Tribune. 2021. "Tracking Chicago shooting victims: 2,021 so far this year, 164 more than in 2020." Chicago Tribune. https://www.chicagotribune.com/data/ct-shooting-victims-map-charts-htmlstory.html.

12. . Washington Post, Griff Witte, and Mark Berman. 2021. "As homicides soar nationwide, mayors see few options for regaining control." *As homicides soar nationwide, mayors see few options for regaining control* (Washington), June 22, 2021. https://www.washingtonpost.com/national/homicides-up-nationwide-mayors/2021/06/21/13e5aa46-d058-11eb-9b7e-e06f6cfdece8_story.html.

13. . Statista.com and Erin Duffin. 2020. "Gender distribution of full-time law enforcement employees in the United States in 2019." Law enforcement. https://www.statista.com/statistics/195324/gender-distribution-of-full-time-law-enforcement-employees-in-the-us/.

14. . COPS, Debra L. Spence, and Jessica Drake. 2021. "Law Enforcement Offcer Suicide 2020 REPORT TO CONGRESS." *Law Enforcement Offcer Suicide 2020 RPORT TO CONGRESS*, (2021), 26. https://cops.usdoj.gov/RIC/Publications/cops-p429-pub.pdf.

CHAPTER 1

1. . Turse, Nick, and The New York Times. 2020. "U.S. Commandos at Risk for Suicide: Is the Military Doing Enough?" *The New York Times* (New York, 1 edition), June 30, 2020. https://www.nytimes.com/2020/06/30/magazine/special-operations-suicide-military.html.

2. . Turse, Nick, and The New York Times. 2020. "U.S. Commandos at Risk for Suicide: Is the Military Doing Enough?" *The New York Times* (New York, 1 edition), June 30, 2020. https://www.nytimes.com/2020/06/30/magazine/special-operations-suicide-military.html.

3. . Turse, Nick, and The New York Times. 2020. "U.S. Commandos at Risk for Suicide: Is the Military Doing Enough?" *The New York Times* (New York, 1 edition), June 30, 2020. https://www.nytimes.com/2020/06/30/magazine/special-operations-suicide-military.html.

4. . Zoyora, Gregg, and USA Today. 2014. "Suicide surpassed war as the military's leading cause of death." *USA Today* (McLean), October 31, 2014. https://www.usatoday.com/story/nation/2014/10/31/suicide-deaths-us-military-war-study/18261185/.

5. . *Ibid.*

6. . *Military Times and Meaghann Myers. n.d. "Four times as many troops and vets have died by suicide as in combat, study finds." Military Times (Alexandria). Accessed August 31, 2021. https://www.militarytimes.com/news/your-military/2021/06/21/four-times-as-many-troops-and-vets-have-died-by-suicide-as-in-combat-study-finds/.*

7. . *Ibid.*

8. . Ruderman Foundation. n.d. "Statements & Press Releases In The News All Inclusive with Jay Ruderman Inclusion In Entertainment Study: Police Officers and Firefighters Are More Likely to Die by Suicide than in Line of Duty." Ruderman Foundation. Accessed August 31, 2021. https://rudermanfoundation.org/white_papers/police-officers-and-firefighters-are-more-likely-to-die-by-suicide-than-in-line-of-duty/.https://rudermanfoundation.org/white_papers/police-officers-and-firefighters-are-more-likely-to-die-by-suicide-than-in-line-of-duty/

NOTES

CHAPTER 3

1. . Journal of the American Medical Association. (JAMA) JAMA Network - Epidemiology of *DSM-5*Drug Use DisorderResults From the National Epidemiologic Survey on Alcohol and Related Conditions–III. https://jamanetwork.com/journals/jamapsychiatry/fullarticle/2470680

2. . National Institute on Alcohol Abuse. n.d. "Alcohol Use in the United States." NIAA.NIH.GOV. Accessed August 31, 2021. https://www.niaaa.nih.gov/publications/brochures-and-fact-sheets/alcohol-facts-and-statistics.

3. . YouTube. 2009. "How Do You LIke Me Now?" YouTube.com. https://www.youtube.com/watch?v=3umaLe37-LE.

CHAPTER 6

1. . NCSL National Conference of State Legislators. 2018. "Possession of Firearms by People With Mental Illness." https://www.ncsl.org/research/civil-and-criminal-justice/possession-of-a-firearm-by-the-mentally-ill.aspx. https://www.ncsl.org/research/civil-and-criminal-justice/possession-of-a-firearm-by-the-mentally-ill.aspx.

2. . Suicide Prevention Resource Center. 2019. "Spousal Attitudes and Suicidal Thoughts." Spousal Attitudes and Suicidal Thoughts. https://www.sprc.org/news/spousal-attitudes-suicidal-thoughts.

CHAPTER 7

1. . PragerU. 2020. "Student Calls Cops on PragerU." YouTube.com. https://www.youtube.com/watch?v=SdrtyVMcH90.

2. . National Public Radio (NPR). 2021. "Study: Body-Worn Camera Research Shows Drop In Police Use of Force." NPR.org. https://www.npr.org/2021/04/26/982391187/study-body-worn-camera-research-shows-drop-in-police-use-of-force.

CHAPTER 9

1. . Genius.com. 1969. *The Boxer*. New York City, NY: Simon & Garfunkel. https://genius.com/Simon-and-garfunkel-the-boxer-lyrics.

2. . PubMedNCHI and Sher L. 2019. *Resilience as a focus of suicide research and prevention*. Bethesda, MD: PubMed. https://pubmed.ncbi.nlm.nih.gov/31150102/.

BONUS CHAPTER: SOUL WRITING

1.   . Psychology Today and Gary Drevitch. 2020. "Reduce Stress and Anxiety Levels with Journaling." PsychologyToday.com. https://www.psychologytoday.com/us/blog/evidence-based-living/202004/reduce-stress-and-anxiety-levels-journaling.

Made in the USA
Middletown, DE
01 May 2022

65025461R00156